The Glass House Boys
# of Pittsburgh

The Glass House Boys
of Pittsburgh

Law, Technology, and Child Labor

JAMES L. FLANNERY

University of Pittsburgh Press

Published by the University of Pittsburgh Press, Pittsburgh, Pa., 15260
Manufactured in the United States of America
Printed on acid-free paper

Frontispiece: The original labeling on this Lewis Hine photograph for the
National Child Labor Committee reads, "Going to their work at 5 P.M.
'Sheeny Joe's' Glass House, January, 1913. Boy to left is 15 years old, can't
speak English." Pittsburgh, Pennsylvania. *NCLC #01303, Hine #3505,
Lot 7478, National Child Labor Committee Collection,
Library of Congress.*

10 9 8 7 6 5 4 3 2 1
Library of Congress Cataloging-in-Publication Data
Flannery, James L.
The glass house boys of Pittsburgh : law, technology, and child labor /
James L. Flannery.
p. cm.
Includes bibliographical references and index.
ISBN-13: 978-0-8229-4377-8 (cloth : alk. paper)
ISBN-10: 0-8229-4377-8 (cloth : alk. paper)
1. Child labor—Pennsylvania—Pittsburgh—History.
2. Child labor—Law and legislation—Pennsylvania—History.
3. Glass trade—Pennsylvania—Pittsburgh—History.
4. Glass trade—Law and legislation—Pennsylvania—History.
5. Educational law and legislation—Pennsylvania—History.
I. Title.
HD6247.G52U545 2009
331.3'10974886—dc22   2009014285

Contents

Illustrations

All photographs are by the noted photographer Lewis Hine, whose work documented social injustice. The photographs are from the Records of the National Child Labor Committee (nclc), Library of Congress, LOC Lot 7478, and the captions replicate the typed information that was originally provided with each photograph, although the authorship of the informational text is unknown.

Preface and Acknowledgments

Because Progressive Era child labor reform was quintessentially based on the power of law, this work is fundamentally a legal history.[1] Any historical research project can encounter myriad challenges in terms of the availability and quality of primary source materials, challenges that can produce both excitement and frustration. One particular challenge that arose during the research for this book dealt with legislative materials. Although the overall sweep of legislative reform regarding child-related issues in Pennsylvania during the late nineteenth and early twentieth centuries could be described as "progressive" in terms of increased educational opportunities and labor protections for children, then as now, the devil is in the details. I investigated these details, in part, by analyzing the particularized legislative history of the state's child labor and education laws. As lawyers, judges, and others in the legal community know, legislative history contains some of the most important evidence for understanding the motivation and intent behind the enactment of a law, information that is not to be found simply in the language of the law itself. The most useful evidence of the legislative history surrounding a statute typically includes the amendments, reports, discussions, and comments offered or prepared by the legislators while the law is under active consideration in the legislative chambers. Today, an investigation into these materials often leads to an embarrassment of riches thanks to the ready availability of textual evidence respecting the intent of lawmakers. A century ago, however, that was not the case; it was certainly not the case at the state level generally and particularly not in Pennsylvania. Perhaps because the stakes in the struggle over the fate of the Pittsburgh glass house boys were so high, or because there was more than a hint of corruption influencing the outcome of that struggle, the legislative record surrounding this aspect of Progressive Era child labor reform in Pennsylvania is at best partial, scattered, and incomplete.

In Pennsylvania, during the period under study here, the state constitution required each chamber of the General Assembly to publish its own journal of proceedings, which recorded its own daily gavel-to-gavel activities as well as a joint legislative record.[2] But if one uses these published records to track the progress of a particular bill as it wends its way through the labyrinthine legislative process, one is struck by the paucity of information presented. Typically, the journals record the introduction of a particular bill by giving its title but only very rarely its initial contents. The record usually indicates to which committee the bill was committed, but only rarely will it shed anything more than inferential light on what happened to that bill behind the doors of the committee room.

In accordance with the state constitution then in force, each bill had to be read and voted on three separate times before it could be sent to the other chamber for action, and final passage required the affirmative vote of a majority of the members elected to each house, not just a majority of those present and voting, even if there was a quorum.[3] Although amendments could be offered, comments made, and discussion undertaken during each of these three (or more) readings, the record is frequently silent as to what was said, the wording of the amendments offered (even when they were approved), and how many yeas and nays the votes produced. The journals typically do not reprint the actual text of a bill until the second reading. If a committee changed the language of a particular bill, as its members did quite frequently, their "editing" was often obscured because the journals might not report the original text or highlight the revised language. Such *sua sponte* "amendments" by committees might come to light only if a member of the full chamber mentioned them when the bill was reported out of committee and even then only if the member's comments were noted in the journal. Finally, while the journals usually recorded the final voting results of the legislative deliberation following the third reading, for example, that a certain bill passed the House by vote of 123 to 45, occasionally even this information is left to historical speculation.

All of these elements presented a challenge to historical statutory investigation, mitigated in part by employing numerous non-legislative sources. But because the specific actions of legislators can still provide critical insight into the legislative process, it was a matter of no small interest when the actual comments of these legislators were noted in the journals, when the language of an amendment was given, or when a verbal exchange providing evidence of disagreement, passion, or emotion was recorded. These relatively rare instances of substantive historical data are like small gems. This project illustrates that, in order to more fully understand the reasons for certain legislative actions, official versions of traditional legislative history must be aligned with analyses of contemporaneous and related non-legislative events. Only then can one bring the history of law into full view.

This microanalysis of the legislative history respecting Pennsylvania's school-related and child labor laws provides the only detailed account available on the legislative struggles to end what was viewed by many progressives as the most onerous form of child labor (night work) in an important national industry (glass-bottle manufacturing) located in the leading industrial center of the country (western Pennsylvania). This analysis is undertaken through a contextualized legal history that weaves together the interrelated stories of progressive reformers, glass house owners, state legislators, and glass house workers, particularly those who were mere boys. A close reading of the legislative record as part of the larger social and political analysis makes clear the relationship between law and society.

This book also brings into view the pivotal actions of both the workers' union (the Glass Bottle Blowers' Association of the United States and Canada, or GBBA) and its president, Denis A. Hayes, in Pennsylvania's child labor struggles. Neither the union nor Hayes has received significant scholarly attention, and this lack of attention is unwarranted.[4] During the late nineteenth century, for example, the GBBA was a powerful and successful union. Its roots predate the Civil War, its members were very well paid, and it was an important affiliate of first the Knights of Labor and then the American Federation of Labor. Hayes was an articulate and forceful union leader. Because of his skill at the bargaining table, his union's members were rarely on strike and were among the most respected skilled workers in the country. At the start of the twentieth century, however, the GBBA faced a virtual sea change in production processes within the glass-bottle industry with the introduction of automated bottle-making technologies, the prospect of a massive de-skilling of the work force, and challenges from reformers committed to restricting child labor. Yet the union survived. Without Hayes's forward-looking leadership, the GBBA might well have collapsed under these pressures.

To understand the responses of Hayes and the GBBA to these challenges, I rely on several sources that have only rarely been tapped by historians of labor and the Progressive Era. These include the GBBA records housed at the Kheel Center for Labor-Management Documentation and Archives at Cornell University and other union papers located at Pennsylvania State University. Materials in both archives include original and carbon copies of thousands of pieces of union correspondence covering all issues of importance to the GBBA. I also rely on the two weekly newspapers representing the major interests in the nation's glass-bottle industry: the *National Glass Budget* and the *Commoner*.[5] Nearly complete runs of both are available for the period under study here, the *Budget* in bound hard-copy form at the Heinz History Center in downtown Pittsburgh and the *Commoner* in the microfilm collection at the Carnegie Library of Pittsburgh's main facility.

Gender (and the way various participants in the Progressive Era's child labor reform debates strategically deployed the term) played a significant role in efforts to regulate the employment of children in western Pennsylvania's glass-bottle factories. Historians such as Maureen A. Flanagan, Alan Davis, and Kathryn Kish Sklar have noted that both male and female reformers lent their voices, energies, and resources to the push for further progressive reforms.[6] As I researched this project, it became apparent that at various points in these struggles over child labor, gender was a critical part of the calculus of reform. Sometimes the part it played was fairly obvious and at other times, quite subdued. Gender, for example, played a subtle and complicated role within the workings of the community of Progressive Era child labor reformers. My project relies heavily on the work of several of these activists. Elizabeth Beardsley Butler, for example, presents in *The Pittsburgh Survey* one of the most detailed views available of the lived experiences of the Pittsburgh glass house boys. Florence Kelley, a founding member of the National Child Labor Committee (NCLC), worked tirelessly to bring these boys under the protection of Pennsylvania law by, among other things, exposing the failures of the state's factory inspector. These women were joined by a number of men, including Owen Lovejoy, Charles Chute, and Herschel H. Jones, who wrote and spoke repeatedly about the need for child labor reform in this particular industry. To their credit I came across no evidence that these, or other activists in the child labor reform movement, made any attempt to parse the value of the contributions made by other reformers along gender lines. But they did appear to make other child labor reform decisions based on gender. For example, while many female progressive activists played a pivotal role in the formation of the NCLC in 1904, when the newly formed organization went about selecting people for public leadership positions, it overwhelmingly chose men. Because the NCLC was designed to foster legislative change, this was, I argue, a strategic decision. It was a decision that, among other things, acknowledged the belief that the political culture of the day was more likely to be persuaded by positions advocated by men than those advanced by women.

When it came to the Pennsylvania legislature, gender's role in the child labor debates was also sometimes obvious and sometimes subtle. It hardly bears mentioning that all of the state legislators at the time were male, as were all of the state voters and virtually all of the industry lobbyists. Thus, the only people who had actual votes and electoral voices in the debates were men. While the natural inclination of these admittedly powerful men might well have been to discount or dismiss reform proposals advanced by women, I found no direct evidence that this was the case. There are no statements in the record of legislative proceedings indicating that political decisions were made purely or even substantially on the basis of the gender of those who advocated for or against reform. That gender was an important factor in the deliberations, however, was apparent in more subtle ways. Opponents of reform would, for example, make reference to the glass house "boys" when they argued that the youths were not hurt by the work, and they would argue that the boys' continued ability to work would be a great economic help to their mothers. Occasionally the lawmakers would be somewhat more direct. In 1909, for instance, they approved certain child labor reforms and made a point to increase the protections for girls but not boys. No girl could, for example, work at night until she was eighteen, whereas for boys the minimum age for nighttime work was sixteen. In dealing with gender in this way, the legislators were, I believe, playing to prevailing gender presumptions or prejudices, for example, that boys were physically and emotionally stronger than girls and that mothers were in greater need of assistance from their children than were their fathers. To argue, as the progressive reformers did, that boys were also vulnerable was then one of the more radical positions in the child labor debates.

I also found substantial evidence that the public discourse on these issues, especially as employed by the opponents of child labor reform, was
infused with negative, gender-based rhetoric. Some of this rhetoric was
subtle and some verged on slander. For example, the glass workers' newspaper, the *Commoner,* would generally use indirect gender associations to
dismiss reform efforts. The newspaper would characterize the child labor
reform proposals as unhelpful "agitation" on the part of progressives while
also noting elsewhere that many women were involved in the reform movement, as if simply mentioning the latter fact was enough to undercut the
validity of the reform effort. The *Commoner* would also argue that the reform proposals were unnecessary because the glass manufacturers (all of
whom were men, as readers well knew) had true progressive principles at
heart. The newspaper would, however, step up the rhetoric as the child
reform challenges continued, especially when the challenges addressed the
"glass house exception." The "exception," as discussed more fully in chapter 6, refers to the central legislative protection for the Pennsylvania glass
industry in the area of child labor reform during this period. It was an exception to the state's general prohibition on night work for children, and it
applied almost exclusively to the western Pennsylvania glass-bottle plants.
In 1909, to help block yet another challenge to the glass house exception,
the *Commoner* first suggested gagging the "bitter tongued, indiscreet female" supporters of child labor reform and then dismissed them as "fussy,
hysterical, impractical, and sentimental."[7]

The glass manufacturers, through their weekly newspaper, the *National
Glass Budget,* were more consistently direct, obvious, and negative in their
gender-based characterizations of the reformers. In the period from 1905
through 1915, as child labor practices in the western Pennsylvania glass
houses came under increased public scrutiny, the *Budget* repeatedly leveled
what were at times blistering ad hominem attacks against the reformers,
attacks couched in overtly sexual and gender-based language. The newspaper tried to dehumanize all reformers by neutering or defeminizing the
women reformers and emasculating the male reformers. The *Budget* did
this by characterizing them variously as "society ladies [and] club women,"
as "motherless mothers and fatherless fathers," as "wealthy spinsters [and]
hen-pecked husbands," and finally as an "association of motherless wives."[8]
Not unlike the media that mounted public attacks on activists in the wom-

en's suffrage movement, both the *Commoner* and the *Budget* often resorted to rants and cruel caricature when discussing the child labor reformers.

Although the glass house boys were for years central to the operation of the nation's factories and at the heart of the controversy over child labor in western Pennsylvania, they are nonetheless almost entirely silent in the historical record of the period. Their words appear only rarely in the debates surrounding the continued existence of the Pennsylvania glass house exception and in the battles over the regulation of child labor in the Pittsburgh glass houses. This silence underscores a rarely acknowledged historical reality. As Steven Mintz explains in his excellent history of American childhood, while children are often the subject of historical inquiry, their actual voices are rarely heard, and they are almost never the authors of their own stories.[9] In part because children lack access to virtually any means of literate production, a crucial form of social power, they almost always leave fewer historical traces than adults, and their actions, perspectives, and understandings are almost always less obvious. The history of the glass house boys is a case in point.

The Pittsburgh glass house boys are not absent from the historical record, however. They are continually being spoken for, referenced, and constructed by each of the other principal participants in the long-running public controversy over child labor. As a result, we know the story of the glass house boys almost exclusively through the words of adults whose discursive patterns simultaneously create the boys as objects of importance and render them mute.

The progressive reformers, the manufacturers, the adult glass workers and their union, the state legislators, and even the glass house boys' families all paint rhetorical pictures of these young workers in support of their own particular positions in the child labor debate. Because the evidentiary purpose of each rhetorical portrait was different, each picture is different as well. The NCLC, for example, as the leading national child labor reform organization of the period, issued hundreds of reports, pamphlets, and brochures depicting what it saw as the horrors of child labor. Many of these publications focused on the glass house boys, and in each the boys were uniformly presented as young, morally impressionable, almost delicate creatures. They were portrayed as children in need of and deserving of special protection. On the other hand, in the pages of the *National Glass*

Budget, the glass house boys appeared in a very different light. When this newspaper ridiculed the reformers and extolled what it saw as the value of child labor, it portrayed the boys as mature participants in the manufacturing enterprise and as hardworking and valued contributors to their families' (often their "widowed mothers'") economic well-being.

This book creates a composite sketch of the glass house boys by overlaying these various, seemingly conflicting images. The "actual" story of these boys can be told only indirectly, by retelling the larger story of child labor reform in the Pittsburgh glass-bottle industry. The recounting of that larger story of reform also underscores the overarching idea behind this book: that the dynamic relationship between law, ideology, and sociocultural change regarding the elimination of child labor in the Pittsburgh glass houses can be made visible only by foregrounding the complex and contradictory forces at work on this particular industry, in this particular locale, at this particular moment in history.

Many people and organizations helped move this project along the road from an early idea to a finished book, and I would like to acknowledge some of them here. First, I would like to thank the University of Pittsburgh School of Law for providing me with financial support to complete this project. The law school was kind enough to provide me with funds over the years to facilitate travel to libraries and archives where pertinent material was located. Its funding also allowed me to hire several law students to act as research assistants. Three of these students in particular provided me with invaluable assistance: Adam Hill, Christopher Gabriel, and Sara Beth Rhem. I also would like to thank Cynthia Miller at the University of Pittsburgh Press for her encouragement of and support for this project, the several anonymous readers of an early version of the manuscript for their very helpful suggestions, and Maureen Creamer Bemko, who did a wonderful job of copy editing.

One of the great rewards of working on this project was seeing the story of the Pittsburgh glass house boys emerge from the historical record. While some parts of that record are fairly robust, other parts are incomplete, and the story of these boys began to materialize only after I had consulted many sources. Some of the most interesting of those sources related to the records of the glass workers' union, the GBBA. I thank the research librarians and archivists at Pennsylvania State University and the Kheel

Center for Labor-Management Documentation and Archives at Cornell University for making their materials available and guiding me to the most useful information. In particular, Patrizia Sione at the Kheel Center was extremely helpful.

Other libraries and archives were helpful as well and deserve special mention. The Pennsylvania State Archives in Harrisburg was a very valuable resource because it has the most complete records for the state's General Assembly for the period under study here. It also has a complete set of reports from the state factory inspector. The Heinz History Center in downtown Pittsburgh possesses a very valuable collection of material on the city's glass industry. The center's collection of Pittsburgh glass from the late nineteenth and early twentieth centuries and the exhibit showcasing them, Glass: Shattering Notions, were particularly helpful. The center also has one of the most complete collections available of the original bound volumes of the *National Glass Budget,* the glass manufacturers' weekly newspaper, from the period. Also in Pittsburgh, the Carnegie Library has available in its microfilm collection a nearly complete set of issues of the *Commoner,* the weekly newspaper of the glass workers. Having such ready access to both of these newspapers was very important. Finally, the Library of Congress in Washington, DC, has two collections that were vital to this project. Its Manuscript Section holds a substantial archive from the National Child Labor Committee, including the several investigative reports on the western Pennsylvania glass houses that I used extensively. The Print and Photograph Section has a large collection of Lewis Hine photographs, including all of those that appear in this book, which the Library of Congress generously made available. These pictures capture something about the glass house boys that words alone cannot express.

The research for this book was used in papers I presented at three professional conferences, and I would like to thank those conference organizers for providing me with the opportunity to engage other conference participants in conversation about Progressive Era child labor. Those conferences were the annual meeting of the Law and Society Association, held in Pittsburgh in 2003; the annual meeting of the American Society for Legal History, held in Cincinnati, Ohio, in 2005; and the Midwest Regional Conference of the Organization of American Historians, held in Lincoln, Nebraska, in 2006. I would especially like to thank my fellow panelists at these conferences, the panel moderators and respondents, and the audience members who provided me with valuable feedback on the project.

I had two mentors in the past who also deserve special mention. They each provided me with encouragement and inspiration. The first is William J. Reese. I met Bill at the School of Education at Indiana University in Bloomington, and conversations with him helped me think about the importance of education, especially when coupled with the law, for effecting social change. I first became interested in studying the relationship between child labor laws and compulsory education laws after working with Bill. The second mentor is the Honorable Judge Ruggero J. Aldisert. After graduating from law school, I was fortunate enough to be a judicial law clerk for two years in Judge Aldisert's chambers in the U.S. Court of Appeals for the Third Circuit. Judge Aldisert remains the single most important legal mentor I have known, and he continually demonstrated for me the power and value of effective writing. He is also living proof of the power of law to effect positive social change.

Last, and most important, I owe an unrepayable debt of gratitude to my life partner, Kathryn. Without her unquestioning encouragement and support, I would never have undertaken the years of research that went into this book. Without her patience to read and reread draft after draft of the developing manuscript, this book would never have taken shape. And without her unequaled ability to edit and offer constructive suggestions, it would never have been completed. For all of this and more, I dedicate this book to her. Kathryn, thank you.

The Glass House Boys
of Pittsburgh

Child Labor Reforms and the National Child Labor Committee

I shall never forget my first visit to a glass factory at night. It was a big wooden structure, so loosely built that it afforded little protection from draughts, surrounded by a high fence with several rows of barbed wire stretched across the top. I went with the foreman of the factory and he explained to me the reasons for the stockade-like fence. "It keeps the young imps inside once we've got 'em in for the night shift," he said. The "young imps" were, of course, the boys employed, about forty in number, at least ten of whom were less than twelve years of age. It was a cheap bottle factory and . . . [c]heapness and child labor go together. . . . The hours of labor for the night shift were from 5.30 P.M. to 3.30 A.M. . . . . That night, for the first time, I realized the tragic significance of cheap bottles.

John Spargo

I N 1913, MICHAEL J. OWENS, a principal figure in the American glass industry, received an unsolicited letter from a "special agent" of the National Child Labor Committee (NCLC). The contents were startling. The NCLC had, since its founding nearly ten years earlier, devoted itself almost exclusively to ending industrial child labor in America and had achieved remarkable success in that arena. Further, the NCLC had focused special attention on the nation's glass-bottle industry, which, with its longstanding practice of employing thousands of children—the so-called glass house boys—had one of the most egregious records of child employment in the country. Yet, notwithstanding these efforts, this letter thanked Owens for accomplishing what the NCLC admitted it had been unable to do: virtually ending the use of child labor in the nation's glass-bottle factories, especially the practice of night labor, for which the glass houses were infamous and which the committee considered particularly odious.[1] The letter Owens received is especially remarkable because he was no progressive reformer. He was the son of a West Virginia coal miner and was himself a former union glass worker who had become one of the leading industrial glass men in the country. What Owens did to generate the letter and earn the praise and respect of the NCLC was to invent, patent, and market the world's first fully automated glass-bottle blowing machine, what came to be known as the "Owens Automatic." Until that time, because of the intricacies of the production process, glass bottles were almost universally made by hand. The Owens Automatic marked the end of a method of glass production that had held sway for thousands of years and had shaped nearly every aspect of the American glass bottle industry.

Yet the triumph heralded by the NCLC letter was not quite complete. Hidden in the shadows of this apparent victory lay one particularly unusual and instructive anomaly. At the time of this correspondence, although the use of child labor in most of the nation's glass houses had been all but eliminated, the glass house boys remained hard at work in one segment of the industry. They continued their unabated toil, day and night, in the glass-bottle factories of western Pennsylvania. This remnant of the centuries-old practice of using child labor in the making of glass would not be eliminated until 1915. The story of Progressive Era efforts to remove these particular child workers from these particular glass-bottle plants is

"Ten Arm Owens Automatic Bottle Machine.
Courtesy of Owen's [sic] Automatic Bottle Machine Co." Toledo, Ohio, ca. 1913

a story of reform that was repeatedly stymied by a unique combination of forces, *sui generis* to Pennsylvania and the Pittsburgh glass houses. It is a story of reform held hostage.

The Pennsylvania legislature had created the "glass house exception" for the use of child labor in 1905, at the same time it enacted a sweeping ban on night work for children under the age of sixteen in virtually all industrial, manufacturing, and mercantile employments. Exceptions to regulatory reforms were not uncommon in the Progressive Era nor are they unheard of today. This particular exception was unusual, however, because it was the only night-work exception created by the Pennsylvania state legislators, it affected only the state's glass industry, and within that industry it applied only to the glass-bottle plants in and around Pittsburgh. The Pennsylvania glass house exception was anathema to the progressive child labor reformers who spent nearly a decade trying to undo it.

Why was the western Pennsylvania glass industry granted this unique legislative dispensation in 1905 and how was it able to rebuff repeated progressive challenges to the glass house exception over the next ten years? Understanding the struggles over the glass house exception requires an analysis of the actions and interactions of several key groups: the glass house boys and their families, the Progressive Era social reformers, the glass manufacturers, the adult glass workers and their union, and the state legislature. Each of these groups had a long history of involvement in the Pittsburgh glass industry, and each had vital, and often competing, interests in this particular child labor issue. Because of these interests, each of these groups played an important and sometimes unique role in the child labor debate, especially when compared with similar reform efforts elsewhere in the country during the early decades of the twentieth century. The particular complex of intersecting, interacting, and overlapping forces—social, political, cultural, economic, and technological—that underpinned the actions of these groups in Pennsylvania gave shape to a child labor struggle that was singular in the annals of Progressive Era reform.

For most of the nation's earlier history, the benefits of employing children, even at a very young age, had been almost universally acknowledged. Not only was it assumed that children needed to learn a useful trade and in the process add to their family's income, but the idleness of unemployed children was thought to lead to "devilment." Child labor was seen as a benefit not only for the child but for the family economy and the larger community as well.[2] During the nineteenth century this view began to change, and by the early twentieth century, the cultural momentum was shifting in favor of the ideal of a more "sheltered" childhood for all children. Under this view, children were seen as being in need of protection and nurturing. It also held that children should not be forced, or even allowed, to enter the adult world of work too early. But what "too early" meant was a subject of much debate.

Progressive Era social reformers embraced the ideal of sheltered childhood and worked tirelessly both to restrict the practice of industrial child labor and to increase the availability of public education. The effect was pronounced. In 1912, the NCLC reported that all forty-eight states plus the District of Columbia had some child labor and/or compulsory education legislation.[3] The number of child workers in the nation peaked in 1910 at nearly 2 million, an increase of almost 20 percent from ten years earlier. After 1910, however, the number steadily dropped until by 1930 it stood at just under 700,000.[4] Sheltered childhood was becoming a reality.

In the country's glass industry, the shift away from child labor (or the "small help," as the children were sometimes called) came even sooner. Official figures show that the number of children under sixteen working in the nation's glass houses peaked fully ten years before the 1910 high-water mark for child labor in industrial employment. In 1880, 5,658 children under the age of sixteen worked in the glass industry. That number peaked in 1899 at 7,116 and then began to fall: to 6,435 in 1904; 3,561 in 1909; and 1,413 in 1919.[5]

But these numbers are deceptive. They obscure at least three important factors related to the Pittsburgh glass house boys. First, because of intense competitive pressures and perhaps a growing sensitivity to the subject of child labor, the Pittsburgh glass-bottle firms had a history of underreporting their child employment. Take, for example, the 1886 federal census publication, *Report on the Statistics of Wages in Manufacturing Industries*, issued under the direction of Joseph D. Weeks. Weeks was a "special agent and expert" for the Census Office. His report addressed the full range of American industry, including glassmaking, at the height of the Industrial Revolution.[6] For his analysis of the nation's glass factories, Weeks studied the four primary manufacturing sectors in the industry: crystal glass, window glass, plate glass, and hand-blown bottles and tumblers. He sent out forty questionnaires to selected glass factories across the country, including several bottle plants in western Pennsylvania. Seventeen of these glass factories returned completed forms, but not a single Pittsburgh glass-bottle manufacturer was among them. This is particularly noteworthy because, at the time, the glass houses of western Pennsylvania made more bottles, and employed more glass house boys, than did plants in any other region of the country.[7]

Second, while the total numbers of children working in all glass factories may well have decreased after 1899, the use of child workers was not uniform across all sectors of the industry. The production processes used in the hand-blown bottle factories required a much higher proportion of "boy help" than did any of the other industry sectors. Further, because the non-bottle sectors required less skilled work than the bottle industry did, the non-bottle factories were more easily adaptable to mechanized techniques. Therefore, when labor-saving technologies began appearing in the industry by the late nineteenth century, they had a far greater impact on reducing all forms of labor (including child labor) in the non-bottle plants, thereby further accentuating the bottle sector's relative reliance on child labor.

Finally, industry-wide child labor employment figures tend to hide geographic differences. Within the bottle-making sector of the glass industry, geography became an increasingly important indicator for the use of child labor by the early twentieth century. As glass-making machines, such as the Owens Automatic, were introduced into these factories, the overall need for labor tended to decrease, thus affecting both the adult glass workers and the glass house boys. However, because the glass workers' union was particularly strong in Pittsburgh, the introduction of these new bottle-making machines to plants in that region took longer than in other areas of the country. Thus, the Pittsburgh glass houses continued to use child labor while the glass house boys were being phased out elsewhere.

As bottle makers in other parts of the country converted to the more efficient automated production technologies, the competitive pressures on the handmade-glass houses in Pittsburgh intensified. In order to survive, the Pittsburgh glass-bottle makers increased production by running their factories both day and night, and they reduced costs by increasing their reliance on cheap child labor. Because younger children tended to work more cheaply than older ones, they also received some hiring preference. In the first decade of the twentieth century, the modal age among *all* glass workers nationally in the bottle sector, for example, was sixteen. In Pennsylvania, it was only fourteen.[8] Thus, early-twentieth-century bottles made in Pittsburgh, more so than anywhere else in the country, continued to be made by hand, and a greater proportion of those hands belonged to young children—the glass house boys of Pittsburgh.

The work of the glass house boys was demanding. In Pittsburgh, the typical handmade-bottle plant was organized around numerous small teams of workers, or shops, who operated simultaneously on the furnace-room floor. The normal shop consisted of two or three skilled adult workers and three or four boys to serve as helpers. The specific jobs for the adult workers

"A midnight scene in More-Jonas Glass Works, Bridgeton, N.J. Four small boys are to be seen in this photo." November 1909

included the "gatherer," the "blower," and the "finisher." The gatherer dipped the blowpipe into the mixture of molten glass. In a series of intricate maneuvers, the master blower then blew into the pipe and began to form the bottle, either free hand or, more frequently, with the use of a mold. During this process the bottle might need to be reheated in the furnace several times before it began to take final shape. When the body of the bottle was formed, it was broken off the blowpipe so that the finisher could complete the neck and top. Then the finished bottle, still very hot, was cooled slowly in a special device called a "lehr oven" to prevent it from splintering. The men were usually equally skilled at each job so that two or three could function as a team and they could switch jobs during the shift.[9]

The glass house boy positions in the typical Pittsburgh bottle shop might include the "snapping-up" boy, who transported the glass-loaded blowpipe

"Glass Works." West Virginia, October 1908

from the gatherer to the blower; the "mold-holding" boy, who stooped at the feet of the blower and repeatedly opened and closed the various metal molds used to give the bottles a uniform shape; the "carrying-in" (or "carrying-off") boy, who transported the bottles back and forth between the blower and the "glory hole" of the reheating furnace, from the blower to the finisher, and then from the finisher to the cooling lehr for the annealing process; and finally the "cleaning-off" boy, who used a small iron tool much like a file to clean off the end of the blowpipe between uses. If the boys were equally skilled at each task, they, like the men, might cover more than one job at a time and they could also trade jobs either during or between shifts.[10] While the men normally remained at their work stations while they performed a particular job, the boys, except for the mold-holding boy (who had to remain at the feet of the master glass blower), scurried around constantly.

Although the work of the glass house boys was difficult and complicated, and although the young workers were key to the industrial production process for glass bottles, the boys were almost universally regarded as unskilled labor. This perception undervalued their abilities. In Pittsburgh, as the intensity of the work escalated, the boys had to negotiate an increasingly cramped and dangerous factory space. They needed to know how to operate quickly the many molds used. They had to carry the partly completed glass objects to the "glory hole" of the furnace to reheat them for final finishing, returning them only when they were hot enough to rework. When the finishing work was done, they had to carry the items to the lehr for cooling. They were expected to perform all of these tasks without breaking the glass or running into the perhaps dozens of other boys scurrying around the furnace floor doing the same things. If a boy got injured, the production process slowed. If a boy stumbled and broke some glass, the factory's output was reduced and the blower, who was paid by the piece, lost a part of his wage. Having skilled, experienced boys was clearly important, yet it was customary for the boys to be poorly treated by the men with whom they worked and poorly paid by the owners who hired them. Even so, in Pittsburgh at least, there was rarely a shortage of boys willing to work in the glass houses.

The Spirit of Reform

Reformers of the Progressive Era focused on reducing an ever-broadening array of social, economic, and political problems linked to the rise of industrialization and the dramatic shifts in economic and political power associated with it. The legacy of reform attributable to progressivism includes the passage of health and safety laws, the creation of settlement houses, and labor and educational improvements, as well as the expansion of voting rights, all of which were intended "to improve the conditions of life and labor and to create as much social stability as possible."[11] Reflecting the breadth of these concerns, the reformers of the period represented many diverse interests, with the reform proposals they advanced addressing an equally broad range of important issues. Because of this diversity, many historians have observed that there was no unified progressive movement. Rather, both the reforms and the reformers of the period were a varied and often contradictory lot. Underscoring their diversity, Arthur S. Link and Richard L. McCormick have observed that "each group of progressives had its own definitions of improvement and stability."[12] And yet, for all the differences within the progressive movement, industrial child labor was a paramount concern. The specter of the glass house boys, hard at work in front of the searing heat of the nation's glass house furnaces, kindled particularly strong fires under the progressive reformers. Given the breadth of the progressive movement, it is all the more significant that eradication of child labor in the glass industry was such an important goal.

Many progressives were members of the rapidly expanding urban middle class. While some of their reform efforts involved large-scale direct action, such as labor agitation or the development of settlement houses, many of their reform programs focused on ameliorating specific problems rather than undertaking more radical systemic change. In particular, they sought to leverage specific social change through the legal system, relying on legislative action to foster particular reforms. Because Americans of the late nineteenth century were just beginning to use federal law to advance reform, most progressive legislative proposals centered on state governmental action.[13] Similar to shifts in the women's suffrage movement, in the early twentieth century differences emerged among child labor reformers about how best to proceed and, in particular, whether to devote more time to individual state-level reforms or to seek a national solution. These differences caused rifts in some progressive organizations and weakened the reform effort.

Significantly, many women were leaders in the fight for progressive causes, including the elimination of industrial child labor. As Nancy S. Dye observes, these female reformers were concerned with "such issues as clean food and pure milk, maternal and infant welfare, industrial pollution, [or] inadequate and highly politicized school systems," and they saw their efforts as having the potential to improve the quality of life not only of the poor but of the whole population.[14] To effect these changes, the female progressives understood that they had to find ways to influence law-based reform. This era was, of course, a period of fundamental changes in the gendered allocation of formal political power and suffrage in the United States. These changes had consequences not only for electoral politics but also for the way men and women jointly inhabited the public sphere. Even though women had been largely denied access to the formal institutions of public governmental as well as private corporate power, they were not excluded from the public sphere. They had historically influenced public and social policy in a variety of ways, perhaps especially through membership in voluntary as-sociations. These associations, however, were also often gender segregated. Kathryn Kish Sklar notes that "although examples to the contrary abound-ed—including churches, trade unions, and schools—sex-segregated social-izing and gatherings in which numbers of one gender greatly outnumbered the other were far more common in the lives of nineteenth-century women than were groups that included men and women in similar proportions."[15] This associational activity continued, and if anything increased, during the Progressive Era as women created or joined groups of other social reformers to effect change.

These groups included charities, local and national welfare organiza-tions, single-issue reform movements, and settlement houses. As historians of the Progressive Era have made clear, the settlement houses are impor-tant sites from which to view progressive reform generally and the role of female progressives in child labor reform in particular. Not only were many settlement house workers female, and not only did these workers tend to be strong advocates for child labor reform, but many of the houses themselves were operated by women, most prominently Jane Addams at Hull House in Chicago and Lillian Wald at the Henry Street settlement in New York. While many female progressives might well have grown up in middle-class households, and as such might be expected to approach reform from the limiting perspective of social class, their lived experience in founding and operating settlement houses complicates any simple, class-based analysis. These women lived and worked on a day-to-day basis in the settlement houses, alongside poor, working-class, often immigrant friends, residents, and neighbors, and from this position they not only organized the activi-ties and programs of the settlement houses but also undertook the active advocacy of a complex social reform agenda. This very active political work was in contrast to the female progressives' lack of official, formal political power, and their lack of such power also caused them to be the object of ridicule and derision directed at them by some who opposed reform. The settlement houses were thus places of refuge not only for the poor but also for some of the female activists as well, providing both a safe haven and an excellent base from which they could develop the skills needed to pursue progressive change. Within this context, the elimination of industrial child labor became one of the principal goals of women progressives.[16]

The female progressives approached child labor reform as a crusade, the intensity of which was similar to that of the antebellum abolitionist movement.[17] Drawing on a cultural valuation of domesticity and motherhood, women could claim a special authority both to speak on social and humanitarian issues affecting working-class women and children and to criticize the indifference of the American political institutions to their plight. Because of their limited access to the official avenues of legal and legislative power, however, their demands could be discounted in the halls of state legislatures as well as in other venues of public discourse, regardless of the strength of their arguments, the precision of their analysis, or the power of their rhetoric. In response to this double positioning, female progressives had to develop less direct means of achieving their ends. One way to do so was to join forces with a variety of male-dominated progressive groups to help push for reform. As a result, female progressives became expert at building broad-based reform coalitions as well as in passionately arguing for reforms and energetically lobbying for related legislative changes.

The effectiveness of such coalitions depended on the actions and contributions of all members, so these groups were not without their own set of pitfalls. Two such difficulties made progressive child labor reform particularly problematic in regard to the Pittsburgh glass houses. First, many of the most successful coalitions forged by progressives around the country to fight for child labor reform involved the active participation of labor unions. These coalitions between unions and progressive activists were based on a symmetry of interests, given the fact that virtually all major unions of the day, either out of economic self-interest or altruism, supported child labor reform. In many instances, labor union assistance in efforts to lobby state legislatures for change was invaluable. In Pennsylvania, however, the progressives were unable to establish this particular alignment of interests for child labor reforms regarding the Pittsburgh glass-bottle plants. Second, some of the male progressives and the male-dominated progressive groups approached reform from a very different perspective from that of the female reformers with whom they had joined forces. Many male progressives preferred to assume the role of the "rational" and "objective" observer when describing or evaluating the social, political, or economic problems associated with industrialization, and they preferred to remain on the political sidelines rather than to get involved in the nitty-gritty process of lawmaking that was a prerequisite for actual social change. These differences in the approach to reform hampered efforts to end child labor in the glass industry in Pittsburgh. The intersection of these several factors came into play in the halls of the Pennsylvania legislature between 1905 and 1915 as the proposals to end night work by children in the Pittsburgh glass houses were repeatedly blocked.

Progressivism Working across/against Gender

Three examples of how gender factored into Progressive Era reform efforts illustrate the complexity of the interactions. The first relates to a pair of related Chicago civic organizations, the second, to two national reform groups based in New York, and the third, to a ground-breaking research survey conducted in Pittsburgh. In her analysis of the two Progressive Era civic reform groups in Chicago, Maureen A. Flanagan identifies significant gender-related differences in the approaches of two organizations. These differences serve to highlight the problems female social reformers of the period experienced in their work with coalitions. Flanagan's study found that the male and female reform organizations in question, although concerned with identical political and public policy questions, generated substantially different proposals for solving those problems. The all-male City Club of Chicago and its female counterpart, the Women's City Club of Chicago, were very similar groups. They were each founded as municipal reform organizations, the men's club in 1903 and the women's, in 1910, on the principle that "the citizens of the city were responsible for the welfare of the community in which they lived."[18] Each club generally drew its membership from the city's white upper-middle-class residents. The members of the City Club tended to work in business and the professions. The members of the Women's City Club, on the other hand, tended to be a bit more diverse. While many, if not most, of its members were the wives and daughters of that same class of business and professional men who peopled the City Club, a significant percentage were also unmarried professional women, including some settlement house staffers and other social workers. As Flanagan points out, however, there is no evidence that the women from these latter organizations "wielded a disproportionate influence over the policies of the club."[19]

On several occasions, these two groups addressed many of the same public or municipal issues. Despite the similarity in their membership, however, they consistently took different, often opposing positions on which reform program should be implemented to address a particular problem. On issues as varied as municipal sanitation, public education, and police activity during labor strikes, the City Club typically advocated reforms that stressed the interests of private business, profit, and limited governmental power. The Women's City Club, on the other hand, consistently supported reform programs that focused on improving the social, environmental, and economic conditions of the city's residents, especially those most directly affected by the municipal issue in question.

In terms of waste management, for example, the City Club supported retaining the existing system of private collection contractors and the system of solid waste "reduction," a process that yielded an oil product, worth up to $150,000 per year, derived from the trash and given to the private contractors. The Women's City Club, on the other hand, advocated municipal ownership of the waste collection process and incineration rather than "reduction" because the former would produce not only electricity but also an inert residue usable in road construction and virtually (it was assumed at the time) no emissions, all of which would have, they reasoned, positive environmental and social attributes.

In terms of educational reforms, while both groups supported instituting a type of vocational education in the public schools, the City Club did so because it would "create a dependable industrial work force" and would therefore increase the "financial reward for business." The Women's City Club supported a vocational education program because its members were concerned about the individual child in school. They wanted to "keep children in school beyond age fourteen ... in order to educate and prepare them for better-paying jobs" and "to provide advice and guidance to school children once they were ready to leave school and seek work."[20]

Thus, the men of the City Club had a vision of Chicago consistent with what might be termed "trickle-down" economics. That is, they saw the city primarily as a place within which private business functioned for the benefit of business leaders and related professionals. Further, they believed, if those business activities were allowed to prosper, then the rest of the city's inhabitants would ultimately prosper as well. The male City Club designed its reform proposals to benefit business first, with the expectation that benefits to the larger citizenry would follow. The urban vision of the Women's City Club started with the well-being of the people who actually made up the city's populace. The solutions they proposed were uniformly intended to maximize direct benefits to city residents, regardless of the immediate economic impact on the city's businesses. Espousing what might be called a "trickle-up" model, they argued that if the general population of the Chicago prospered, then its businesses would eventually prosper as well.[21]

A similar situation regarding the differences in approach taken by male and female groups existed in regard to two progressive reform organizations more closely tied to the child labor issue: the National Consumers' League (NCL), headed by Florence Kelley, and the American Association for Labor Legislation (AALL), headed by John R. Commons. Both Kelley and Commons had superlative progressive credentials, and the similarities between the two groups are striking, but so too were the differences in their approaches to reform. The two organizations were formed within less than a decade of each other, and they each sought the passage of reform labor legislation as one of their primary goals. Both also drew their membership largely from the middle class, each had national offices, and both relied on professional expertise to advance their programs for progressive reform.

The NCL was organized first, in 1898, by a small group of already active local consumers' organizations. Both the local organizations and the NCL were overwhelmingly female in membership, and, under Kelley's leadership, the NCL strove, in her words, to "moralize" consumer purchasing decisions made by women by providing them with "knowledge" so that the purchasing "decision when made shall be a righteous one."[22] Kelley worked tirelessly to build up the grassroots basis of the organization. In 1901, the NCL had 30 local chapters, and by 1906, it had 63. This growth continued, and by 1913, individual memberships, virtually all with local chapter affiliations, had grown to more than 30,000. The NCL also worked to build alliances with other groups. In 1903, for example, to broaden the influence and extend the reach of the NCL, Kelley chaired the child labor committees for both the National Congress of Mothers and the National American Women's Suffrage Association. For specific legislative programs, the NCL worked with local labor and other progressive organizations. Kelley also affiliated the NCL with the General Federation of Women's Clubs, which, in 1900, had more than 2,675 local groups and a membership list that exceeded 155,000 names.[23]

The AALL, on the other hand, was formed in 1906, not as the outgrowth of local labor reform groups but as the American branch of the International Association for Labor Legislation, headquartered in Paris. The AALL membership, while middle class, was almost entirely male, and the group approached reform from what might be characterized as a respectful distance. According to Sklar, the "AALL leaders treated knowledge as professional, not personal." That is, they "exercised power through the prestige of their position and expertise, not through [the organization's] members." Further, "rather than seeing government as a democratic extension of the popular will, the AALL viewed the state as a vehicle of enlightened administration." In keeping with this general philosophy, the AALL eschewed organizing or affiliating with local chapters. It also exhibited few populist tendencies; its general membership remained at about two hundred through 1909 and barely topped three thousand in 1913. It considered itself an elite organization of experts rather than a broadly based group of activists, generally seeing its political role as one of advising others on matters of labor law and expecting that those others would "carry their advice forward into the political arena."[24] When it came to specific labor legislation, such as the fight to enact state-level minimum wage laws, the NCL actively and directly lobbied for these measures in several states while the AALL declined to enter the fray. Remaining cautious and reserved, the AALL refused to give direct, public support to such efforts because it believed that, if new, progressive laws were challenged in court, the judges of the day would probably strike down the legislation.[25]

As an activist, politically astute, largely female organization that engaged in extensive coalition building to support direct political action, the NCL established local, grassroots organizations with links to labor and other progressive groups to actively lobby for reform. The AALL, on the other hand, saw itself as a detached, intellectual association of rational elites, disdaining local affiliates and preferring to comment on, rather than to endorse, specific legislative reforms. It generally refused to become involved in the messy business of state lawmaking. These two reform organizations exemplified the dilemma facing many female progressives. Whereas the women reformers might take on the role of political and legislative activists, their efforts could be limited, or at least not furthered, by their associated male reformers who preferred to be distant and disinterested legislative observers. To be sure, not all male progressives were cut from the same cloth as those of the City Club of Chicago or the AALL, but the danger in forming coalitions with male-dominated groups was clear. If the activist women wanted the help of male progressives in their battles for reform before the state legislatures, they needed to construct their coalitions with care.[26]

Kelley and Commons worked together on another major Progressive Era project that focused directly on the glass house boys of Pittsburgh and reflected, to an even more acute degree, the political limitations of an effort centered on these gender-based differences in approaching reform. Kelley and Commons were among a group of prominent progressives who were principal investigators for *The Pittsburgh Survey*, one of the first large-scale urban studies in the country. The *Survey* began in June 1906 when Alice B. Montgomery, the chief probation officer in the Allegheny County Juvenile Court in Pittsburgh, wrote a letter to Paul Kellogg at the Charity Organization Society in New York. In the letter Montgomery asked Kellogg if his organization could conduct an investigation into social conditions in and around Pittsburgh. Kellogg agreed and, with the financial support of the newly formed Russell Sage Foundation, the project was launched.[27] Kellogg was named the *Survey's* general editor, Lewis W. Hine was enlisted to take documentary photographs, and Commons, Kelley, and Elizabeth Beardsley Butler were among those asked to conduct research. As Margo Anderson and Maurine W. Greenwald have noted, the *Survey* was "one of the most extensive social research and reform efforts of the twentieth century. In all, over seventy researchers—a veritable who's who of early twentieth-century Progressive thought—lent their efforts and expertise.... The reform proposals listed in the pages of the Pittsburgh Survey reports provided much of the blueprint for reforming urban industrial society—including introduction of workers' compensation systems, pollution controls, civic reform, protective legislation, and a shorter work week."[28] The *Survey's* impact on the nascent field of urban sociology, as well as its effect on some of its contributors, was dramatic. After Paul Kellogg, Margaret Byington, John Fitch, Crystal Eastman, Butler, and other researchers for the *Survey* finished their fieldwork, "[t]hey set off immediately not only to write articles ... and book-length studies of what they had discovered and learned in Pittsburgh, but also to continue their work of Progressive reform in journalism, in university teaching and research, on public commissions, and in state and national politics."[29] The research was published in six volumes that analyzed and found substantial fault with the city's economic, labor, health, housing, and educational systems.

Despite its descriptions of social, political, and environmental degradation in Pittsburgh, a city at the very heart of industrial America, the *Survey* had very little immediate or practical effect. After the findings were made public, they were roundly criticized by local politicians, business leaders, and Pittsburgh newspapers and then largely ignored or dismissed. Under a banner headline, "The Pittsburgh Survey's Appalling Disclosures," the city's leading general circulation newspaper, the *Pittsburgh Gazette*, featured on its front page a large cartoon mocking what it portrayed as the exaggerated claims offered by the *Survey*. The cartoon shows pages from a report falling to the floor at the feet of a gentleman dressed in colonial garb—the personification of the city—each page indicting the city for some alleged failure: "Labor Conditions, Bad; Charity Work, Bad; Housing, Bad; Just About Everything, Bad." The bewigged figure scratches his chin and muses, "Who'd a Thunk I Was Such a Sick Man?"[30] In the 1909 mayoral election, conducted just after the first installments of the *Survey* were issued, the progressive reform candidate William Stevenson was defeated by Republican William Magee, but neither candidate even mentioned the *Survey*'s results during the campaign. To provide some research support for an official rebuttal to the *Survey*, the Pittsburgh City Council and the local chamber of commerce sponsored a cursory economic review in 1911 in order to emphasize the "good side of Pittsburgh life." The report that followed noted blandly that if any reforms were needed, they were not pressing and would come in due time. In short, "the Survey failed to arouse Pittsburghers—either influential citizens or the middle class—to improve everyday life for workers in Pittsburgh, solve environmental problems of the area, or meet the immediate 'needs of the poor' at the time." Although Pittsburgh did have some local progressive organizations, such as the Civic Club (discussed in chapter 3), in the early twentieth century it was still largely a working-class city, and not many residents or leaders found any part of the Progressive Era reform agenda appealing.[31]

Two key factors seemed to have played a part in the failure of the *Survey* to directly effect reform. Although initiated by an inquiry from a local public official, the study had no local sponsorship, and virtually all of the work was done by principal researchers drawn from places other than western Pennsylvania. It was, therefore, not inaccurately perceived to be the work of "outsiders." But insularity and suspicion of outsiders was only part of the problem. The approach taken by the researchers themselves also seems to have been a factor. Although the tradition of muckraking and investigative journalism was fairly well established by 1907, Paul Kellogg, the *Survey*'s principal editor, feared, ironically as it turns out, that if the researchers took that sort of approach, they might very well anger and alienate the civic leaders of Pittsburgh. He wanted to avoid negative and hostile reactions from local officials. He hoped to use the researchers' status as "unbiased" outside observers to "elevate their research to a scientific, if reform-minded, stance." The result was consciously intended to be more academic than polemical, and this focus, it was hoped, would be more likely to persuade local decision makers of the need for reform. Thus, while the rhetoric used in the reports and monographs that constituted the *Survey* was by no means disinterested, it was characterized by a more methodical, research-based style. The authors and editors sought to paint a portrait of the social and environmental decay that they saw amid substantial industrial power and wealth by using intense and thorough description rather than words of anger and outrage. This rhetorical attitude was emblematic of the male-oriented progressive organizational approach that, in Pittsburgh at least, failed to produce the desired political results.[32]

These examples—the City Club and the Women's City Club of Chicago, the National Consumers' League and the American Association for Labor Legislation, and *The Pittsburgh Survey*—suggest some differences between male and female reform groups and how those differences influenced the content of reform proposals, modes of persuasion, political tactics employed, and the results obtained by progressives in the early twentieth century. Although the political climate of the time may have limited the ability of female progressives to directly effect social change, it did not dampen their desire for and efforts to effect reform. The work of Florence Kelley, within the child labor reform movement generally and regarding the Pittsburgh glass house boys in particular, exemplifies the resilience and determination of the progressive reformers.

Florence Kelley and Child Labor

Florence Kelley was perhaps the most prominent, vocal, and determined social activist advocating for the rights of American children during the period. Her actions and accomplishments also serve to complicate any easy categorization of the reformers, their motives, their power, and their effectiveness. Although middle class by birth, she did not fully fit the cultural expectations for women of her class. Neither in her life nor in her political commitments can she be easily read as a domesticated or domesticating reformer. She was college educated, with graduate education in law. She studied and lived in Europe, where she was an active member of the Socialist Party. She returned to the United States, where, as a divorced woman with children, she became actively engaged in progressive politics while maintaining her ties to socialist friends, including a decades-long correspondence with Frederick Engels. As one of her biographers notes, "In the long history of the struggle against child labor in America, the person who made the most consistent and effective contributions was Florence Kelley."[33]

Kelley worked diligently not only to establish the legal scaffolding needed to eliminate children's factory employment and expand their educational opportunities but also to change the public's view on the subject of reform because she realized that public opinion, and not law alone, was key for effective social change. As her work with the National Consumers' League attests, Kelley was by no means a disinterested social observer and commentator. She was an active, passionate force in legislative lobbying; she was the first female chief factory inspector in the country; and she worked for numerous private social service as well as state and federal administrative agencies. She was an active member of such progressive organizations as the NCL and the National American Women's Suffrage Association. She was also a founding member of the National Association for the Advancement of Colored People (NAACP) and, central to this study, the National Child Labor Committee.

Because her life and work stand at the center of child labor reform in the United States during the period of its most fervent activity, she provides a particularly useful case for considering the complex questions surrounding reform and the glass industry in western Pennsylvania. Kelley's background and activism are especially instructive because, even though she devoted considerable energy to the national child labor problem and gave special attention to the situation in Pennsylvania, her efforts to remove the thousands of child workers from the state's worst offending industry, the glass-bottle factories of the Pittsburgh district, were only partly effective. Considering the strength of Kelley's record and the evidence of her effectiveness elsewhere in the field, the failure to more decisively effect change in Pennsylvania, especially in the creation and enforcement of regulatory legislation, stands as a disquieting testament to the limits of progressive reform and the indifference to reform of early-twentieth-century Pennsylvania legislators.

Born in 1859, Florence Kelley grew up in a politically active Philadelphia family, within a solid reformist tradition. Her great-aunt, Sara Pugh, and her father, William Darrah Kelley, were especially powerful models of active, progressive, and effective political involvement. Florence Kelley's mother, Catherine Bonsall, had been orphaned in 1838 and adopted by Isaac and Elizabeth Kay Pugh, Quakers of Germantown, Pennsylvania, near Philadelphia. Florence considered them her grandparents. Sarah Pugh, Isaac's sister, lived with her brother and his family and had considerable influence over Kelley as a young girl. A Quaker schoolteacher, Sarah was active in the Female Anti-Slavery Society, founded by her close friend, Lucretia Mott. Representing the Pennsylvania branch of the society at the World Anti-Slavery Convention in London in 1840, Sarah, together with the other female delegates, was forced to sit in a gender-segregated gallery, to be joined in protest later by an angry William Lloyd Garrison. Like many other abolitionist women, Sarah Pugh was also a supporter of women's rights and a friend of Susan B. Anthony. As late as her seventy-fourth year, she led a successful petition drive to persuade the Pennsylvania state legislature not to legalize prostitution. Florence Kelley's longstanding support of women's suffrage and her membership in the NAACP can be understood in part as reflections of her great-aunt's influence.[34]

Florence Kelley's father provided her with another model for progressive reform. William Kelley's life is something of a rags-to-riches story. Shortly after he was born in 1814, his father died, forcing William's mother to open a boardinghouse to support the family. As in many families that could not afford to have their children continue formal education, William quit school at the age of eleven to apprentice as a jeweler, following in his father's footsteps. After practicing his trade in Boston, he returned to Philadelphia and began a career in politics. He read law, was admitted to the bar in 1841, and became increasingly active in local Democratic Party politics. By 1844, he was appointed a local prosecutor, and by 1847, he was a local trial judge. In 1854, he left the Democratic Party in protest over its support of the Kansas-Nebraska Act, which he and many others saw as a sellout to the interests of slavery. He returned briefly to the practice of law and soon became actively involved in the newly formed Republican Party. In 1860, as a strong supporter of Abraham Lincoln's bid for the presidency, he ran for and was elected to Congress. He served there for the next thirty years, championing many progressive causes.[35]

Florence Kelley took a formative trip with her father in 1871. That autumn, William Kelley took his then twelve-year-old daughter with him to the Alleghenies in western Pennsylvania to introduce Florence "to the romance of industrialization as manifested in the iron and steel industry." He took her first to see the newly introduced Bessemer steel-making process in action. She later recounted that they arrived at the mill at "nearly two o'clock in the morning, the first time I had ever consciously been awake at that hour, when the steel was turned out into the molds." She found this to be a "terrifying sight" replete with the "presence and activity of boys smaller than myself—and I was barely twelve years old"—darting about in the fitful light and flaming heat, "carrying heavy pails of water and tin dippers, from which the men drank eagerly." She vividly recalled that the focus of everyone else's attention was on industrial production and that "the little boys were not more important than so many grains of sand in the molds."[36]

A few weeks later, her father took her to visit a glass factory near Pittsburgh. Again, this was a night visit, and "[t]he only light was the glare from the furnaces."[37] While the two industrial processes she had viewed seemed similar to the twelve-year-old, she was struck by the fact that the number of boys in the glass factory was far greater than in the steel mill. In front of each furnace stood a glass blower with his long blowpipe, and around each blower were his "dogs," as Kelley remembered the boys were called. She later described how the mold-holding boy sitting right in front of the blower had to take "the blower's mold the instant the bottle or tumbler was

"Blower and Mold Boy, Seneca Glass Works." Morgantown,
West Virginia, October 1908

removed from it, scrape it and replace it perfectly smooth and clean for the next bottle or tumbler which the blower was already shaping in his pipe." This visit confirmed her "astonished impression of the utter unimportance of children compared with products, in the minds of the people whom I am among."[38] These images of the small glass house boys working at night in Pittsburgh would stay with Kelley for the rest of her life.

By providing the young Kelley with a firsthand, unvarnished glimpse of late-nineteenth-century American industrial power, William Kelley gave his daughter, perhaps inadvertently, a core of material experiences around which to focus what would become a burning, lifelong desire for social change. He also provided her with the power to act on that desire by encouraging her to go to college. Such an education was seen as crucial for middle-class men and women concerned about the course of social change. Education increased their ability to influence public policy, to process new forms of information, to create new modes of communication, and to devise new answers to social problems. With such tools, they might hope to counterbalance the fact that they lacked control of an economy dominated by industrial capitalists, were unable to directly master chaotic urban growth, or were often stymied by a legislative process dominated by male voters, by male politicians, and by male-controlled party machines. With her father's encouragement, Kelley matriculated in 1876 to Cornell University, where she excelled. Her senior thesis, "On Some Changes in the Legal Status of the Child since Blackstone," was both a reflection of her maturing social conscience and a sign of her interest in the role of law in shaping the lived experience of childhood. After graduating in 1882, with honors, she applied to the University of Pennsylvania for graduate school, intending to study law. The university, however, felt differently and denied her application because, as it told her in the rejection letter, it found the prospect of men and women taking classes together "abhorrent."[39]

Rejected by the University of Pennsylvania, Kelley began her turn to activism, joining the Philadelphia New Century Club, a women's organization founded in 1877 by a family friend. The club, formed by women who had been active in the antebellum antislavery movement, attracted many middle-class women to its social activist program. Kelley established a very successful evening school for working girls and women under the club's auspices and taught there for two years. In addition, she established the

"Night Scene[,] Cumberland Glass Works." Bridgeton, New Jersey, November 1909

New Century Working Women's Guild, which proved to be "one of the most progressive societies for women in the United States in the 1880s." But her budding activism was cut short when her older brother, Will, became ill in 1884, and the family called on Florence to accompany him to Europe to try to nurse him back to health. The strategy worked, and he began to stabilize and recover. Within a year, Florence had enrolled in the University of Zurich to begin graduate study in government. There, her politics took a somewhat more radical turn. Most of the female students at the university were in the medical school, and many of them were Russian. She cultivated friendships among this group of women, who introduced her to German socialism. She met and married Lazare Wischnewetsky, a Russian medical student who also attended the university and, with Lazare, joined the Socialist Party of Zurich. They had their first child and Florence began an

Child Labor Reforms and the NCLC   25

English translation of Frederick Engels's *The Condition of the Working Class in England* in 1844. Her translation, completed in 1887, remained the only English version of the work until 1958. While she worked on the translation, she began what would become nearly a lifelong correspondence with Engels.[40]

In 1886, Florence, Lazare, and their son moved to New York City, where they had two more children as Lazare tried to establish a medical practice, without success. In financial trouble and with three small children, Florence continually sought help, financial and otherwise, from her own family. But mounting money troubles led to conflicts, and the marriage began to fall apart. As Sklar notes, by "early January 1891, the couple's quarrels had erupted into physical violence."[41] Florence took the three children with her to Chicago, in a state that had more liberal divorce laws than New York, and succeeded in formally ending the marriage. In Chicago she and her children took up residence in Jane Addams's Hull House, where she would later recall being "welcomed as if [she] had been invited." She remained a resident at Hull House for "seven, happy, active years."[42]

While living in Chicago, Kelley was able to focus her commitment to social justice, especially for women and children, into an effective, practical political ideology. Working with the newly elected reform governor of Illinois, John Altgeld, she helped develop the most progressive child labor law in the state's history and one of the most progressive in the country. She was buoyed by the fact that it passed into law with "suspiciously little opposition in the press or the legislature."[43] The law included as one of its principal features the creation of the position of factory inspector. With the law's enactment in 1893, Kelley accepted Governor Altgeld's offer to be the state's first chief factory inspector, a position she would hold for nearly four years. In the midst of this activity, Kelley earned her law degree from Northwestern University in 1894, crediting her accomplishment to "my reading law with Father in Washington in 1882, my study in Zurich, [in addition to the] one year in the senior class in Chicago." Rather conscientiously, she also noted that because the law lectures were given in the evening, they did not interfere with her administrative work as chief factory inspector.[44]

During her tenure as the Illinois factory inspector, Kelley "unrelentingly prosecuted employers of child labor, obtaining convictions against tailors, bakers, meatpackers, and makers of cigars, candy, shoes, pails, pickles, rattan items, electrical machinery, paper boxes, cutlery, baking powder, chemicals, sewing machines, and chairs." In 1895, Kelley launched an attack on the child labor practices of the Illinois Glass Company in Alton, Illinois, then the "state's single largest employer of children." In her 1895 assessment of the glass industry, she remarked, "The sustained speed required of the children and the heated atmosphere rendered continuous trotting most exhausting ... but these little lads trotted hour after hour, day after day, month after month in the heat and dust." Sklar notes that "chronic illness, frequent night work, serious burns, and illiteracy prevented the glass house boys from being self-supporting in later life, ruining them (as Kelley reported) 'in body and mind before they entered upon the long adolescence known to happier children.'"[45] Because of this campaign, a local Alton newspaper castigated her in language that highlighted the way industrial interests and their apologists condescended to female reformers. The newspaper complained that "Mrs. Florence Kelley ... seems to be as arbitrary and unreasoning as any other woman with an alleged mission." During her tenure as chief factory inspector, she sued many employers in court, prosecuting 542 violations of the child labor law in 1895 and another 520 in 1896. In November 1896, however, the Republicans swept the state elections. Governor Altgeld lost to an opponent of reform, and Kelley was quickly replaced as the state's factory inspector. The new inspector was a man who had been on the payroll of the Illinois Glass Company for twenty-seven years.[46]

In 1899, Florence Kelley and her children moved to New York, where she become the general secretary for the newly created National Consumers' League. Under her leadership, the NCL would become one of the premiere progressive organizations in the nation, active in the fight to improve the political and economic rights of women and children. While in New York, she took up residence in Lillian D. Wald's Henry Street settlement house, and she and Wald became lifelong friends and allies in progressive causes. Kelley's NCL office was in the Charities Building at Twenty-second Street and Fourth Avenue, the same building that would house a number of other progressive agencies over the next several years, including the Charity Organization Society (which spearheaded *The Pittsburgh Survey*), headed by Edward T. Devine; the National Child Labor Committee, which Kelley helped found and which would be headed by Samuel McCune Lindsay and Owen Lovejoy; the New York Child Labor Committee led by George

Hall; the publication *Charities*, edited by Arthur Kellogg and Paul Kellogg; and the American Association for Labor Legislation, with John R. Commons at the helm.

This was an intensely synergistic environment, and Kelley both influenced and was influenced by each of these other progressive organizations. The progressives with whom Kelley came into contact had many interests, but chief among them were the problems associated with industrial child labor. Kelley's motivations as a reformer were multilayered, and she was particularly effective in gathering others together in coalitions to work on a wide range of progressive concerns. This talent was perhaps most evident in her work with the National Child Labor Committee.

The National Child Labor Committee

The National Child Labor Committee did not spring to life ab initio in 1904. Rather, much like the National Consumers' League, with which it was closely associated, the NCLC could trace its origins to the efforts of numerous other reform organizations and countless child labor advocates who had been hard at work around the country over the previous several decades. Although the NCLC did not start the work of child labor reform, the organization came into being in order to provide that effort with a national focus and national leadership. Perhaps the earliest groups to speak out against the practice of industrial child labor, although not initially in conversation with each other, were the voluntary women's associations and the male-dominated industrial trade and craft unions in the middle of the nineteenth century. In the second half of the century, as national unions began to emerge, virtually all of them included "provisions calling for the abolition of child labor" as part of their agendas.[47] These unions were invaluable in working with other progressive groups to realize many child labor reforms, but because they could be seen as having a direct economic interest in the issue, they typically remained in the background, working behind the scenes when legislative or other policy changes were sought. Social welfare and other reform organizations thus took the lead in public for the battle to abolish child labor.

Under Florence Kelley, the National Consumers' League became a leading force in child labor reform. In the spring of 1902, Kelley, as the general secretary for the NCL, worked with her friend, Lillian Wald, as well as with several other progressive activists, including Mary K. Simkovitch, Pauline Goldmark, and Robert Hunter, to form the New York Child Labor Committee to lead the efforts on behalf of child labor reform in the New York area. In addition to these reformers, the charter members of the New York group included such well-established male civic leaders as Felix Adler of Columbia University; James G. Phelps Stokes of the Hartly House Settlement; William H. Baldwin, president of the Long Island Railroad; V. Everit Macy, director of the Title Guarantee & Trust Company; and Paul M. Warburg and Jacob A. Schiff of Kuhn, Loeb, an investment banking company. The New York Child Labor Committee was the second such organization in the country created specifically to advance child labor reform, the first having been organized the prior year in Alabama under the direction of Edgar Gardner Murphy, an Episcopal rector from Montgomery.[48]

Soon after starting the New York Child Labor Committee, Adler, Baldwin, Kelley, and Murphy began work to form a national committee to provide further organization to the growing number of state-level child labor initiatives. On April 15, 1904, they convened the first general meeting of the National Child Labor Committee at Carnegie Hall in New York. Adler presided, explaining to the gathering that the purpose of the NCLC would be to act as "a great moral force for the protection of children." He asserted that the organization's goal was to "combat the danger in which childhood is placed by greed and rapacity." Specifically, Adler contended that because "[c]heap labor means child labor[,] consequently there results a holocaust of the children—a condition which is intolerable." The organizers wished to develop "enlightened public opinion" on the issue of child labor and to work for the passage of state child labor laws.[49] The initial executive committee consisted of several members from the already established New York committee, including Adler, Baldwin, Kelley, Macy, and Warburg, together with Murphy, attorney Robert W. de Forest, Edward T. Devine of the Charity Organization Society, John S. Huyler of the Huyler Candy Company, investment banker Isaac N. Seligman, and John W. Wood. Dr. Samuel McCune Lindsay, a native of Pittsburgh and a faculty member at the University of Pennsylvania, was chosen as the permanent general secretary, and two ministers, Owen R. Lovejoy and Alexander J. McKelway, were selected as assistant secretaries.

Thus, although a set of strong, able women with reform experience, including Lillian Wald, Florence Kelley, Pauline Goldmark, and Jane Addams, were key to the formation of the NCLC, the visible leadership was almost entirely male. Further, the men selected to head up the NCLC came disproportionately from the academic, business, and professional ranks rather than from the activist ranks such as settlement house workers. This was undoubtedly a conscious decision on the part of Kelley and the other founders because they knew from the start that the NCLC was going to be heavily involved in both public persuasion and political lobbying. They were clearly trying to create an official profile that would maximize the organization's credibility and effectiveness. Florence Kelley was, as we have seen, a seasoned veteran of numerous battles to push for progressive labor reform, and she undoubtedly knew the value of having a cadre of prominent men in the high-profile front ranks of any reform organization advocating for change. Whatever the motives, the body of work the NCLC generated during the Progressive Era was formidable. As part of its educative mission, the committee published hundreds of handbills, pamphlets, bulletins, investigative reports, books, and articles as well as numerous speeches and presentations from its annual meetings. Virtually all of these texts addressed problems associated with industrial child labor, and many dealt specifically with the problem of children in the nation's glass houses, especially the bottle factories in western Pennsylvania.

By the spring of 1905, the NCLC was fully operational, with offices in lower Manhattan. Its goals and direction were reaffirmed at its second annual meeting, held in Washington, DC, December 8–9, 1905. The Honorable B. F. Macfarland, a commissioner of the District of Columbia, greeted the gathering and told them that their work was particularly valuable and would benefit not only the country's children but also the nation as a whole. Speaking on behalf of the entire membership and indicating that the emerging notions of sheltered childhood were being fully embraced by the NCLC, he said, "We want the child to have a full childhood." Referring to a theme familiar to most reformers, he asserted that premature entry into factory work had serious negative developmental consequences for the child: "Stunted children make stunted citizens ... [a]nd stunted citizens make a stunted state." Thus, he continued, "[a]ll our material wealth would be dearly purchased at the price of the labor of the children."[50]

Felix Adler addressed the gathering next. He was in many ways characteristic of the articulate, thoughtful, and rhetorically passionate advocates who worked for the early NCLC. In words chosen more to speak to the faithful than to convert the skeptics, he noted that child labor was still on the rise: "It is no luke warm, tepid interest, that brings us here, it is a feeling that we have to strangle a snake that is coiling around the neck of the young child, that we have to abolish a new kind of slavery, that we have got to take action, not only to check a retreating evil, a retreating and diminishing force, but we have got to use every power at our command to prevent the steady increase, the steady and ominous increase of this disastrous and dangerous thing." He concluded that if they were going to succeed, the NCLC needed to make plain to the nation "the necessity of the abolition, the total abolition, of child labor."[51]

Dr. Lindsay, the agency's general secretary, then addressed the group and alluded to the gendered nature of the reform movement for child labor. While he may have recognized the irony of being the male figurehead of a newly formed organization whose board was dominated by other males but that owed much of its existence to the tireless work of numerous women activists, he did not mention it. Nor did he directly state that both he and the other men stood on the shoulders of these female social reformers. He did acknowledge those women by noting that "[b]efore there was a National Child Labor Committee, or any state child labor committees, before there were any committees . . . the women of the country took [up] the matter and throughout most of our states in their numerous organizations we found looming up gradually child labor committees."[52] Implicit in his speech was the assumption that he felt there was something very "natural" about the country's women rising up to defend children and something equally "natural" about the country's men leading that fight when it assumed a national character. Lindsay observed, but did not dwell on, the foundational work of women activists because it was simply an assumed social and political reality, one that could remain hidden in plain view: while women had a certain moral authority to work on behalf of children, men were expected to lead the child-centered progressive organizations.

A different problem, however, confronted the NCLC from the start. All of the principals agreed that one of the committee's main goals would be to fight for child labor legislation, but they did not at all agree on the proper forum, state or federal, where those battles should take place. In 1906, the issue came to a head when a U.S. senator from Indiana, Albert Beveridge, was preparing to introduce federal legislation to ban the interstate shipment of goods produced by child labor. Beveridge naturally asked for the endorsement of the NCLC, but the executive board was deeply split. While many members, including Kelley, Baldwin, Lovejoy, and Adler, were willing to embrace a larger, national approach to eradicating industrial child labor, others, most notably Edgar Murphy, saw a federally imposed cure as potentially worse than the disease. When, after a bitter series of debates, the board voted to support Beveridge's legislation, Murphy, a founding member, quit the NCLC along with several of his southern colleagues. This split reflected deep-seated differences in regionally acceptable approaches to government-sponsored reform.

Initially, this split was more symbolic than actual because for the next several years the NCLC worked almost exclusively on state-level child labor solutions. But as the difficulty in obtaining uniformity among the several states on the issue of child labor reform became more evident, and as Beveridge's efforts began to take legislative shape in the U.S. Congress in the form of the Keatings-Owens Child Labor Bill, the NCLC placed more and more effort into lobbying for a federal solution. As early as 1907, for instance, Jane Addams said that she found it "difficult . . . to understand that the federal government should be willing to spend time and money to establish and maintain departments related to the breeding . . . of cattle, sheep and hogs, and that as yet the federal government has done nothing to see to it that the children are properly protected."[53] The effort to find a national solution to ending child labor, however, was frustrated for some thirty years by the Supreme Court of the United States, until *United States v. Darby Lumber Co.*, when, after the Court had reversed its longstanding narrow interpretation of the U.S. Constitution's "commerce clause," it allowed for federal child labor regulations.[54] In that case, the Court unanimously upheld the constitutionality of the Fair Labor Standards Act of 1938, which included a federal child labor provision. However, because federal action on the child labor issue was effectively unavailable throughout the Progressive Era, the energy expended by the NCLC and other reform organizations seeking national legislative solutions to the problem of child labor was energy diverted from, and therefore a weakening of, state reform efforts.[55]

Internal conflicts notwithstanding, the NCLC recognized that it would have a difficult time eradicating industrial child labor. From a legislative point of view, the state laws were complex and locally specific. There were questions about what minimum age to establish, how it could be certified, which occupations to cover, how to coordinate with the compulsory education laws (and if there were none, how to enact them), how to limit night work, and whether girls and boys should be treated the same. Then, even if a good, progressive law was successfully enacted, it could easily become a dead letter if there were no means established for its effective enforcement. Aside from technical, statutory details, the NCLC realized that any effective ban on child labor also had to be supported by the general public. To address this latter challenge, the NCLC saw a tremendous need to educate the American people about the evils of child labor in order to enlist the political power of their support in the cause. In fact, at least as much of the energy of the NCLC in its first several decades was devoted to educating the public as it was toward direct legislative lobbying. To this end, the NCLC prepared pamphlets, reports, and other documents that focused on the glass industry in general and the western Pennsylvania factories in particular. These publications, discussed in chapter 2, were designed to describe the nature of child labor in the state's factories and to expose the extent to which the state's factory inspectors failed to uncover and prosecute child labor violations.

The NCLC, as the premiere organization fighting for child labor reform during the Progressive Era, brought together a diverse and largely effective coalition of male and female reformers who played important roles in many progressive, state-level, child labor legislative reforms. As we shall see, however, effecting these reforms for the glass house boys of Pittsburgh proved uniquely difficult.

Progressive Reform and Child Labor in the Pennsylvania Glass Industry

It was in the iron mill, stove factory, shovel factory, but especially in the glass-houses that boys were to be found at work in the occupations characteristic of the Pittsburgh District. Big and black as the iron mill might loom in the imagination . . . it was the glass-houses which were suzerain over childhood in the town.

Elizabeth Beardsley Butler

D ESPITE THE health dangers, the low pay, and the abusive working conditions, the late-nineteenth- and early-twentieth-century glass houses seemed to draw young boys into their confines with a power that even Progressive Era reformers characterized as nothing short of magical. As one progressive noted, using the flowery language of a fairy tale that might appeal to a vulnerable, impressionable child, "The molten wax-like glass in the furnace, the skillful twist and turn which prepares the embryonic bottle for the mold, the speed with which the wax bubble is made a thing of use, the white light, red glare, and shifting shadow, the dexterity of the bare-armed men, combine to cast a spell over the gaping youngsters."[1] This environment was special in other respects as well because the lives of these working children straddled two very different spheres, one resting on the outer edges of recently emerging notions of childhood and the other entering into the adult working world of industrial America. Although many glass house boys were not yet fourteen years of age, they worked long hours, they were regularly exposed to alcohol as well as foul and abusive language, and, at least in Pittsburgh, almost all of them worked at night. In their various publications, the progressive reformers very carefully described these conditions in order to persuade the larger public that these particular children were in need of increased protection under state child labor laws.

The child-adult duality was associated with many forms of child labor of the time, but the glass house environment was unusual. Unlike other industrial workplaces employing children, the glass house boys worked side-by-side with the adult glass men; the boys were thus integral, almost equal members of the glass-making team. They were paid as children but worked the same hours and under the same conditions as the adults. The influence of the men on the behaviors and development of these children was substantial. Many investigators reported that after a short time in the glass factory, the glass house "boys" quite naturally began to act very much like the adults with whom they so closely worked. In arguing for reform, however, the progressives made a strategic decision and chose to emphasize the "child" in the glass house boy. In their stories, in their descriptions of the boys' work, and in their arguments concerning the ill effects of glass house employment, the reformers characterized the boys as young, almost delicate, impressionable, and in need of adult protection, protection that, the reformers conceded, all too often the parents of the boys were not providing.[2]

The decision to characterize these young workers as boys was strategic. The progressives wanted to persuade both the public and the state policy makers that these children, these glass house boys, were not adults, not yet "responsible" for themselves, and thus were desperately in need of legal protection. That protection, they argued, should be child labor laws to prevent these children from working at night until they were at least sixteen years of age. It would be easier, the progressives reasoned, to persuade people that these boys needed this protection if they could still be seen as children in the sense of being physically and emotionally vulnerable and thus potentially responsive to the positive effects of nurturing and education. If, on the other hand, the boys were seen primarily as already hardened adults, the job of passing child labor legislation would be much more difficult. With this in mind, the progressives carefully constructed an image of the glass house boy as a "child" and used the language of newly emerging cultural ideals to serve the needs of reform.

Determining who and what a child was, of course, was and perhaps still is a tricky business. Legal, biological, and social/cultural standards can change over time, some of which lead to different conclusions and many of which can operate simultaneously and even contradictorily. The law may define the age of majority, that is the age at which a person attains all adult rights and responsibilities, as twenty-one (as was the case during most of the Progressive Era), but it may also allow that same person to marry at the age of eighteen. A boy of fifteen who is financially independent and emancipated from parental supervision may act and be treated in many respects like an adult, while a college student of twenty may engage in behaviors much more characteristic of a child and may even be protected as such under doctrines such as *in loco parentis*. Child labor reformers of the Progressive Era tried to avoid the ambiguities and pitfalls of these shifting legal and cultural definitions of childhood. They sought to stabilize the moving target of what a "child" was by couching their arguments for child labor reform in terms of specific ages. They uniformly lobbied for state laws, for example, that would prohibit any child under sixteen years of age from working at night and any under fourteen from working at all.

In order to have these legal reforms accepted, however, the reformers knew that the general population would need to accept the underlying notions of childhood upon which the age standards were based. The reformers were attempting to extend to working-class boys through law the protections afforded to middle- and upper-class children through economic privilege. Their efforts were thus potentially in conflict not only with longstanding ideas about the value of work for children but also with the economic circumstances of working-class children and their parents.

For much of the nineteenth century, the nearly unchallenged view was that most children should work. Such work was seen as beneficial not only for reasons related to the family economy but also because it was generally believed that children needed to learn how to earn a livelihood early in life, both for their own good and so as not to become a burden on their community. Idle children were seen as more likely to cause trouble for themselves and others as well.[3] A sheltered and protected childhood was a luxury available primarily to the wealthy and upper classes, whose children rarely needed to work. Thus, these families could afford to shelter their children. As the nineteenth century progressed, however, the growth in the national economy (evidenced by the increasing number of merchants, lawyers, and other professionals occupying new positions generated by industrialization) freed women and children of the expanding middle classes from the necessity of engaging in paid work. Urban middle-class mothers, because they no longer had to work outside the home, began to devote themselves largely if not exclusively to the responsibilities of child rearing and household management. That their children could also remain outside the work force came to be seen not only as a sign of the economic well-being of the family but also as necessary for proper moral development.

These ideas about sheltered childhood also drew on older cultural concepts derived from Enlightenment ideals and Protestant beliefs that considered children as possessing "innocent" souls and assigned parents the responsibility of turning their souls toward God.[4] Children were no longer seen as simply small adults but as nascent individuals requiring protection and direction if they were to develop to their fullest potential.

Attempts to purify the environments of the young, and to limit and/or reorganize their networks of association, were made manifest in a stunning effusion of new reform sentiments, strategies, and structural rearrangements of childhood experience between 1830 and 1870. An almost obsessive attention to sources of moral corruption appears to have inspired a preoccupation with the means of moral education during that period. The commitment to purity involved the promotion both of women as proper guardians of moral sensibility in the young and of families as moral refuges from the corrupting influences of strangers and workplaces. It united a co-alition of physicians, ministers, and middle-class women.[5] Children, it was felt, simply could not be allowed to partake freely of their surroundings. Not only did they need to be removed from the industrial workplace but they also needed supervision by and guidance from caring adults. And if working-class parents could not be relied on to provide the proper "sheltered" environment for their children, then the progressives were not opposed to marshaling the force of the law to do so in their stead.

The ideal of the economically worthless but emotionally priceless child, extending beyond the upper classes, thus began to take shape.[6] Many of the social programs of Progressive Era reformers, including the movement to strictly regulate industrial child labor, were an important part of the process of extending the ideal of sheltered childhood to all children, even those of the nation's poorest working-class families. All children, the progressives believed, should be sheltered from the pressures and influences of the outside world, be freed from the responsibility of augmenting the family economy, and should receive the benefits of both home-centered and formal education.[7]

The Pittsburgh Survey and the Glass House Boys

A Progressive Era portrait of the Pittsburgh glass house boys, constructed with these ideals of childhood in mind, was sketched by Elizabeth Beardsley Butler. In 1907–1908, Butler investigated the life of working-class children in Sharpsburg, Pennsylvania, a small borough immediately east of Pittsburgh along the Allegheny River.[8] As noted earlier, Butler, together with Florence Kelley and John R. Commons, among others, helped prepare The Pittsburgh Survey. Butler's analysis of the Sharpsburg glass house boys appeared in Wage-Earning Pittsburgh, one of the six published volumes that made up the Survey.

As with much of the rest of the Survey, Butler's writing contains very little in the way of fiery rhetoric.[9] Rather, she depends on seemingly straight-forward descriptions. Butler spent the winter in Sharpsburg developing a multilayered portrait of what it was like for these particular children to grow up in what was then the heart of industrial America. At that time, few would have characterized the environment around Pittsburgh as either visually aesthetic or healthful.[10] In 1868, James Parton, the American author and biographer, after seeing Pittsburgh's factory-strewn landscape at night with the steel mills all ablaze, offered the now familiar observation that it looked like "hell with the lid taken off."[11] Only a few years earlier, the British novelist Anthony Trollope, on an American tour, similarly described Pittsburgh's industrial landscape as "without a doubt the blackest place which I ever saw."[12]

Although *The Pittsburgh Survey* was prepared some forty years after these observations, not much had changed. Butler, working in the midst of this sooty tumult, produced what amounts to an ethnographic analysis of the societal effects of industrialization, nearly a half century before such ethnographies became common. Her portrait of the glass house boys, while by no means disinterested, follows the spare, research-based style typical of *The Pittsburgh Survey*. In conducting her research, she talked with residents, met with school and public officials, and questioned factory owners. She investigated the quality of housing, the availability of health services, and the life of work and play experienced by the children of this small, working-class, urban community. She prepared what anthropologists would now call a "thick description" of one type of childhood. Her descriptions of the lives of the glass house boys are particularly instructive, designed as they are to present a sympathetic and compelling portrait of children in need of, and who should have had the advantages of, protection.

Take, for example, "John C.," who was fifteen years old at the time of the interviews. Butler used only first names and initials for living children in an attempt to preserve a modicum of privacy for them and their families. She observed that John "had first gone to the parochial school, then to the public school as far as grade two. At the age of eight he had gone to work first in one glass-house, then another; then in a shovel factory, and again in a glass-house." A glass house clerk at John's latest place of employment observed, "He's a hard one, . . . he's learned it all in his fifteen years. The boys work for two or three days, then loaf; then come back and work awhile. Friday nights half the boys don't go home at all; they hang around [the glass factory] until the next morning. What becomes of them, do you say, by the time they are twenty-two or twenty-three? The workhouse. They are no good to us anymore."[13]

In many of the country's glass-producing areas, especially those located away from larger industrial cities, the supply of glass house boys could be very limited. But Pittsburgh was different. Many of the city's working-class families were recent immigrants, drawn to the United States by the promise of economic opportunity offered under the expansive umbrella of industrialization. But because this promise was honored more often in the breach than the observance, many of these families had to send their children to work at early ages to augment the family income. Because the glass houses in Pittsburgh offered ready employment for legions of un-skilled male children, even as young as nine or ten, many child workers became glass house boys. The vast majority of these glass house boys had little or no formal schooling, virtually all worked both day and night shifts, extremely few earned even a dollar a day, and, because of union rules, virtu-ally all of them were effectively prohibited from progressing to any of the higher-paying skilled glass-making positions available in those same glass factories. The pace of work was always relentless; the factory conditions were usually dangerous; the adult glass men were often abusive. Regard-less, the Pittsburgh glass houses rarely had difficulty filling the "boy" posi-tions.

The ready supply of boys acted to depress their already meager wages and provided some elasticity in their employment. As such, the boys' work in the glass houses could be either very regular or sporadic. The boys were largely fungible goods from the perspective of the factory owners, who would tend to hire the help they needed from the pool of boys who hap-pened to show up at the start of the shift. Some boys, either because of their own initiative or because of their reputation for dependable work, would be hired very regularly. These boys, especially if they agreed to work both day and night shifts, could expect to work for six days, and up to fifty hours, each week. Others, however, could easily drift in and out of the glass house labor force, working when they or their families needed the money and "loafing" when they did not.

Although child workers in many industries at the time might expect to stay employed in that industry for a substantial part of their adult working life, such stability was not the case in the glass houses. The only link between the boy positions in the glass factories and the skilled adult glass-worker jobs was the apprenticeship system, and the unions exercised tight control over the number of apprentices. While the number of these slots varied depending on the specific items being produced and the general economic conditions of the time, typically there was only one apprentice for every ten to twenty-five journeyman glass blowers. Either officially or unofficially, the glass blowers' sons had the inside track for these admittedly scarce apprenticeships, even though these same sons rarely if ever worked as glass house boys. This made the prospects for advancement from a boy job to an apprentice position fairly bleak indeed.[14]

If, as was entirely likely, a glass house boy did not become an apprentice, as he became older his only options were to remain in the glass house in one of the boy positions, as long as there was work, or to leave and find work in another industry. A number of the glass house boys continued to work at "boy" positions well into their late teens and beyond, but because their value to the owners did not appreciably change just because they happened to be older; they still earned "boy" wages. Butler tells of one such "boy," described to her by a glass factory manager as one who at "seventeen had worked at intervals for five years in a glass-house." This particular boy had gone to a parochial school for a while but had never progressed beyond one of the "lower grades." At seventeen years of age he was still a glass house "boy" earning just ninety cents a day. "He'll never amount to anything," the manager told Butler. "He's no good."[15]

With such a limited future in the glass houses, many of the boys left by their late teens, although their prospects for employment outside the glass factories were hardly bright either. Working, as many boys did, between forty and fifty hours per week in the glass house from the age of twelve or younger, they had lost any chance either to complete what formal schooling might be available or to learn an adult trade in another industry and move up in that industry's hierarchy of jobs.[16] The "skills" they had learned as glass house boys, such as the ability to carry trays of hot glass bottles, to open and close a bottle mold on command, or to clean off the end of a blowpipe, were not particularly transferable to other industrial employments. Further, the intermittent work habits engaged in by many of the glass house boys were less likely to be tolerated in other jobs. All the glass house boy could realistically look forward to upon leaving the glass plant was to remain an unskilled laborer or start some new trade from the bottom of the ladder, or, as prophesied by Butler's glass house clerk, end up in the workhouse.[17]

As evidenced in Butler's descriptions of the boys, schooling and work were often in conflict, with both the boys and their parents favoring work over school. Although some children managed to stay in school while working, most of those who worked did not. The Pennsylvania child labor and compulsory education laws in force at the time nominally required that all children under fourteen be in school. Children between fourteen and sixteen could leave school to go to work, but only if they had a valid permit or certificate attesting to both their age and the fact that they could read and write the English language.[18] For most employments, boys sixteen and over were considered adults, at least as far as these special labor and education regulations were concerned. Working children fell under the jurisdiction of both the state factory inspector, charged with enforcing the full array of state labor and workplace safety laws, and local school officials, charged with enforcing the attendance laws. Enforcement of child protective legislation, however, in Pennsylvania as elsewhere, was cursory at best. Factory inspectors were notorious for their failure to enforce child labor laws vigorously, and school officials, at least in the Pittsburgh district, were not much better. When Butler talked with the Sharpsburg school officers, she found that they made very little effort to find children who should have been, but were not, attending classes; the exception was children who were already enrolled in school. Of those actually enrolled in the Sharpsburg schools, the district officials managed to keep up to 95 percent in attendance. When Butler asked how many eligible children were in the district but not enrolled in school, "the educational authorities," she reported, simply "did not know."[19]

Butler found that, for most of the glass house boys, the permits or certificates "required" for them to work proved to be no obstacle at all. The boys and their families found it easy to either satisfy or circumvent the requirements of the law. Satisfying the requirement for the age certificate, for example, required only the word of the parent and occasionally only that of the child. And, as Butler suggests, enforcement of even these minimal standards was lax. Given this, it was not surprising that Butler found many boys as young as ten or twelve working in the glass factories in direct violation of state law. Robert B., for instance, was eleven years old when Butler interviewed his family. She found that he had worked in a nearby glass factory "nearly every Friday and Saturday for a year past," and his family said that "20 others" of similar age "were doing the same." None of these boys had age certificates. A Polish mother whose ten-year-old son worked in a glass factory told Butler quite frankly that she "had never heard of a certificate or legal working age." Neither the state factory inspector nor any school official had ever informed her of such. Another underage glass house boy, Charlie L., who at thirteen "was one of the older sons in a family of nine . . . had stopped going to school in grade one, and had worked seven years" in the glass factory, all without being detected by the authorities. Then there was John V., "twelve years old, an Italian boy who . . . had been working in the . . . [glass] factory [next to his house] for a year." When his mother took him to a notary to get his age certificate, the notary refused to issue it because the boy was not yet fourteen. Undeterred, she simply sent him to work without one rather than have him go to school. No school or state official intervened.[20]

The literacy certification was not difficult to avoid or satisfy either. When, for example, under earlier statutes, the law allowed these certificates to be issued by a notary public, the glass houses routinely kept notaries on staff who issued the certificate as a matter of course upon the request of a boy or his parents. When the law was strengthened to require a more disinterested issuing officer, these new officers were willing to approve the certificate on very minimal evidence. As explained to Butler by one glass factory manager, if "you talk to these little Italian chaps[,] they're the brightest fellows I have. One came here the other day and couldn't write his name, and I told him he'd have to learn how or the factory inspector would turn him out. Well, if he didn't go home and practice over night, and the next morning he could write his name well enough to pass anywhere." As with the age requirements, if the literacy certificate could not be obtained, most of the time the children worked anyway without legal penalty.[21]

While glass house work was perhaps not as dangerous as some other industrial employments, Butler's report confirmed that it was nonetheless demanding and not without risk. In Pittsburgh, most glass houses operated around the clock, and those boys willing to work both the day and night shifts with the men were given preference. The floor of the glass house furnace room was typically strewn with broken glass, and those rooms were extremely hot in summer and often drafty in winter. The boys were invariably poor, and many worked barefoot, suffering innumerable cuts on their feet. Danger also came from the "blow over," the fine glass dust that continuously floated in the air and would "lodge in the eyes and nostrils of men and boys, causing great pain." The boys working in the furnace rooms also risked dehydration in the hundred-degree heat.[22] While water was "the most common replacement fluid, . . . reports note that in many workshops, beer was the replacement fluid of choice."[23] Further, as a result of the extremes in temperature between the factory interior and exterior, especially in winter, the boys tended to suffer from a variety of respiratory illnesses. In summer, the intensity of the heat was such that virtually all glass houses closed for July and August. The heat affected all workers, but the pace of the boys' work added additional strain. Finally, because the skilled adult glass workers were usually paid by the piece and thus had to rely on the speed of the boys for their earnings, they were particularly demanding. To facilitate production, for instance, the mold-holding boy usually had to sit in a stooped position by the blower's feet for his entire shift. As a result, many boys developed a slightly stooped posture that followed them into adulthood. The carrying-in boys had to run back and forth constantly with trays of hot glass in the often cramped factory space; even the slightest misstep could be costly.

These conditions were not conducive to good health for men or boys, but the health effects were most serious for the young. Butler reported on one boy, Willie App, who in July 1907, at the age of fourteen, "died of rheumatism of the heart." He had worked in a local glass house both day and night for a year and a half, and she noted that while "his death may not have been due wholly to the conditions of his work, his physician was confident that it was hastened by them."[24] Or take the case of Roy H., whose bad eyesight and resultant headaches had forced him "away from his studies at eleven years of age, and the family council had put him into the glasshouse." Roy could no longer read but his family, in Butler's words, "had never had his eyes examined nor done anything except put him to work." Butler's phrasing implies that his family had a realistic choice to make, al-

"Three years in the Glass House and no chance of promotion yet. Boy in foreground
[has] been 'carry-in' since he was 14 years old. Wormser's Glass House."
Pittsburgh, Pennsylvania, January 1913

though if asked, the family might well have disagreed. Other families, like
that of fifteen-year-old Frank S., relied on the kindness of strangers to look
out for their children. Frank, Butler learned, had had epilepsy from the age
of ten. When Frank was thirteen, a physician had told the family he should
leave school, and he was immediately put to work in a glass factory. When
questioned about the possible danger, his mother replied, "Oh, the men
look after him and see that he doesn't hurt himself."[25]

One of the primary aims of Butler's contribution to *The Pittsburgh Survey* was to help persuade policy makers, legislators, and even the general
public of the need for improving child labor regulations for the benefit
of the Pittsburgh glass house boys. To accomplish this goal, Butler recounted story after story describing these boys as vulnerable children who
suffered from their work in the Pittsburgh glass houses. The persuasive-

ness of her stories depended on her audiences' sympathy for the children of these poor working-class families and the public's perception that such children should be afforded a sheltered and protected childhood. Through her stories she hoped to make the boys compelling and worthy objects for progressive reform legislation. Unfortunately, there was a gap between the image of the boys created by the rhetoric of reformers such as Butler and the image of the boys in the minds of their families. It may have been, as the reformers described, the "magical allure" of the glass houses that kept these impressionable boys coming to the furnace rooms to work, but it was also economic necessity. For most of the families of the glass house boys, the economic realities were clear. These families felt that they needed all of the income that all of their members, children and adults alike, were able to earn. Time and again the glass house boys and their parents demonstrated a willingness to evade the law or exploit its loopholes to enable the boys to continue to work. In so doing, these children and their families were exercising a type of class-driven agency. By taking advantage of the "flexibility" in enforcement and gaps in the structure of the law, the families rather easily managed to have the boys fully, even if quite illegally, employed in spite of the existing child labor regulations.

The Problem of Factory Inspection in Pennsylvania

In Pennsylvania, as in other states, the job of enforcing child labor laws typically fell on the shoulders of a designated factory inspector. Progressive reformers became increasingly aware that even the strongest law could become a dead letter in the hands of a weak, reluctant, or corrupt inspector. Even an inspector committed to the full and effective enforcement of the state's child labor laws faced serious obstacles. First, child labor laws were but one of a growing list of progressive industrial reform measures that came under the factory inspector's jurisdiction. In Pennsylvania, for example, the factory inspector oversaw fire, safety, wage equity, and even elevator safety regulations in addition to child labor concerns. Second, considering the breadth of the inspector's charge, many inspection departments were seriously understaffed and underfunded. During the period covered by this study, for example, in spite of the fact that western Pennsylvania ranked among the nation's, if not the world's, leading industrial centers, it never had more than five factory inspectors assigned to the region. Third, the heads of many if not all factory inspection departments served at the pleasure of the state's governor. Thus, both the technical qualifications and enforcement efforts of the inspectors were subject to political influence. Finally, while all state child labor laws set some minimum age or educational requirements for employment, not all required that they be supported by an independent authenticating certificate.[26] If no certificate was legally required, the inspector was severely hampered in any effort to enforce the age restrictions. Even where certificates were required, as in Pennsylvania, depending on who was empowered to issue them and what documentation was required, the certification process, as evidenced in Butler's contribution to *The Pittsburgh Survey*, was also subject to abuse.

Glass factories presented yet additional difficulties for factory inspectors. In many locations, particularly older glass centers such as western Pennsylvania, the glass industry tended to be made up of a multitude of small, separate factories. In the Pittsburgh district, for example, at the start of the twentieth century, there may have been more than one hundred operational glass houses at any one time. With no more than five inspectors assigned to the area, each charged with enforcing the full range of factory laws against every existing employer, inspecting the glass houses for child labor violations was almost impossible. In other states, where glass production typically occurred in fewer, but larger, factories, a different set of inspection challenges existed. Alton, Illinois, for example, had the Illinois Glass Company, reportedly the single largest glass factory in the world. Edgar T. Davis, the Illinois chief factory inspector, told the National Child Labor Committee in 1906 that the prospect of an unannounced or surprise visit to the Alton plant was simply not possible. The moment an inspector entered town, he told the gathered committee members, the factory knew about it: "Should an inspector pass a saloon or any of the stores [in Alton], someone telephones [the glass factory]; if you stop at a hotel the glass companies' officials knew." Because the Illinois Glass Company plant covered "many acres," he explained, "they have a complete telephone system . . . [and t]his great piece of territory is all fenced in with a huge fence surmounted with barbed wire; two gates for the inspector to get in and lots of holes for the kids to get out."[27] The factory could thus easily hide anything it did not want even a diligent inspector to find.

The factory inspector in Pennsylvania thus faced a considerable challenge. In 1889, when the state created the office of factory inspector, the concept of an inspector as the chief enforcement agent for a set of regulatory laws was not entirely new in Pennsylvania. Four years earlier the state had established a similar office of inspector to enforce laws related to anthracite and bituminous coal mining.[28] With the 1889 legislation, the state set its new factory inspector's salary at fifteen hundred dollars per year. The inspector was authorized to hire up to six deputies for the entire state, "one-half of whom shall be females," at an annual salary of one thousand dollars each.[29] The factory inspectors were "empowered to visit and inspect, at all reasonable hours and as often as practicable, the factories, workshops and other establishments in the State employing women and children ... [and] to enforce the provisions of this [child labor] act and to prosecute all violations of the same before any magistrate or any court of competent jurisdiction in the State."[30]

The legislative history behind the 1889 law is instructive, as was the actual operation of the office. The law was introduced in the Pennsylvania Senate on January 24, 1889, and committed to the Committee on Corporations. When the bill came up for consideration on the Senate floor, its three required readings yielded barely a comment, criticism, or alteration from any of the senators.[31] The text of the bill under consideration by the Senate, as recorded in that body's official journal, was virtually identical to the enacted law except that the Senate version included section 14, which expressly empowered county district attorneys (in addition to the factory inspector) to sue any violators of the state's child labor and factory laws. The potential effectiveness of the factory inspector law would have been substantially strengthened with the addition of so many possible enforcers. On March 12, by a 37-to-0 vote, the Senate approved the bill, including section 14, and sent it over to the House chamber.[32]

On March 22, the bill was introduced into the Pennsylvania House of Representatives and sent to the Committee on Manufactures. After being approved on its first reading, the bill returned to the House on April 18 for its second reading; as usual, it was read to the representatives and voted on, section by section. Three items are of interest. First, Representative C. Harry Fletcher of Philadelphia tried twice to insert a type of whistle-blower protection clause into the law, but to no avail. His unsuccessful amendment would have provided that "any person ... shall have the right ... without danger of publicity, to report ... any violation ... of this ... act."[33] Second, Representative John M. Rose of Cambria County complained at some length (but never offered any specific amendment) that the bill gave too much discretionary power to the factory inspector. Third, on second reading the bill still included section 14, as it had when approved by the Senate. The comments recorded in the House journal for the second reading, together with the attempted amendments, indicate that the legislators knew full well that they were creating a potentially powerful office.

While some legislators, like Representative Rose, may have been concerned that the proposed inspector might go on a rampage against the state's factory owners, the office also had its supporters. Representative Henry Hall (Mercer County), for example, quickly responded to the concerns expressed by colleagues such as Rose, asking rhetorically, "Is it not reasonable to suppose that the Governor will exercise his reason and judgment in selecting a proper person for this position? Will he not endeavor to find a man suited for the position and who will exercise the power vested in him with prudence and common sense?"[34] That said, the remainder of the bill was fully approved without further comment and scheduled for its third and final reading two weeks later.

The final action by the House on the factory inspector bill was uneventful except for the insight it provides on the power of committees in the Pennsylvania legislature of the time. As alluded to earlier, the only part of the final law that significantly differed from the bill approved by the Senate was section 14, which expressly allowed the county-level district attorneys of the state to prosecute violators of the law. This section had been in the bill from its inception in the Senate and had received the positive vote of both legislative houses, without any negative or qualifying comments of record, during every prior reading. Yet, when the bill arrived for final House action on May 2, 1889, this section was marked for deletion by action of the House Committee on Manufactures. Perhaps even more interesting, this unexplained, committee-generated deletion generated not a ripple of concern among those state representatives present and voting. The House approved the bill, with section 14 deleted, by a 107-to-18 vote, without a single recorded comment, even though the deletion of section 14 seriously compromised the enforcement potential of the factory inspector law.[35]

Progressive Reform and Child Labor   49

The creation of the position of factory inspector with the express (and now sole) authority to enforce the ever-increasing array of child labor and safety regulations was an important chapter in the story of progressive reform in Pennsylvania. The general fear of possible abuse of discretion was misplaced. The inspectors were rarely zealous in carrying out their duties, using discretion more often than prosecution to "enforce" the regulations. Especially after 1903, the factory inspector in Pennsylvania acquired a national reputation for, at best, nonchalant enforcement of the state's child labor laws and, at worst, active obstructionism. As a detailed analysis of the history of the actual operations of the factory inspection department shows, the inspector, it turned out, very consciously exercised his discretion *not* to enforce the law.

Beginning in 1889, the statute called for the factory inspector to submit an annual report on the activities of his department. The first two such reports went to the relatively obscure Pennsylvania Bureau of Industrial Statistics. In recognition of their potential political significance, however, all subsequent reports, at least during the period under study here, went directly to the governor. This redirection also made sense because the factory inspector was a direct gubernatorial appointee. Inspectors remained in office at the pleasure of the governor, and no other executive or legislative bureau or department had any oversight function regarding their work. The content of the factory inspectors' reports gives some insight into the operations of the office in general and its impact on the Pittsburgh glass houses in particular.

The first factory inspector, William H. Martins, submitted a 138-page report on June 1, 1891, for the period ending November 30, 1890—the first full year of departmental operations. He noted a total of 2,087 inspections, covering about 30,437 child workers under the age of sixteen, with 264 underage worker violations being discovered. Despite this substantial violation rate, he stated that "I take pleasure in saying that we have not been compelled to take a single case into court and but two arrests have been made." The first was a neckwear manufacturer who simply attempted to bar the inspector from entering his factory. The second case "was a firm in the city of Pittsburgh engaged in the manufacture of glass," and here the charges were the employment of children under twelve years of age. A footnote in the report indicates that this second arrest led to a trial the following year, which resulted in a courtroom victory for the department. Martins also notes that he hired two deputy inspectors for the Pittsburgh district: Mr. M. N. Baker, stationed in Corry, Pennsylvania, and Mrs. Nan Y. Leslie in Titusville, each more than seventy-five miles from Pittsburgh.[36]

Over the next dozen years, these reports grew in size from the initial 138 pages to more than 1,200 pages in 1902. They all followed a similar organizational pattern, with two principal sections. The first was a narrative from the chief factory inspector, supplemented occasionally with narratives from deputies, generally describing their activities, together with a listing of the relevant statutes and any interpretive rulings or letters from, for example, the state attorney general. The second section consisted of statistical data concerning the factories inspected over the course of the year. This latter section took up the bulk of the report, and it alone accounted for more than a thousand pages by the turn of the century.[37] The data included, among other things, the names and types of establishments inspected, the number of employees, the number of child and women workers, and the number and description of the legal violations. The statistical tables were generally organized by political units and, within those units, by a fluid set of industrial classifications.

The opening section of these annual reports contained narrative descriptions of the inspectors' activities, and these were relatively brief. Nevertheless, several things may be noted. While child labor was one of the principal statutory concerns of the inspectors, most of their time and effort, as evidenced by the reports, was spent on other health and safety issues, such as fire escapes and fire safety laws, the fair-pay laws, and elevator safety regulations.[38] A common complaint in the reports was the lack of staff. In the 1893 report, Chief Factory Inspector Robert Watchorn complained about "the imperfections of the law of 1889, under which we were working, and the inadequacy of the force of inspectors employed under its provisions."[39] In the 1901 report, George Rudolph, a deputy inspector who had been assigned to Allegheny County (the seat of which was Pittsburgh) for the previous six years, commented that "[t]his, the largest manufacturing district in the world, is badly in need of more inspectors."[40] And again, in 1902, Chief Factory Inspector James Campbell noted that "[o]wing to the insufficient number of deputies, all the places amenable to the law were not inspected."[41]

A recurring complaint by the factory inspectors had to do with the issuance of the several types of certificates required to legally employ child workers. As early as 1894, for example, Chief Factory Inspector Watchorn complained about "[t]he improper manner in which some few notaries public have in some instances issued [erroneous] certificates to children, leaving no room for any other conclusion on the subject than that they were influenced by only one consideration, and that, the notary fee."[42] In 1902, Chief Inspector Campbell commented that, in an attempt to crack down on fraud, "[a] number of aldermen and notaries public have been prosecuted and fined for issuing certificates in violation of the factory law."[43]

Notwithstanding these comments regarding prosecutions of certain public officials in the 1902 report, references to judicial enforcement actions of any kind against factory owners are rare. The factory inspectors, as shown in the very first report by Factory Inspector Martins, seemed to take pride in the fact that they garnered compliance more through persuasion than prosecution. As noted above, Martins stated that during the first year of the law his department made but two arrests, with no prosecution that year whatsoever.[44] In 1896, Chief Factory Inspector Campbell noted, "I call special attention to the . . . fact that we were not required to prosecute but one case during the year."[45] In 1906, Chief Factory Inspector J. C. Delaney recorded only fourteen prosecutions, statewide, for age violations.[46]

Although rooting out child labor violations was a principal part of the activities of the office, rarely can one find any direct reference to child labor violations in the narrative parts of the reports in the first dozen or so years. Aside from the mention in the first factory inspection report (1890) of the Pittsburgh glass house owner arrested (and later prosecuted) and an occasional line in a statistical table, there is only one direct mention linking the Pittsburgh glass industry with child labor in any of the reports up to 1903. That was in 1893, when M. N. Baker, still one of the deputy inspectors for western Pennsylvania and sounding more sympathetic than prosecutorial, stated that "[c]hild labor is undoubtedly necessary in some industries, such as . . . at work in the glass houses."[47] In a state with the industrial strength of Pennsylvania and for an industry like glass manufacturing with a national reputation for hiring very young child workers, this dearth of textual references, much less prosecutorial activity, is striking.

After 1903, what some saw as deference on the part of the factory inspectors toward employers on the child labor question and special treatment for the glass industry became formalized as official practice. A new governor was in the state capitol, Samuel W. Pennypacker, and he installed a new chief factory inspector, Captain J. C. Delaney, a decorated Civil War veteran who had himself begun work in the Pennsylvania mines at age eight.[48] Delaney instituted something of a sea change in the reports coming out of the inspector's office. The size of the annual reports plummeted, from more than 1,200 pages in 1902 to 190 pages in 1903, to 78 pages in 1904, and to just 56 pages in 1905. Within these reports, the narrative summary by the chief factory inspector grew substantially from previous years' reports, in both relative and actual terms, and the statistical summaries shrank to almost nothing. The changes did not go unnoticed. In an editorial published in late 1904, the *National Glass Budget*, the glass manufacturers' weekly newspaper, called the attention of its readers to the "little volume" prepared by Delaney as his first annual report. At this point, the *Budget* was not quite sure what to make of Delaney and cautioned its readers that it was "a bold and reckless man who would contend that he could squeeze as much solid information into 190 pages as another able, painstaking and conscientious public official [former inspector Campbell] had presented in 1165 pages, but such is the reckless and unwarranted claim made by J. C. Delaney." The newspaper concluded that "[s]uch factory reports or statistics are not worth the paper they are printed on."[49] Later, once the *Budget* realized that the glass industry had a real friend in Delaney, their criticism would turn to praise.

The social progressives harbored no illusions about inspector Delaney, however, and almost immediately both he and the state of Pennsylvania became the object of their intense criticism. They argued that the superficiality of Delaney's annual reports mirrored the attitude of his department on the issue of child labor. One of the earliest critiques of Delaney came from Florence Kelley. In 1905, during the second annual meeting of the National Child Labor Committee in Washington, DC, Kelley brought the weight of her authority to bear on the issue of child labor law enforcement when she presented a paper in which she criticized the general state of factory inspections in the nation's top ten industrialized states, Pennsylvania in particular. As noted in chapter 1, no member of the NCLC, and in fact virtually no other progressive social reformer in the country, could match Florence Kelley for firsthand knowledge and credibility concerning factory inspection. She began by linking child labor laws with schooling, the simple logic being that if children were working, they were almost never attending school. Kelley noted that of all the major industrial states she was analyzing, Pennsylvania had, according to the 1900 Census, by far the highest rate of childhood illiteracy, with at least 6,326 illiterate children between the ages of fourteen and sixteen, or about one-third of the total number of such children in all ten of the industrial states in her report. This situation existed in spite of the fact that Pennsylvania, along with at least seven of the other ten states, had a compulsory education law on the books ostensibly requiring that many of those same children either had to attend school or had to be able to prove their ability to read and write.[50]

She attributed Pennsylvania's unenviable position at the bottom of the child literacy scale to the state's seemingly insatiable thirst for child labor and a political attitude that favored work over school for those same children.[51] Kelley stated that Pennsylvania had "on a large scale, all the industries," and here she included glass works, "which call for the labor of children," and therefore that it was hardly accidental "that the number of children at work under the age of sixteen years is larger, by some thousands, in this state than in any other, or that the opposition of employers to legislation for the effective restriction of the employment of boys and girls is more stubborn and more effective here than elsewhere in the North."[52] At the next year's meeting, Kelley broadened her complaint about enforcement. In a paper included in the published materials for the third annual meeting of the NCLC, she noted that an effective child labor regulatory system depended not solely upon "the quality of the men to whom the work of enforcing it is entrusted; it depends far more largely on the quality of the community in which those men hold office."[53] She then highlighted the critical importance of public education to the child labor and child education reform efforts.

Inspector Delaney responded defensively to Kelley's and other, similar critiques. In 1904, for example, Delaney assured the readers of his annual report that he had "urgently reminded" his deputy inspectors "of their duties respecting the employment of children . . . that they should make a searching and rigid examination as to the number of children employed and the legality of their employment." He then went on to say that he did this not to ensure the firm and fair enforcement of the state's child labor laws but simply as a way of "disproving oft-repeated allegations to the effect that, the factories, workshops and mercantile establishments in Pennsylvania were 'literally crowded' with children under the age of thirteen years."[54]

In 1905, Delaney again complained that "[s]o much has been written and said by magazines and newspaper critics about the millions of under-sized and underfed children swarming in the factories and workshops ... of Pennsylvania, that a rigid and searching inquiry into the truth or falsity of these statements was deemed timely and necessary." He then went on, without any specific offer of proof, to assert that his inquiry proved all of the allegations false.[55] As discussed in chapter 5, in 1906, the legislature debated strengthening the state's compulsory education law, which would likely have a direct negative impact on the pool of child workers available to industries such as the western Pennsylvania glass houses. In response to the proposed legislation, Delaney stated that, although he thought educating children was a good idea, he did not "see the connection between the 'three R's' and the necessity for seeking employment and the ability to do the work."[56] Because of comments like these, reformers viewed Delaney's attitude toward industrial child labor as callous. Because of the way he ran the inspection office, critics viewed his enforcement of the state's child labor laws as bordering on negligent. He was stung by the charges that progressives leveled at him, and he used the pages of his annual reports more to fight back at his critics than to demonstrate the details of his or his deputies' regulatory enforcement work.

Fred S. Hall, secretary of the Pennsylvania Child Labor Association, added to the chorus of concern about Delaney in 1910 when, at the NCLC's sixth annual meeting, he reported that Delaney had stated flatly that no child under fourteen was then employed in the state. Hall was dumbfounded and believed this assertion to be facially absurd. To prove his point, he compared Pennsylvania with New York, both states having established fourteen as the minimum age for child workers. By comparing published employment statistics for a similar set of industries in each state, Hall found that, in New York, children ages fourteen and fifteen made up about 3 percent of the total number of workers in those industries. In Pennsylvania, such children accounted for almost 21 percent of the total employment in those industries. Hall reasoned that, assuming the economic and demographic profiles of the two states were similar, "the conclusion was unavoidable that hundreds of our 11, 12, and 13-year old children have been recorded statistically by the Pennsylvania [factory] inspectors as being between 14 and 16 years old."[57]

In a separate section of the published report from that same annual meeting, Hall reported that the Pennsylvania Child Labor Association had campaigned unsuccessfully against the reappointment of Delaney as factory inspector. They did so not only because of his historic insensitivity to the issue of child labor reform but also because he had recently "interpreted the exception in our [child labor] night work prohibition clause— the exception which, it was assumed, allowed night work only in the glass industry—to be broad enough to cover the messenger service and so allow all-night work in that demoralizing occupation." To Hall, not only was Delaney lax in his inspection duties but he was in fact actively seeking to further undermine an already compromised child labor law.[58]

The most scathing criticism of Delaney came in 1911, at the end of his tenure as the state's factory inspector, with the publication of *Wage-Earning Pittsburgh* as part of *The Pittsburgh Survey*. In it, Florence Kelley, herself the former chief factory inspector for Illinois, took Delaney to task. Kelley characterized the Pennsylvania inspector as ineffectual, in part because he acted like a "remote and inaccessible dignitary," far removed from the factories and the children of Pittsburgh. This distancing was both metaphoric and actual because, as she noted, at that time the factory inspector still maintained no offices in Pittsburgh and there was no place in Pittsburgh to access any of the records relating to his or his deputies' inspections. She pointed out that while the office of the factory inspector was intended to be an advocate for the protection of the interests of children and the furthering of reform, it was in fact being operated by Delaney as an ally of the state's powerful industrial interests. He was, as Kelley pointed out, a political appointee, he had no civil service protection, and he had no particular technical expertise in either industrial technologies or labor practices. He was, quite simply, a minion of the political and industrial interests.[59]

Kelley characterized Delaney's annual reports as models of ineffective leadership. Because he had taken pains to slash the length of the reports and thereby truncate virtually all of the statistical data, the employment figures were presented in such a way as to obscure rather than highlight specific industrial profiles. She noted that even though night work by children under fourteen was specifically banned in 1905 in all industries except glass, Delaney chose not to report night employment by children in *any* industry in Pittsburgh or to indicate *any* prosecutions for same. There were no night-time employment statistics in part because the deputy inspector in charge of the Pittsburgh region had decided, with Delaney's approval, that neither he nor his deputies needed to work at night! If they did not work at night, they obviously could not discover firsthand any evidence of violations of the night work employment ban for child workers. Further, Kelley noted that even though there was greater interest concerning child employment in the glass houses "than in any other manufacturing industry employing children in Pennsylvania," glass house employment figures for Pittsburgh were virtually inaccessible in the reports. They were lumped together with "Miscellaneous Manufactures," an industrial category that totaled nearly forty-seven thousand employees in 1907.[60]

Kelley's gravest concern about Delaney, however, was not merely that his enforcement of child labor laws was inept but rather that he seemed actively antagonistic to the law. Reiterating the concerns she had registered in 1905, she again pointed out that in Pennsylvania, the "employment of an illiterate child . . . was very common," even though state law required that all working children under sixteen had to be able to read and write "intelligently." The source of this problem was laid at the door of the factory inspector because, as Kelley notes, Delaney had decided, on his own motion, that this statuto-rily required literacy standard simply should not be enforced. In his annual report of 1906, for example, he had asked, rhetorically, "[W]hy should boys and girls fourteen years of age and in good physical condition be withheld from learning a useful trade or from earning a necessary livelihood simply because they cannot read and write, or cannot explain sums in arithmetic, or tell the difference between a transitive and intransitive verb?"[61]

Kelley's criticism of Delaney was reinforced in 1912 by Charles Chute, a longtime child labor reform advocate and a "special agent" investigator for the National Child Labor Committee. He had recently been appointed sec-retary of the Pennsylvania Child Labor Association, and in a report for the NCLC, he commented at length on the subject of child labor law enforce-ment. He argued that in virtually all areas of social reform, the reformers too quickly aimed toward legislative solutions without adequately consid-ering the question of enforcement. "Nowhere," he stated, "is this seen more strongly than in the field of child labor legislation." The key to enforcement, he urged, was the factory inspection system, but in only a handful of states in the nation did he see that such a system was even "fairly good." Among states with factory inspectors, Chute concluded that only New York provided anything close to an adequate number of inspectors, with eighty-one on the job. On the other hand, Pennsylvania, as late as 1912, had about one-half that number. Further, because of the systematic underfunding of the inspection departments and because in virtually all states the chief factory inspector was a political appointee, "men qualified neither by nature, experience, or education, become inspectors, [with] their appointments and terms of office depending rather on 'pull' and 'politics' than on any merit."[62]

Chute argued that politics had weakened the factory inspection departments and made them much less aggressive in enforcing the law. To support this claim, he compared enforcement practices in factory inspection departments in Great Britain, another major industrial power, with those in the United States. He noted that in a recent year the factory inspector in Great Britain reported "approximately 4000 prosecutions" for violations of its protective labor laws, with fines being imposed in 95 percent of the cases. In New York, on the other hand, the best state Chute could find for child labor law enforcement, while the factory inspector brought approximately 1,065 prosecutions in 1910, fines were imposed in only 30 percent of the cases. In that same year, the Pennsylvania factory inspector, J. C. Delaney, reported that his office had brought a total of only 26 prosecutions and imposed only 9 fines. Even without a detailed discussion of the similarities of the various schemes for protective legislation in force in each jurisdiction or the relative size of the work force at issue, the import of Chute's rhetorical condemnation was clear: enforcement of child labor protective legislation in Pennsylvania under Delaney was all but nonexistent.[63]

Thus, at the height of the Progressive Era, Pennsylvania's child labor laws were being widely and systematically ignored by the very people charged with their enforcement, and the social progressives could do little more than complain. As chapter 6 explains, although Pennsylvania may not have been, in the early twentieth century, at the forefront of progressive reform respecting child labor laws, it did have a set of significant regulations respecting working children. The law provided that all children under fourteen were prohibited from engaging in virtually any industrial or factory labor; that all working children under sixteen had to be able to read and write intelligently before they could work; and that children under sixteen were barred from night work in virtually every industrial establishment in the state (except the Pittsburgh glass houses). But the state seriously blunted the force of these regulations by placing their enforcement in the hands of a politically appointed state factory inspector. Especially under the leadership of J. C. Delaney, the inspection department in Pennsylvania was much more responsive to the industrial interests of the state than it was in actively enforcing the letter, much less the spirit, of the law.

Delaney was eventually removed from office in 1912, when he admitted to his involvement in a political scandal a few years earlier, one that was unrelated to the factory inspection department. As he was being forced out, the glass manufacturers acknowledged how valuable he had been to their industrial interests. The *National Glass Budget* editorialized that "[t]he removal of State Factory Inspector Delaney by Governor Tener will be regretted by employers generally who had come to look upon him as a very competent public official, who, without fear or favor, devoted his energies to the enforcement of factory laws and child labor legislation." The newspaper went on to characterize his critics, with clear though unacknowledged references to Charles Chute and Florence Kelley, as a group of "labor fakirs, consumer leaguers, and child labor fanatics." Delaney, the newspaper concluded, was a valuable public servant, and his detractors were nothing more than a "pack of hoodlums."[64]

The NCLC Critique of the Pittsburgh Glass Houses

The ineffectiveness of the factory inspection system, especially in the glass-producing states, heightened the NCLC's determination to create a system of even stronger reforms affecting the glass house boys. As part of its effort to marshal public opinion and lobby for legislative change to address the problems of child labor in the Pittsburgh glass houses, the NCLC issued a wide variety of publications, from summary pamphlets to larger-scale research studies.

The first of these publications was a small pamphlet focused exclusively on child labor in the Pennsylvania glass industry. Prepared by Owen Lovejoy, then one of the NCLC's assistant secretaries, it combined a brief summary of relevant facts and figures along with some rather straightforward descriptive prose as he sketched the dimensions of the problem. In 1900, he noted, Pennsylvania had some seventy-three glass factories, which employed a total of 12,961 workers, at least 2,677 of whom were children under sixteen years of age. In the pamphlet, Lovejoy observed that even though there had been a "marked tendency of the industry to move west and southwest," growing demand for glass had still allowed the Pennsylvania plants to expand, and as they did they also increased the number of boys employed. Because a large part of the growth in western Pennsylvania glass production was also attributable to round-the-clock operations, Lovejoy complained that "[n]o modern industry makes a stronger demand for child labor than does the manufacture of glass" and that the "employment of children at night is the chief offense of [the glass] industry."[65] The negative health and developmental effects of such work on the glass house boys were clear to Lovejoy. Not only was there the tremendous heat of the furnaces and the "nervous strain" of the repetitive yet fast-paced work, there was also the loss of appetite and sleep among the boys as a result of irregular hours and night-time shifts. Lovejoy pointed out that all of this labor was unnecessary because of inventions such as the Owens Automatic. He observed that "[t]he glass industry is not compelled to employ little children, either for the benefit of the children or from the necessities of the industry ... [because] this work ... could be as well done by machines."[66]

Lovejoy's little pamphlet was intended primarily for and circulated among NCLC members. As such, it was probably effective at strengthening their belief that the western Pennsylvania glass houses had unconscionable child labor practices. The language of the pamphlet is matter-of-fact rather than polemical or even particularly passionate and tended to confirm or solidify the beliefs of those who already considered themselves strong proponents of child labor reform. In contrast, to convert opponents of progressivism, industrial apologists, or state legislatures, the NCLC prepared "investigative reports." These were longer, research-intensive, narrative descriptions of various groups of child workers. The NCLC began issuing these reports shortly after its founding in 1904. No fewer than a dozen of them directly concerned the glass industry, and several of these focused specifically on the Pittsburgh glass house boys. The reports usually included statistical data on wages, numbers of employees, numbers of child workers, and the products made in those factories. The investigators typically visited a large number

"Scene from Woodbury Bottle Works. They work nights."
Woodbury, New Jersey, November 1909

of manufacturing sites during various hours of operation. They interviewed the adult workers, industrial managers, school personnel, other public officials, and the families of the child workers. The NCLC hoped to increase the persuasive value of these investigations by presenting them as well-researched, objective pictures of child labor conditions in the subject industry. With regard to the western Pennsylvania glass industry, the NCLC used these investigative reports to create a sympathetic image of the glass house boy so as to further the organization's reform proposals. But, like *The Pittsburgh Survey*, the NCLC's efforts met with only limited success, at least with regard to the glass house boys in western Pennsylvania.

To the extent that the NCLC reports had persuasive value, it was because most were produced by reformers who, on the basis of experience or credentials, had significant authority to speak on the subject. The reports uniformly present scathing indictments of the child labor practices in the industry under investigation, and those dealing with glass factories are no exception. But the NCLC glass house investigatory reports also provide something unique in the history of the glass house boys. Many of the investigators, as part of their research, arranged to talk with the parents of the boys in their homes. When they did so, they occasionally interviewed the glass house boys themselves. In these occasional interviews with the children, the reports are one of the very few places where the voices of the glass house boys themselves can be heard, however quietly and briefly. Even though the few words quoted from the boys were being deployed by the authors of the reports for a particular persuasive purpose, they are also some of the only surviving firsthand, contemporaneous accounts of what these boys may have felt about their work.

The very first NCLC investigative report, prepared in 1904 by Harriet M. Van der Vaart, then the secretary of the Illinois Consumers' League, reported on the Illinois glass industry. In 1908, Lewis W. Hine, former teacher at the progressive Ethical Culture School in New York City and recently employed as an investigative photographer for the NCLC, prepared a similar report on the glass industry in West Virginia. Of particular interest for the present study are Charles Chute's 1911 comparative study of the glass manufacturers in the five principal glass-producing states (Illinois, Indiana, Ohio, West Virginia, and Pennsylvania) and Herschel H. Jones's 1912–1913 investigation, which focused solely on the glass houses in western Pennsylvania. Each of these two latter reports offers a detailed picture of the child labor practices of the Pittsburgh glass industry in a rational, descriptive, researched-based, almost scientifically analytical style. Again, while not disinterested, each author nonetheless tried to present a self-consciously, and in their words, "unexaggerated" appraisal of the industry's child employment practices, the absolute abolition of which was the acknowledged goal of the sponsoring agency.

Charles Chute began his report with a general introduction of glassmaking in the United States, and he reiterated its historic reliance on child workers. He then moved quickly to a methodical description of the typical jobs the glass house boys perform, the factory conditions under which they work, their probable future (or lack of same) for advanced employment in the glass industry, their ages, and the hours they work in a typical day or week. Chute devoted a large part of the report to the issue of night work by children in the glass factories, which reflects the NCLC's special concern with this element of the child labor puzzle in western Pennsylvania. He concluded with a discussion of how the glass industry's child labor practices affected schooling and their impact on the economic situation of the children's families.

To frame the importance of his particular study, Chute noted that while the NCLC had had a special interest in child labor in glass factories "ever since it began its work in 1904," this interest had been addressed "more or less unsystematically" until his project was initiated. To better focus the NCLC approach to the problem, Chute undertook a "comparative investigation" of the glass-making establishments in the "leading 'glass' states." He confessed that, in an effort to hide the true nature of his inquiries from the glass companies under investigation and in order to gain the necessary access to their factories, he was not above using deception. He wrote that in order to undertake his investigation and raise as little concern among the glass house owners as possible, he "enrolled as a graduate student in Ohio State University and carried letters of introduction [to the glass houses] from its faculty." No comment was made as to whether the university was complicit in, or even aware of, Chute's deception.[67] Of the five states he investigated, he characterized "Pennsylvania, Indiana and West Virginia . . . [as] representative of States having backward and weak . . . child labor laws."[68] From the NCLC perspective, because the "child labor problem and the glass industry [had] long been inseparably related," weak child labor laws meant that the reformers had to work much harder to effect change. To emphasize how deeply entrenched the problem in these states was, Chute noted that "[f]rom time immemorial the [glass] industry" in each of these states "has employed young children."[69]

Chute quickly turned to the adverse health and developmental effects of such work on the children. On the positive side, he acknowledged that the factories normally had "abundant fresh air" (largely from drafts that resulted from hasty, haphazard construction) and that the production process necessitated "a certain co-operation and team-work" among the workers. These benefits notwithstanding, Chute concluded that the work was "hard and generally injurious for such boys." Chute confirmed previously described concerns that the glass factories were very hot, that while "a great deal of water is consumed," the boys were also regularly exposed to beer, and that winter and night work increased the likelihood of certain respiratory diseases. Chute noted, for example, that tuberculosis was "nearly twice as prevalent" among workers in glass factories as in any other industry.[70]

Then Chute turned to the strain of the physical labor. He characterized the work expected of the boys as repetitive, monotonous, and (according to the factory owners) unskilled. Chute noted that most of the boy jobs required constant movement back and forth across the work floor, and he cited one study that found that the typical glass house boy might walk (or more likely jog) between ten and twenty miles in a single shift of work. Many people testified to Chute that the work was increasingly more taxing due to greater competitive pressures. Because of the effects of automation, the hand-blown glass factories were under continuous pressure to increase output, and thus "bottles [had to be] produced many times faster than they used to be." Also, because "blowers all work on a piece-work basis," their pay was directly dependent on what they were able to produce, which in turn depended on the speed and agility of the boys. Chute noted that the "men frequently make as high as $12 a day" but that the boys' daily wage was only "about $1."[71]

Chute emphasized that job insecurity for the boys also added to the stress of the labor. He described the problem with the apprenticeship system and noted that it had become especially acute as automated glass-making techniques made inroads into the industry. As the Owens Automatic spread through the glass houses, the number of unemployed adult glass blowers increased, the competition for a skilled job opening became even more intense, and apprenticeships were even fewer in number. In 1909–1910, for example, Chute reported that the GBBA allowed "no apprentices at all . . . in union bottle factories." Even so, the number of children at work in the glass factories who were directly affected by these working conditions was substantial. Chute estimated that for the five-state area, the total number of glass house boys was 5,240, with Pennsylvania accounting for the greatest number by far. The rate of child labor among the glass houses in Pennsylvania—that is, the relative percentage of boys employed to total employment—was more than twice the rate for any of the other five states.[72]

Reflecting the NCLC's particular concern about night work by children, Chute dedicated about sixteen of his report's fifty-seven typescript pages almost exclusively to the deleterious consequences of such work for the children. As noted earlier, the prevalence of night work in the glass industry had been increasing, and of the ninety-nine factories Chute investigated, eighty-nine worked day and night shifts. Union rules dictated that these glass houses operate with two work shifts per day, each of eight and one-half hours plus an hour for lunch (even on the night shift) and two fifteen-minute breaks. The day shift generally went from 7:00 A.M. to 5:00 P.M. and the night shift, from 5:00 P.M. to 3:00 A.M. Because the children worked side-by-side with the men, these were their working conditions as well.[73]

Although Chute noted that direct data on health problems for boys under sixteen years of age attributable to night work were "difficult" to get, he nonetheless concluded, based almost entirely on home interviews, that such work "in all glass factories, is injurious to men and boys alike." Chute reported that for those boys who worked at night, sleep was the major concern. When the night shift ended, public transportation, if available at all, would have shut down for the night, so the boys either would have to stay at the factory or walk home in the dark. Many chose the former. Of those who did go home, Chute stated that many had to walk several miles, the vast majority went to bed without eating, and few slept well. Their sleep was usually irregular, and their home conditions were not quiet. During home interviews, the boys' families attributed various additional problems to the night work, including headaches, colds, stunted growth, anemia, pale color, bad eyesight, fainting, bad eating habits, and use of chewing tobacco. Acknowledging class differences, Chute reported that because "most of these boys come from poor families, and are blessed (or cursed) with numerous brothers and sisters ... they do not receive the care at home that children differently circumstanced enjoy."[74]

Chute devoted several pages of his report about the difficulties of night work in the glass houses to "direct evidence" that he "secured by visits to the homes of [forty-eight of the] working boys." On these home visits he usually talked with the boys' mothers, but occasionally he spoke with the boys themselves. When referring to the boys' responses, Chute usually paraphrased their comments, writing, for example, that "[s]even boys (or their mothers) confessed to not having any place where their sleep could be undisturbed" or that the "[b]oy said he couldn't sleep as well by day." When he did quote the boys directly, Chute provided only snippets. Chute quoted one boy as saying that he had "bad eyes" from the glass plant. Another offered that "[t]he work is hard." A boy stated that after his night shift, "I usually goes down town and 'bums' around a while" until the streetcars began to run and then he could get home by 6:00 A.M. Several boys offered

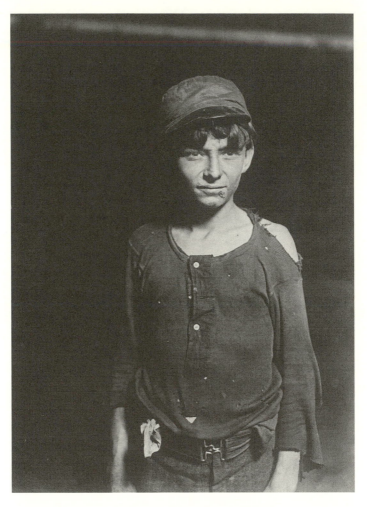

"A Typical Glass Works Boy, Indiana, Night Shift. Said he was 16 years old. 1 A.M." August 1908

the identical statement that "I can't sleep in the day time," and one boy in particular told Chute that "[s]ometimes [at work] we get sleepin' and they pour water on us, and everythin.'"[75]

These are boys of few words. Perhaps they were tired when Chute visited their homes, perhaps Chute made them uncomfortable (or vice versa), or perhaps Chute was not a probing interviewer. In any event, the boys' comments did not give Chute much firsthand information. But Chute, assuming that he is quoting from the boys' statements faithfully, used what they did say to his advantage. Quoting the several boys claiming to suffer from bad sleeping habits as a result of night work supported the NCLC's case on the ill effects of such work. Similarly, by providing a presumably natural and authentic rendition of the boys' spoken comments demonstrated that they had only a tentative grasp of standard English usage and grammar ("I goes down town," or "sleepin' . . . and everythin'"), which supported the contention that work in the glass houses interfered with schooling.

Chute also included slightly more extensive comments from factory managers, adult glass workers, and others, the vast majority of whom, according to Chute, freely supported his conclusion that such night work was harmful. Most are straightforward, simple statements, such as "boys ought not work at night" or "such work is bad." Perhaps recognizing that their comments would be particularly persuasive on issues pertaining to the health of the glass house boys, Chute quoted physicians more extensively. Even so, he could not report unanimity among the medical doctors interviewed. He wrote that while there was "some difference of opinion," most of the physicians "condemn[ed]" the practice of night work "when faced with the facts." Dr. Frank Le M. Hupp of Wheeling, West Virginia, for example, said, "It cannot be satisfactorily denied, that the evolution of both mind and body, so active at the age of 14 and 15, is dwarfed and blighted because of strenuous night duty." Harriet B. Jones, M.D., of Fairmont, West Virginia, told Chute that "it is very injurious for children to do night work" and that "[m]any bright little boys who worked at night have made very stupid men and at twenty-one years of age do not compare with their companions who had their regular night's rest." Other physicians whom Chute cited concurred with that opinion.[76]

The NCLC reports, like this one by Charles Chute, have been lauded as providing invaluable insight into "the evils of child labor in the glasshouses and on the particular evil of night work."[77] While the NCLC may have hoped that these reports would persuade the public of the problems associated with night work for the glass house boys of western Pennsylvania, not everyone was convinced. Concluding his report with a discussion of the need for stronger laws, especially laws prohibiting night work, Chute offered this explanation for why the western Pennsylvania glass industry remained outside the purview of such laws: "Indiana, following this investigation, passed a night law similar to that of Illinois, and in Pennsylvania a strenuous campaign to compel the legislature to do away with the clause in the sixteen year night law which excepts 'continuous industries' [i.e., the glass factories] was unsuccessful not because the people were opposed to the change but because of a confessed alliance between politicians and glass manufacturers."[78] Here, Chute understated the problem because, as discussed in chapter 6, the opposition to child labor reform in Pennsylvania extended beyond just the politicians and glass manufacturers.

Two years after the publication of Chute's study, the NCLC funded a similar report by Herschel H. Jones, who focused his investigation specifically on the western Pennsylvania glass industry. The NCLC designated Jones, like Chute, to be a "special agent" of the committee. His commission was to report on "night work by boys under sixteen" in the Pittsburgh area's glass-bottle factories, and he stated that his work was intended to supplement the "very thorough investigation of the Glass Industry" prepared by Chute. Toward that end, Jones consciously followed much the same research protocol as Chute: he visited some thirty-three glass factories in the Pittsburgh district, "by day and by night"; he talked with factory managers and workers; he conducted numerous interviews in the homes of approximately seventy-five of the glass house boys he encountered in the factories; and he discussed the problems of night work with school officials and physicians. Of the more than twelve hundred boys under sixteen that Jones determined were working in the Pittsburgh glass factories at the time, the vast majority worked both day and night shifts, and he tried to make the deleterious effects of such labor abundantly clear in his findings.[79]

Although Jones's factual descriptions continued to paint a troubling portrait of the working life of the glass house boys, the fact that he was so closely following in Chute's footsteps meant that little in the report was really new in terms of the facts presented. Where Jones's report does differ

"Glass works. Midnight." Indiana, August 1908

from Chute's, and from many other NCLC investigative reports, is in those several places where Jones allowed his personal reflections and observations to speak to the reader. At these places, in contrast to the rather straightforward recitation of research and interview-based facts and method more typical of other NCLC investigative reports, the prose becomes more compelling. Jones seemed to slip almost effortlessly into the role of storyteller used so effectively by other progressives, such as Butler in *The Pittsburgh Study*. In these few sections, Jones relied on the power of his prose to give an emotional sense of how the glass house work affected the boys.

Two of Jones's reflections are especially illuminating. The first comes in the midst of reporting on a series of home visits conducted to document the adverse effects that night work had on the sleeping habits of the boys. Almost as an aside, Jones remarked that he

was in a number of homes just as the boys were getting up in the evening and starting off to the factory. Their [*sic*] was something dull and lifeless about them that is hard to describe. They seemed to have no interest in anything or anybody. To understand it one must think what it means for a boy of fourteen or fifteen to be sleeping in a blind darkened room while the sun is shining and other children are playing in the streets or going to school, and to get up just as darkness comes again and start out with his dinner for the factory again. It is depressing to the boy's spirits; he feels that he is no longer a boy but a laborer; other things being shut out of his life, the factory environment becomes the moulding force.[80]

Here Jones was clearly contrasting the life of the glass house boy with the ideals of sheltered childhood. He was trying to develop a sympathetic portrait of the working-class glass house boy to help persuade his readers that such boys should, along with the children of middle- and upper-class families, have this type of childhood as their birthright.

Later, Jones tried to explain why the "moulding force" of the glass factories was particularly problematic for the moral habits and well-being of the boys. He observed,

The boy enters the glass house at a most plastic period of his life. He associates with men whose language is vulgar, whose personal habits are dissolute, who drink, who use tobacco, who swear at them, and in some factories, even strike them if they do not keep up the pace. It is the delight of the gang of boys to "break in" a tenderfoot. A little Polish boy who had quit his job at a glass factory on the South Side, Pittsburgh, because he "couldn't stand the night work," says, "They try to *make you tough* down there." . . . A number of times the boys were cursed viciously for stopping for a few seconds to answer the questions of the investigator. The relations between the blower or presser and the boys are often very intimate, however, and the men exert a great influence over them. That this close association with men and older boys is not the best thing for the young boys just out of school is putting it very mildly.[81]

In these brief passages, Jones provided evidence of what drove reformers to work so tirelessly to improve the lives of the glass house boys. We also get a glimpse of what made the reformers' goals so difficult to achieve.

Jones and the other progressive reformers were fully aware of the developing cultural view concerning the value of sheltered childhood—the ideal of the economically worthless but emotionally priceless child. Progressive social reformers believed in the plasticity—and thus vulnerability—of childhood, and given this understanding, it is little wonder that Jones's report showed a heightened level of frustration with the persistence of child labor, especially night work, in the Pittsburgh glass houses. Night work by children had already been successfully eliminated in almost all other

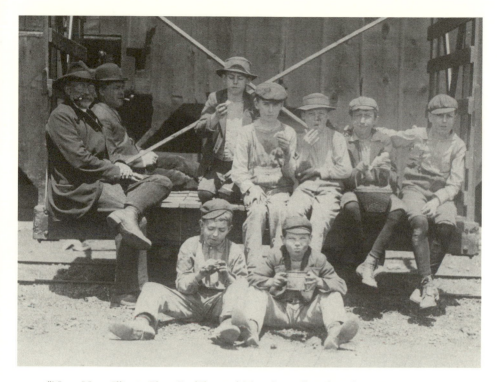

"Noon Hour. Illinois Glass Co. (Shop #7.) These boys all work in above glass company. Tuesday noon." Alton, Illinois, May 1910

glass-producing states (only Pennsylvania and West Virginia had not enacted such legislation), but it remained particularly intractable in western Pennsylvania, where progressives found it unusually difficult to shift the tide in favor of reform.

One of the problems with the portrait that progressives painted of the glass house boys was that it was at odds with the demands and circumstances of the working-class families in Pittsburgh who depended on their children's wages to augment the family economy. Charles Chute noted as much toward the end of his 1911 report when, after detailing the myriad negative health effects on the boys from glass house work, he stated almost as an aside that "the *majority* of parents as well as *most* of the boys themselves refused to see *any* injury in night work, no doubt fearing to loose [*sic*] their chance of work altogether."[82] The families in Pittsburgh were no

Progressive Reform and Child Labor   71

different. They tended to be poor, working-class, and largely immigrant families, and one of the only means they had for cushioning the harshness of their condition was to augment the family income through the employment of their children.[83] Acting in what they reasonably perceived to be their own best interest, these families used what limited power they had at their disposal to further their economic survival, even if it meant possibly sacrificing the long-term health and economic well-being of their children. The resistance to reform among these boys and their families was a significant obstacle to the progressives. Not only did their acts of resistance undercut the effectiveness of existing child labor laws but the families' need to have the boys work undercut the political support for any new child labor regulations designed with the boys' protection in mind.

The NCLC, on the other hand, viewed industrial child labor, and especially night work, as an "unquestionably inhumane" practice that simply had to be outlawed.[84] The committee was "opposed to any employment outside the home which interfered with the child's physical, mental, or moral growth."[85] When reformers considered the array of well-documented health and developmental problems associated with child labor, to say nothing of the additional problems for both the child and society from the concomitant loss of formal education, they considered the case for reform to be irrefutable. Many of the progressives simply could not comprehend that working-class families might see the situation differently, and one reason for the great failure of their reform efforts in Pennsylvania was that the reformers could not articulate just how the families might make up for the loss of the children's wages should the reform proposals be enacted. In other words, the reformers did not adequately understand that, "[g]iven the precarious finances of working-class families and the necessity of pooling wages of as many family members as possible in order to make ends meet, immigrant, working-class families viewed the passage of child labor statutes as a personal economic disaster and made strenuous efforts to circumvent child labor laws."[86] The resistance of the glass house boys and their families to reform was a serious problem for the progressives. It was made more serious when this resistance was added to the reform opposition coming from the western Pennsylvania glass industry.

3

Glass House Owners and
the Politics of Glass

*Almost without exception the [glass] factories are well lighted and
ventilated, both by day and by night and only through carelessness
need the juvenile help employed therein meet disaster.... [T]hey
are contented and happy, and the fact that many of the successful
[glass] manufacturers of the present day began work as carrying-in
boys before they had reached the age of 10 years exposes the false
pretense which is now being worked off by the daily press at the
instigation of freak reformers.*

National Glass Budget editorial, 1909

THE EARLY TWENTIETH CENTURY was a time of great change and uncertainty for the glass-bottle producers in western Pennsylvania. Their position of dominance in the glass industry, which had developed over the previous fifty years, was diminishing. Natural gas fields producing cheap and clean fuel for glass furnaces were being discovered in Ohio, Indiana, and Illinois, and glass factories were relocating there in larger and larger numbers. The economic foundation of the Pittsburgh manufacturers was further eroded by newly developing technological innovations in glass production, including the Owens Automatic. These machines used far less labor than the traditional methods of glass production on which Pittsburgh manufacturers continued to rely, and the economic advantages of using these new mechanized processes could be dramatic. At the same time, the Pittsburgh glass factory owners found themselves repeatedly attacked by Progressive Era reformers because of their child labor practices. The traditional hand-blown glass methods used in Pittsburgh required large numbers of glass house boys, and the proposed reforms sought to put an end to their use by eliminating the glass house exception in child labor laws and prohibiting the boys from working at night. Despite these challenges to their power, however, the Pittsburgh glass manufacturers still exercised considerable political influence within the corridors of the state legislature, where they sought to block virtually every effort to regulate child labor in their factories. In the process of opposing the child labor agenda, these manufacturers developed a unique set of alliances that helped shape the face of progressive reform in the state.

How Glass Came to Pittsburgh

The history of glass reaches back to the beginnings of recorded history. The early Roman historian Pliny, in a technologically unlikely but nevertheless romantic story, credited the discovery of glassmaking to early Phoenician sailors seated around a fire built on blocks of soda or natron, on a sandy beach by the Mediterranean. Somehow, as if by magic, these basic elements—the wood ashes, the sand, and the soda—were commingled and melted by the heat from the fire to produce a small rivulet of molten glass.[1] More reliable sources identify the Egyptians as the first to use glass, and other evidence points to the development of several critical glass technologies, such as the use of the blowpipe, by the Romans.[2]

The basic process had changed little by the time the English brought their glass-making skills to the American colonies in the early seventeenth century. Records of the settlement at Jamestown indicate that the colonists built a glass furnace as early as 1608. It was used for the production of beads for trade and bottles for domestic use. Most glass furnaces at the time used wood for fuel, but as that resource became scarce in England, other fuels were sought. In 1610, Sir William Slingsby developed and was granted a royal patent for a glass furnace that used coal as its primary fuel.[3] Although Slingsby's invention would not have an immediate impact on colonial glassmaking, it would prove decisive in the establishment of Pittsburgh glass houses some two hundred years later.

Even though glass was among the very first colonial industries, glass production in the colonies under the English mercantile system was generally subordinated to production in the mother country. Thus, the level of colonial glass manufacturing remained low throughout much of the seventeenth century.[4] By the beginning of the eighteenth century, however, because of continuously expanding colonial demand for utilitarian objects such as bottles and windows and a weakening of the mercantile bonds with the mother country, colonial glassmaking achieved greater stability as Massachusetts, New York, New Jersey, and eastern Pennsylvania became glass centers.[5]

Because of the relative abundance of forests on the eastern seaboard, wood rather than coal was the principal fuel for the glass furnaces in these areas at the beginning of the colonial period. It remained the preferred fuel there, even after coal became an option, because it had several advantages over coal. Not only were coal furnaces somewhat more expensive to build but the increased soot from burning coal affected the color of the glass unless special hoods were used to shield the molten glass from contaminants. Where coal was plentiful, however, it had one important advantage: it was cheap. At the start of the nineteenth century, coal was especially plentiful and cheap in western Pennsylvania. Largely because of the easy availability of very inexpensive coal, in 1797, Revolutionary War veterans General Isaac Craig and his quartermaster, James O'Hara, opened the first glass factory in Pittsburgh. They located their factory on the south side of Pittsburgh, not far from the "Point," the origin of the Ohio River at the confluence of the Monongahela and Allegheny rivers.[6] The men called their new factory the Pittsburgh Glass Works, and it was one of the first in the country to rely exclusively on soft coal for fuel.

Pittsburgh was an attractive location for the production of glass for several reasons. The basic ingredients of utilitarian glass—silica (in the form of Oriskany quartzite or sandstone), lime, and potash—were all readily available, and an expanding regional population was generating a demand for glass.[7] In fact, situated as it was at the headwaters of the Ohio River, Pittsburgh was particularly well positioned to serve both the growing regional population and the new settlements farther west. As all of these areas grew in population, so did the demand for glass, especially windows and bottles. Because transportation of glass from eastern factories over the Allegheny Mountains was difficult and expensive, a Pittsburgh glass house could have a significant competitive advantage in serving the demand from the western Pennsylvania region and beyond. Further, western Pennsylvania was a strong market for alcohol. The production of beer and whiskey in western Pennsylvania was well established by the start of the eighteenth century (as evidenced by the Whiskey Rebellion from the early years of the republic), and glass bottles were the container of choice. Whiskey was so plentiful, in fact, that it was often used in place of hard currency, which was always in short supply as a medium of exchange. There is, for example, a record of one John Bedollet of Greensburg, Pennsylvania, just east of Pittsburgh, selling a piece of property for "1600 gallons of whiskey to be paid in four installments."[8] Geography, resources, the westward expansion of the country, and whiskey all combined to make Pittsburgh well suited to become an important glass center not only for utilitarian glass—especially bottles and windows—but for more specialized glass products as well.

One of Pittsburgh's most successful early glass houses was formed in 1808 by Benjamin Bakewell, and it specialized in flint or lead crystal glass rather than more utilitarian wares. Indeed, at the time, the Bakewell glass factory was one of the only commercial producers of this type of high-end glassware in the country. Bakewell utilized pressing techniques whereby the hot molten glass was forced into a mold to produce objects resembling cut glass—usually plates, tableware, doorknobs, or drawer pulls. It was a uniquely American technology, perfected if not invented in Pittsburgh, and it was John P. Bakewell of the Bakewell company who received, on September 9, 1825, the first patent for a pressed-glass manufacturing process.[9]

The success of the Bakewell enterprise is evidenced not only by its list of customers and awards but also by its recognition of the importance of political influence. In 1817, President James Monroe visited Pittsburgh and was presented with two cut-glass Bakewell decanters. In 1825, the Bakewell firm presented Senator Henry Clay in Washington with a set of Bakewell decanters to thank him for his work on the tariff bills. Also that year, the former Revolutionary War general, the Marquis de Lafayette, received a set of Bakewell decanters when he visited Pittsburgh, and the firm was awarded a gold medal at the Franklin Institute competition in Philadelphia. In 1829, Bakewell made a full table service of glassware for President Andrew Jackson. Through such gifts to influential private parties and governmental leaders, the Bakewell company demonstrated what would become a hallmark of the western Pennsylvania glass interests: the linking of glass-making interests with politics.[10]

Work Redefined and Child Labor Reconsidered

The Bakewell enterprise was, as noted, something of an exception, since most Pittsburgh glass houses made glass for more general use. Most Pittsburgh glass factories employed production techniques that were labor intensive, requiring teams of both skilled adult workers and glass house boys. These glass workers operated in an environment in which the laws that circumscribed their labor had, within the last generation or two, undergone some radical changes. Although these changes worked to the benefit of both the workers and the employers, they primarily benefited the employers, especially with regard to their child workers. The nineteenth century saw the ascendancy in the United States of "free" labor as the norm of the marketplace. This was a significant change from earlier dominance of "unfree" labor in both England and the colonies.

Most forms of unfree labor included work under a formal indenture as well as almost all forms of more informal labor for hire. Both were essentially contractual in nature, and the legal structures that defined them prior to the nineteenth century gave the employer tremendous physical as well as economic power over the contracting worker, whether an adult or child, essentially binding the worker to the job. In the early colonial period, under American law, based directly on English law, if a worker violated a labor agreement, he or she could be subjected to criminal as well as civil penalties. That is, in addition to being liable for any monetary damages that might result, the "worker who agreed to work for a period of time or to perform some particular piece of work in exchange for either wages, or training, or for transatlantic transportation expenses was subject to imprisonment for failure to fulfill the agreement."[11] These restrictions applied to servants and apprentices as well as laborers and artificers. With the tremendous labor shortage that characterized the early American labor markets, however, the country could ill afford to have part of the available workforce sitting in jail. Thus, the criminal penalties for breach of a labor contract were eventually eliminated in the United States, not only in their application to adult workers but for children as well.

The most common forms of labor restriction applicable to children in the early years of the republic were contractual apprenticeships, binding out, and indentured servitude. Prevalent in the colonies, these labor systems had several shared features. Apprenticeship was a fairly common way for a father or guardian to augment the family's income and to ensure that (usually) his son learned a useful trade. Young children were contracted into the care of an adult employer skilled in a line of work that the child then learned. Typically the child lived with, and was under the direct supervision of, the adult employer for a set period of time. The contract was between the employer and the father, with the child representing the property or the subject of the agreement. The wages earned by the child belonged, by law, to the father. The employer not only taught the child a trade but also was responsible for more general, quasi-parental supervision and discipline. Binding out was a similar arrangement except that it was generally reserved for orphans and children otherwise removed from their homes by force of law. Indentured servitude was also contractually similar to apprenticeship but was primarily a financing arrangement without the express requirement or expectation that the child would learn a useful skill or trade as a result of the employment.[12]

Each of these forms of unfree child labor fell into disuse during the nineteenth century, to be replaced by free, contractual labor for children, much as for adults, except that the nineteenth-century father retained the legal right to the child's contract wages until the child reached the age of majority. But even after the decline of unfree labor, the power of the employers, while changed at law, was not substantially reduced in practice, whether the worker was an adult or a child. For all workers, the end of imprisonment for violating a labor contract gave those workers technical legal autonomy over the value of their labor. This was not unimportant, but the employer nevertheless retained an enormous advantage in economic power over the worker, especially where, as in the United States for much of the nineteenth century, many forms of unionization were either illegal, unavailable, or otherwise restricted. The employer still exercised nearly full control over the means of production—that is, the employer owned and controlled the factories, the equipment, and the capital. While changes in the legal relationship between worker and employer gave some measure of control to the laborer over his or her work, "it also helped to obscure the systematic ways in which law continued to contribute to their oppression through the operation of the ordinary rules of property and contract in a world in which productive assets were unequally distributed."[13]

This general disparity in power between the employer and employee was accentuated in the case of most child workers and especially the glass house boys of Pittsburgh. In Pennsylvania, as in most states in the late nineteenth century, the legal environment had evolved to allow children like the glass house boys to contract their labor "freely." The possibility of criminal penalties if they failed to fulfill these contractual agreements no longer existed, but the glass manufacturers still owned the means of production—the glass houses—and thus they exercised significant control over the terms and conditions of employment.[14] Also, unlike in some other glass centers located in more rural areas, Pittsburgh had a dependable supply of potential glass house boys. This surplus gave the employers additional leverage in the hiring process. Further, while the bottle or green-glass industry in the Pittsburgh district had a very active union presence, these unions were open only to the skilled adult glass worker. Thus, although the boys followed many of the same work practices as the adult glass workers, especially in terms of the physical conditions of employment, they did not have a direct, officially acknowledged, or organized way to participate in the structures that created these practices and conditions. These boys worked side by side with the skilled adult glass men, they labored in the same shops, they were to be found next (and often closer) to the same furnaces, they kept the same shift hours both night and day, but they had only a muted voice in structuring their work life.

Glass and Politics in Western Pennsylvania

From the late eighteenth century until the Civil War, the glass houses in western Pennsylvania, like those founded by Craig, O'Hara, and Bakewell, expanded and contracted in response to the ebbs and flows of national economic policies and cycles. Overall, however, glass experienced a general if uncertain growth in response to expanding demand. Nationally, while there were about 10 glass factories in 1800, there were 20 by 1810 and 30 by 1820. The pace of growth then quickened a bit, and by midcentury the nation had some 94 glass factories.[15] By 1880, there were at least 169 glass houses in operation and another 42 were being built. The Pittsburgh glass-bottle industry tended to mirror these national patterns of growth.[16]

During this period, the American glass industry in general, and the western Pennsylvania glass houses in particular, benefited (and occasionally suffered) from governmental actions. Because of these influences, the glass manufacturers in Pittsburgh, as illustrated by the Bakewell company, learned to meld politics and business to their economic advantage. One of the first "political" benefits bestowed on the glass industry came with the embargo of 1807. The embargo, coupled with the Non-Intercourse Act and the eventual War of 1812, effectively cut off virtually all English imports, including glass. To meet the domestic demand for glass products, the market turned to domestic suppliers, and glass production increased. This surge in demand was reversed in the years immediately after the war. The postwar flood of imports and the related economic depression hit the glass factories in Pittsburgh hard, with several of the newly formed producers closing down. By 1819, however, these economic troubles led to the passage of the first federal protective tariff, and glass production again increased. The glass manufacturers in Pittsburgh immediately recognized the beneficial effects of this type of federal legislation, and they worked with western Pennsylvania's congressional representative, Henry Baldwin, to strengthen glass-related protections under the 1824 tariff. The influence of the Pittsburgh glass interests on this tariff law was so substantial that it became known, at least locally, as the "Pittsburgh cut glass bill." The tariff's principal sponsor, Senator Henry Clay, received Bakewell decanters in recognition of his support for the glass manufacturers' efforts.[17]

It is important to note how the issue of child labor (intertwined with the importance of whiskey) was brought to the public's attention during congressional action on the 1824 tariff legislation. In an earlier election, Representative Henry Baldwin, a federalist, defeated his Republican challenger, Samuel Douglas, in large part because Baldwin supported the tariff that was one of the principal campaign issues. Later, Baldwin, who was on the committee in the U.S. House of Representatives that drafted the 1824 bill, responded to the lobbying efforts of the western Pennsylvania glass interests and expanded the tariff's protections to include glass bottles as well as flint/crystal glass, which was already under the protection of the 1819 law. As the bill was being debated in the House, Baldwin argued that the expanded protection was necessary because "the greater proportion of the raw materials necessary in the manufacture of [glass bottles] came from domestic sources, while the demand for the manufactured product created a market for the products of the farmer [i.e., whiskey] and gave employment not only to laboring men, *but also to boys who would otherwise contract habits of idleness and vice.*"[18] Baldwin's comments tell us several important things about the western Pennsylvania glass industry in the early years of the nineteenth century. His words provide direct evidence that, even by 1820, the production technologies for glass bottles in western Pennsylvania required the use of child labor. Not only were these factories using boy help but they were also employing enough boys to allow Baldwin to leverage some political advantage out of that fact. The basis for this political capital was the view, which was held by many in the early nineteenth century, that industrial labor was actually beneficial rather than harmful for a young child. Finally, the federal tariff legislation evidenced the importance of the glass industry to the Pittsburgh economy and the developing ability of the area's glass interests to favorably influence federal legislation.

After the 1830s, the western Pennsylvania glass men used their developing political lobbying skills to generate benefits from state legislative action as well. Transportation in particular was a problem; because of the fragility of the product, shipping glass any distance was of special concern to the Pittsburgh glass manufacturers.[19] The Allegheny Mountains, which had made it difficult to ship eastern Pennsylvania glass to Pittsburgh and thus given rise to a western Pennsylvania glass industry, also made it difficult for Pittsburgh producers to expand their markets by shipping glass across the mountains to eastern areas. One of the first major transportation improvement projects sponsored by the Pennsylvania legislature was the construction of the Pennsylvania Canal, which opened in 1834 and linked Pittsburgh with Philadelphia. The impact of the canal on the glass producers of Pittsburgh was startling. In 1834, during the first year of the canal's operation, Pittsburgh window glass firms shipped 3,212 boxes of product east. The next year this figure increased to 5,908 boxes, and the next year, to 6,650. This change represented more than a doubling of production in two years.[20]

With this level of increased production, the Pittsburgh glass men clearly realized the potential economic impact of state legislation and the importance of state-level political lobbying. They began advocating for other state-sponsored infrastructure improvements because, while significant, the canal did not solve all of their transportation problems. Pittsburgh, for example, relied heavily on its rivers for moving its industrial products, but because of low water levels for much of the summer, commercial traffic on the rivers was not always possible. To compensate for navigability problems on the Ohio River, the western Pennsylvania glass men lobbied the state for and won a canal connection to Lake Erie. To help access markets to the south, they sought and received improved navigation on the Monongahela River.[21]

Because water transportation, even with canal and river improvements, was not unproblematic, the glass men also lobbied for and played a principal role in establishing the extension of the railroad to western Pennsylvania. When one of the first western Pennsylvania railroad ventures, the Pittsburgh & Connellsville Railroad Company, was incorporated in 1837, its commissioners included four men with ties to Pittsburgh glass companies: Benjamin Bakewell, William Ripley, William Davidson, and Andrew Stewart. Then, on April 14, 1846, when the state legislature granted the charter for the Pennsylvania Railroad Commission, the first set of commissioners included five men prominent in the western Pennsylvania glass industry: Harmar Denny, of Pittsburgh's H. Denny & Company glassworks; Thomas Bakewell, son of Benjamin Bakewell and a principal in Bakewell,

Page & Bakewell; William Eichbaum, who had been the principal glass man in the very first Pittsburgh glass house started by Craig and O'Hara; John Hay, of the Pittsburgh-based Hay & McCully glass enterprise; and Samuel W. Black, a principal in a Williamsport, Pennsylvania, glass factory. By 1857, the Pennsylvania Railroad had acquired all of the property of the Pennsylvania Canal system, thereby effectively ending the canal's existence as a competing means of transport and ensuring the railroad's position, for the foreseeable future, as the primary commercial transportation system serving western Pennsylvania.[22]

Thus, by the start of the Civil War, Pittsburgh was very well situated to assert dominance in many industrial ventures, especially in glass. After the war, glass manufacturing was established on such a firm foundation that periodic economic depressions had no radical effect on it. Many factors had created a permanent demand for glass. Since the inception of the glass industry in western Pennsylvania, the population of the United States had increased tremendously. This increase, together with rising standards of living, resulted in an extensive market for everyday necessities. The improvements in transportation facilities, including new roads, canals, and railroads, permitted western Pennsylvania glassmakers to ship their products to all parts of America, and even to Europe.[23]

In 1860, there were as many as thirty western Pennsylvania glass houses, together producing windows and other glass wares worth approximately $2.3 million. The rest of Pennsylvania accounted for only about $1.2 million in glass production, while the two other principal glass-manufacturing states, Massachusetts and New Jersey, accounted for just $2,004,500 and $1,098,000, respectively. Thus, the Pittsburgh region produced nearly two-thirds of Pennsylvania's glass and nearly a quarter of the nation's. This represented substantial growth since 1820, when Pittsburgh accounted for only slightly more than 15 percent of the nation's glass factories, or even 1840, when Pittsburgh accounted for little more than 20 percent of the nation's total value of glass product.[24]

After the Civil War, production from western Pennsylvania glass houses continued to expand to meet the demands of the nation's rapidly growing population. By 1880, Pittsburgh had nearly 30 percent (61 of 211) of the country's glass factories and accounted for more than 31 percent of the dollar value of production, with an annual output in excess of $6.6 million.

After 1880, however, conditions began to change. The newly discovered natural gas fields in Ohio, Indiana, and Illinois lured factories away from Pittsburgh, and the locus of glass production began to shift westward. New technological developments also increased competitive pressures on the western Pennsylvania manufacturers, further reducing their leadership position in the industry. Progressive Era reform proposals put pressure on the child labor practices that formed the backbone of glass production techniques used in the Pittsburgh area glass houses. The full impact of these and other developments was not realized for some years, and at least at the end of the nineteenth century, the Pittsburgh glass men were still in an enviable position. They were the nation's leading producers in a growing national industry, they were well connected in state and federal political circles, and they were located in the principal industrial region in the nation, where they enjoyed substantial benefits both from the easy availability of natural resources and from a well-developed transportation network.[25]

Glass Manufacturers and Early Technological Change

Up until the last decades of the nineteenth century, the glass-bottle factories in and around Pittsburgh used the same process for making bottles as had been in use for several thousand years. Bottle production was organized around the "pot" system, and work was conducted during a typical ten- to twelve-hour work day. Bottle glass was typically made with a mixture of sand, potash, and lime, which was placed in special clay pots, each standing several feet high, and then put in a furnace to melt. While any given glass factory might operate several furnaces at once and while each furnace might have room for several pots, any one pot was always worked by a single crew of workers, or "shop," which made their bottles from the molten glass inside. The contents of one pot tended to keep one shop busy for a single work day. At the end of the day, the furnaces would be shut down, and the process would resume the next morning from scratch. When smaller pots were used, the shop might consist of a single adult glass blower and two boy assistants; with larger pots, there might be up to three adults and up to four boys. An experienced shop of this sort might produce about forty dozen eight-ounce bottles per day.[26]

Because production levels under the pot system were restricted by the size and number of pots that could be placed in a furnace, manufacturers sought other ways of preparing the raw glass for use in their factories. This research led to the most significant technological advance to affect the glass-bottle plants in the United States during the nineteenth century: the development of the continuous tank system for melting glass. This invention did not change how glass bottles were formed, but it dramatically altered the way molten glass was prepared. The continuous tank process was relatively simple, but it revolutionized glassmaking and replaced the traditional pot system in virtually every commercial glass-bottle factory in the United States. Under the tank system, the desired proportions of raw materials for the glass were fed into one end of a large vat or tank. The raw materials were then mixed, heated, and melted as they were slowly moved to the other end of the tank. By the time the now-molten glass reached the far end of the tank, it was ready to be worked. Unlike the pot system, if the tank was continuously supplied with raw materials on the one end, it never went dry at the other. The work of making glass, therefore, never needed to stop. The first continuous tank furnace was put into operation in Poughkeepsie, New York, in 1879, and it was first put to large-scale commercial use in the mid-1880s at a massive new glassworks in Jeannette, Pennsylvania, just a few miles east of Pittsburgh. By the 1890s, the continuous tank system had become the standard way to melt glass in the hand-blown bottle sector of the industry.[27]

The continuous tank technology was particularly well suited to the Pittsburgh glass-bottle industry, and the Pittsburgh producers did not find conversion to the tank system to be either unusually expensive or difficult. The new system still required the traditional hand-blowing process to form the bottles, and, as such, it did not disturb the importance of the glass blowers in the production process; if anything, the new system increased their importance. Because the tank system enabled the Pittsburgh glass houses to operate around the clock, it allowed for a substantial increase in the number of bottles that could be made, which in turn greatly increased the demand for skilled glass blowers. The increase in production was also easily absorbed by the nation's growing demand for glass. Because of the demand for more glass workers, both the skilled glass blowers and their union encouraged the region's factories to convert from the older, history-laden pot system to the new tanks. As both the number of conversions and the number of skilled glass blower positions grew, so did the demand for glass house boys. In Pittsburgh, the demand for boy help was easily met, and by the early twentieth century, most western Pennsylvania bottle plants were operating round-the-clock shifts and most glass house boys worked day and night. As the reformers made clear, the increased demands on the glass house boys for night work further exacerbated the strains on their health and made it increasingly difficult for them to go to school.

Bottle making under either the pot or continuous tank systems was both a labor-intensive and skill-dependent operation. Multiple, intricate production steps were required to form the base, sides, and neck of the bottle, and each step needed to be accomplished with great precision if the finished object was to function properly. The skill involved in crafting hand-blown bottles had, by the late nineteenth century, enabled the adult glass blowers to be among the highest paid workers in American industry, even as the glass house boys were among the lowest. At this time a Pittsburgh glass blower could expect to earn at least between $3.52 and $3.63 per day, while the average glass house boy could expect only between $0.72 and $0.84.[28]

With the introduction of the continuous tank system and the increased demand for glass blowers, glass manufacturers faced what they perceived as ever-increasing demands from the skilled blowers for higher wages and more control over the production process. The manufacturers began to search for labor-saving machinery to replace at least some of these workers in order to fight both union militancy and rising labor costs.[29] Because of the difficulties in making bottles, however, the introduction of machines into this sector of the industry was slow. Fewer patents, for example, were filed for bottle-making processes between 1850 and 1890 than in any other area of glass production.[30]

Because bottle manufacturing was the largest part of the glass industry, however, it continued to provide an appealing target for the inventors of automated technologies. Some of the earliest mechanical devices to be developed for this sector were molds for forming the bottles. These allowed for visually identical bottles to be made one after the other by blowing glass into a mold that was opened and closed by a glass house boy crouching at the feet of the glass blower. One of the first mold-related patents was

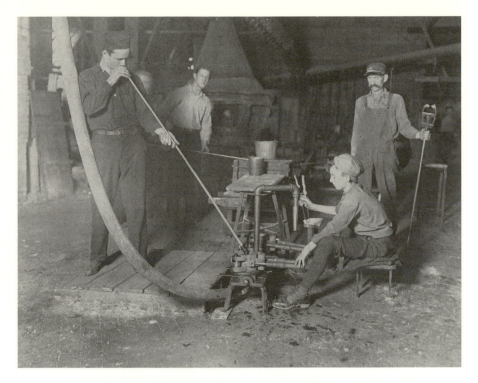

"Glass Blower and Mold Boy. Boy has 4½ hours of this at a stretch, then an hour's rest and 4½ more: cramped position. Day shift one week: night shift next." Grafton, West Virginia, October 1908

awarded to Gustavus Storm in 1875, when he developed a detachable plate to be fitted inside a regular bottle mold so that a flask could be made with a name, symbol, or other personalized image to meet the needs of the purchaser. This was primarily a way to add ornamentation to a bottle that was otherwise being blown by hand, an effect that was particularly popular with the patent medicine trade and with political parties, which used the bottles as campaign souvenirs.[31]

In 1880, a more significant development occurred. William L. Libbey, of the New England Glass Company, developed a patented mold that could be used to form a more complete bottle by uniting several of the separate bottle-making steps into one operation. In 1882, Philip Arbogast of Pittsburgh built on the Libbey invention and patented a two-mold sys-

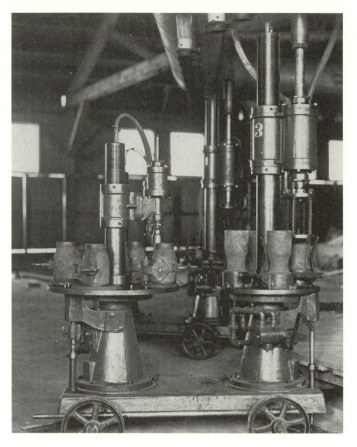

"Machine that blows 4 milk bottles at a time. No 'lung blowers' employed. Travis Glass Co., Clarksburg, W.Va. Manager says machines are fast coming into play in bottle industry, plans eventually to have machines in place of 'carrying in boys.'" October 1908

tem that accomplished a similar, though somewhat more refined result. The Libbey and Arbogast inventions marked the first time that mechanical devices could be used to replicate a significant part of the hand-blown bottle-making process. To the extent that "beginnings" can be identified, together these two inventions started the automated (or at this point, the semi-automated) bottle-making process. In the 1890s, the Ball brothers in Muncie, Indiana, purchased the rights to the Arbogast patent for ten thousand dollars, and by the turn of the century, the Ball company had developed its own version of a bottle-making machine that could actually blow the molten glass into the mold and automatically make wide-mouth jars. By 1905, more than 250 of the Ball machines were in use, producing the vast majority of what are now familiar as canning jars.[32]

The Libbey and Arbogast inventions also inspired Michael J. Owens in 1894–1895 to develop a series of paste mold machines that could mechanically produce lightbulbs, lamp chimneys, and tumblers with no visible lines where the mold sections joined. A single automatic Owens paste mold machine could be operated by just two men, with no particular glass-making skills, to produce up to forty-three hundred items per day, whereas three skilled hand-blowers with their several assistants and boy helpers could expect to produce only thirty-six hundred similar items in the same period. The potential savings in labor costs were thus substantial.[33]

These and similar labor-saving machines tended to operate at the margins of the glass-bottle sector, and they initially had little adverse impact on the industry's demand for either skilled glass blowers or glass house boys.[34] Ball jars, for example, while an important product, were a relatively small part of the bottle business. Their production could be fully automated, and with the still-increasing demand for other types of bottles, the glass blowers who had made Ball jars could readily find work producing some other line of ware. The other inventions in the bottle sector, like that of Gustavus Storm, did not really operate as labor-saving devices either. To the extent that they increased demand for a particular type of product, they actually increased the demand for skilled glass blowers and for glass house boys. These mechanical devices also increased jobs in other glass-related industries. By the end of the nineteenth century, for example, W. S. McKee of Pittsburgh, whose family had started making glass in 1842, got into the mold-making business with the purchase of the P. Smith & Company machine shop. McKee was soon joined in Pittsburgh by Fischer Foundry & Machine Company, the William Hirth blacksmith shop, and a machine plant operated by Charles Leng, who was formerly with Pittsburgh's D. O. Cunningham glass factory. These and similar glass-making machine shops were appearing in virtually every glass-producing area in the country to service the needs of manufacturers using the new automated technologies.

As with any technological changes in an established industry, these mechanical inventions were viewed by some glass-bottle manufacturers as great improvements for their sector of the industry and by others as a source of great anxiety and uncertainty. The *National Glass Budget*, the glass manufacturers' newspaper published in Pittsburgh, reflected these conflicting perspectives as it reported on these early efforts at mechanization in the industry. Stressing the advantages of automation, the *Budget* stated that "[m]achine made goods . . . now have the call and preference over inferior and often indifferently made handmade goods, because of their absolute cleanliness, perfect finish and unvarying uniformity."[35] Observing the influx of mechanical devices in the industry, the *Budget* also predicted that "during the next five years, the American glass industry will be more mightily impulsed by the introduction of glass-working machinery, than it has during the last half century."[36] The newspaper later noted approvingly that one of the Owens paste mold machines had been seen to produce as many as two thousand tumblers in five hours.[37] This particular machine, treated as a mechanical marvel, was built with a rotating table attached to a multi-pipe blowing apparatus, which allowed sequential blowing and finishing operations to be performed in a precisely timed sequence. This system could produce multiple identical copies of the desired object simultaneously. The end product was of very high quality, and, the newspaper noted, the machines had proven to be very successful.

But the *National Glass Budget* also tried to reflect the concerns of the glass manufacturers who feared that these machines would drive them out of business. Speaking for these interests, the newspaper told its readers that the glass manufacturers faced a "present emergency" created by the introduction of glass-producing machines, acknowledging that the "manufacturers are at their wits end to know what to do." The machines that were in use prior to the start of the twentieth century tended to be product specific and, when introduced in any significant numbers, tended to dominate production in that sector of the industry. Thus, they generated massive restructuring in the affected sectors. Using the language of a military conflict, the *Budget* noted that the machines had "invaded" branch after branch of the trade with the same result: while production had been "immensely increased," prices had also dropped "below the living point," and the industry was "being concentrated."[38]

It was this last point that was foremost in the minds of many glass manufacturers because "concentration" meant consolidation, and consolidation (they feared) meant that not everyone would survive the "invasion." The *National Glass Budget* observed that prior to the introduction of the automatic tumbler machine in the 1890s, a great many glass factories in the country made that line of ware. But following the introduction of the tumbler machine, only a very few glass houses were needed to make "all the common pressed tumblers and goblets required" by the nation. The same was true of "vaseline jars, fruit jars and all wide mouth ware." This understandably worried some of the owners of handmade glass–bottle factories. When mechanization occurred, they wondered whether they would be among the few survivors or among the many left behind. The *Budget*, looking at the benefits of automation to the industry as a whole, counseled the owners, albeit cautiously, to "do their utmost to obtain, as early as possible, the best labor saving machinery perfected by man, at home or abroad, [or] . . . be ground to pieces in the merciless competitive struggle."[39]

The "invasion" of machines into the glass-bottle factories, of course, did not abate. And, so long as there were significant numbers of glass houses that had not yet converted from hand-blown to mechanical processes, the tension within the glass-bottle manufacturing community did not abate either. As the glass-making machines became more sophisticated and costly, not all manufacturers were equally able to afford the expense of conversion, and the tensions increased proportionately.

The Development and Impact of the Owens Automatic

The several mold and semi-automatic machines developed toward the end of the nineteenth century were very important for the bottle-making sector of the glass industry, but without question, the most significant invention for these manufacturers during the period under study here was the Owens Automatic developed by Michael J. Owens in 1903–1904. The Owens Automatic, more so than any other previously developed mechanical glass-making device, could do it all and, in the process, replace virtually all adult and child labor associated with glass-bottle manufacturing. As one contemporary described it, the Owens Automatic was in a class by itself: "It gathers its glass, forms its blanks, transfers the blank from the gathering mold to the blow mold with a finishing lip and ring, blows the bottle and delivers the finished bottle automatically without the touch of the human hand . . . and puts the same amount of glass into every bottle, makes every bottle the same length, finish, weight, and capacity, it wastes no glass, uses no pipes, snaps, finishing tools, glory holes, rosin, [or] charcoal."[40] While its development was predicated on prior mechanical inventions in the glass industry, the Owens Automatic was singular in its operational characteristics and in its impact. Not only did it change the lives of the laborers involved in making glass bottles—the skilled glass blowers and their boy helpers—but it also changed the lives of the manufacturers.

It was ironic that the Owens Automatic, the quintessential labor-saving machine in the glass-bottle industry, had been developed by Michael J. Owens, who was himself a former union glass blower. Owens was born in Mason County, Virginia (now West Virginia), on January 1, 1859. The son of a coal miner, he started work as a glass house boy and advanced to become an apprentice in the Hobbs and Brockunier glass works in Wheeling, West Virginia. After becoming a journeyman glass blower, he joined the American Flint Glass Workers Union. In 1888, Owens moved to Toledo, Ohio, to begin work for Edward D. Libbey. Libbey had taken over the New England Glass Company in 1883, when his father died. Just prior to joining forces with Owens, and shortly after receiving his patent for the semi-automatic bottle mold device, Libbey had moved his company to Toledo to take advantage of the newly discovered natural gas fields in northwestern Ohio. In the process, he changed his firm's name to the Libbey Glass Company. With Libbey's financial backing and encouragement, Owens moved from making glass to making machines that made glass. It was under Libbey's sponsorship that he designed in the 1890s the previously described set of lightbulb, chimney, and tumbler paste mold machines that dramatically changed glassmaking in those sectors. Largely because of these inventions, he was singled out for special praise in the *National Glass Budget*, which noted that, while most of the inventors of labor-saving, glass-making machinery were not men who had come out of the glass factories, "Michael Owens is one of the exceptions," and what set him apart from the others was the "practical knowledge" he had acquired as a glass worker.[41]

Owens put this practical knowledge to use in creating and perfecting the Owens Automatic. The first indication of the scope of his new invention came in early 1903, when the *Budget*, in one of the numerous articles it ran summarizing the list of mechanical inventions available, noted almost in passing that "the [forthcoming] Owens machine . . . will not only make narrow neck bottles but will [do so] . . . automatically."[42] A few months later, as more of the details of what the Owens Automatic might be able to do became known, the newspaper's praise of Owens's invention increased. Owens, the newspaper reported, had invented a "world-beater down in Toledo that bids fair not only to take away the breath, but it will paralyze any glass worker who has a nervous system." The *Budget* then predicted that when the machine was fully operational, "there will be no gatherers, pressers, blowers, stick-ups, finishers, carrying-in boys, or laying-in boys, no learsmen, batch wheelers, teasers or infillers—only one man with a monkey wrench, and he will wear a white collar and linen duster."[43] Later, because of the reluctance of some glass-bottle manufacturers, particularly those in Pittsburgh, to convert their factories from hand-blown production methods to the Owens Automatic, the *Budget*'s early advocacy of automated machinery and support for the Owens invention would be slightly tempered. But its initial praise was effusive.

The economic advantages of operating the Owens machine were impressive. In the early twentieth century, labor amounted to about 60 percent of the production cost of bottles. Because the Owens Automatic eliminated the need for virtually all human labor, it was not surprising that significant economies could be realized from using the machine.[44] Distribution of the Owens machine was handled by the Owens Bottle Machine Company (Owens Company), which estimated that in 1905, the labor cost for making a gross of beer bottles by hand was about $1.47. The labor cost was $0.75 for bottles blown on any one of the several semi-automatic machines on the market but only $0.10 for bottles made with the Owens Automatic. With an annual production of at least 2.5 million gross of beer bottles nationally, the total potential cost savings was nothing short of staggering.[45]

The Owens Company realized that the price for glass bottles might well collapse if this machine were introduced too fast, so it acted with caution. By the end of 1905, it had licensed the operation of just 4 machines, to glass factories in Toledo and in Newark, New Jersey. This licensing figure expanded to 14 in 1906, 22 in 1907, and 46 in 1908.[46] By 1911, at least 103 Owens Automatic machines were in operation, and these machines had a total capacity of about 4.2 million gross of bottles per year. By 1912, there were 133 machines installed, and the annual capacity topped 7 million gross. In 1914, the number of machines swelled to 172.[47] Such results no doubt explain why, in 1915, Owens was awarded the Eliot Cresson Gold Medal by the Franklin Institute of Philadelphia for his work in the promotion of the mechanical arts. The effect of the Owens machine on employment of glass workers matched the pace of its introduction. In 1905, when it was first introduced, the total number of workers employed in bottle factories was approximately ten thousand. But by 1924, after the vast majority of hand-blown factories had converted to mechanical processes and more than 18 million gross of bottles were being made by automatic and semi-automatic machines, the number of workers had dropped by 75 percent.[48]

What made the Owens Automatic noteworthy was that it posed a serious threat to the economic well-being of not only the glass house workers but also many of the glass-bottle manufacturers. Individual manufacturers used a complicated calculus to decide when and if a transition to the Owens machine was possible: Did they need to build a new factory or substantially remodel an existing one? How much would the machine cost to purchase or lease? What were their competitors doing? What was the availability of child labor? Could they risk losing skilled glass workers in the event of a union boycott? Because of the uncertainty attached to each of these questions, the position of the individual glass-bottle manufacturer might well be conflicted. The calculation was not a trivial matter because the likely results of switching to the Owens Automatic were such that those who used it might well be able to put those who did not out of business.

When the *Budget* reported on problems with automation, it was careful not to criticize the glass manufacturers who were reluctant to adopt machines such as the Owens Automatic. Instead, it questioned the actions of others. For example, when the *Budget* ran stories and editorials critical of the slow pace of adopting the new mechanized processes, it would usually not mention those manufacturers who had not yet automated their plants but would instead castigate either the Owens Company or the glass workers' union for being obstacles to modernization. The Owens Company came under attack by the *Budget* because of the way it licensed the Owens Automatic. The company had set the licensing fee both to reflect the savings potential available to the machine's users and to regulate the speed of the machine's introduction into the industry. As noted above, the company was concerned that the aggressive introduction of the Owens Automatic might have negative impacts on the price, and thus the profitability, of glass. While the Owens Company kept specifics about its licensing practices secret, it was not too difficult for observers to determine what the fees were. Early on it was reported that the company had sold the right to make milk bottles with the Owens Automatic to the Thatcher Manufacturing Company of Potsdam, New York, for an estimated $250,000 and that it had made a similar deal with a foreign syndicate to have bottles made in England and France.[49]

The National Glass Budget used this information on the licensing fees as an opportunity to criticize the Owens Company's business judgment. The newspaper complained that because of the high licensing costs, the "Owens bottle blowing machine, the wonderful performance of which has been heralded to the world in various forms during the past two years, has not yet been put into practical operation for the commercial mass-production of bottles." The newspaper then said that the Owens Company had simply failed to properly market the machine and that "the prospect of efficiently utilizing the Owens machine seems to be too big for the hands that hold the controlling stock. . . . They have up till now hesitated to grapple firmly with the problem, and are, in the judgment of the best informed glassmen, frittering away valuable time and wasting their opportunities to make money and get control of the bottle trade." This, the newspaper concluded, had been a matter of "real genuine surprise to interested observers, and a disappointment."[50]

The Budget also liked to repeatedly remind its readers that the principle glass-bottle union, the Glass Bottle Blowers' Association, and its president, Denis A. Hayes, were also major obstacles to mechanization. Hayes's basic position was that modernization was acceptable so long as the glass-bottle plants still employed his union glass men and so long as the mechanized shops did not produce so much glassware that they drove the remaining handmade bottle shops out of business. The Budget, needless to say, found several problems with this stance. In an editorial run during the summer of 1903, when the first prototype of the Owens Automatic was being completed, the newspaper asserted that the only place for such a sophisticated piece of automated glass-blowing machinery would be "in a non-union factory; [because] it takes more ... brains" to run a single nonunion shop "than it takes to run a half dozen union factories." The problem with union factories, the *Budget* contended, was that they were run according to union rules and not intelligent decision making. As the *National Glass Budget* saw it, because of the stranglehold the GBBA had over the production process, installing labor-saving machinery in its plants would require "not only genius but diplomacy of the highest order to ... make quality and quantity satisfactory to union workmen working under union rules."[51]

This characterization of the union as obstructionist and fostering narrow thinking was not new. But, in a very rare move, the *Budget* also extended its critique to include some manufacturers as well. Addressing the manufacturers, the same editorial noted that they had been complicit with the union's obstructionist tactics because for many years they could be "depended on to yield" to union demands "rather than have trouble." The editorial's rhetoric grew sharper, stating that "[e]ver do they [the manufacturers] duck to the shallow pate and thereby encourage what they most despise."[52] In such passages one can see the newspaper engaging in the delicate task of trying to rouse manufacturers to modernize without alienating them.

Hayes also provided an easy target for the *Budget* because of his response to the Owens Automatic in particular. In early 1905, in an unprecedented move, Hayes was invited visit Toledo to observe firsthand the Owens Automatic making bottles in the Owens/Libbey factory. The *Budget* took this opportunity to remind its readers that it had been "goading and prodding President Hayes for more than a year about his duty to see the Owens machine in operation." Then, after he finally made the trip and saw the machine in action, the newspaper complained that Hayes was too slow in issuing a promised circular sharing his appraisal of it.[53] Two weeks later, while still complaining about Hayes's tardiness in preparing the circular, the *Budget* took the opportunity to direct more ridicule at Hayes, asserting that "a circular on the subject would really not be necessary if the members of the bottle blowers' union were all readers of The Budget," but they were not, according to the *Budget*, because Hayes "does not allow them to be." Offering no specific support, the editorial simply asserted that Hayes "requires all who wish to remain in touch with the throne and in grace with its occupant"—that is, with Hayes—"to cut out The Budget."[54] When the newspaper finally got a copy of the Hayes circular, it reprinted it in full. In it, Hayes both recognized the potential impact of the Owens Automatic and outlined a plan in which the union would gradually accommodate the new machine. He told his union members that "we cannot ignore its existence or belittle its importance without doing injustice to ourselves," and from that day forward, he noted, "such machinery must of necessity become a very prominent factor in all our calculations."[55] The *Budget*, however, was not satisfied, and it used more than three full-length editorial columns to respond to the circular and rake the GBBA president over the coals. In what could be viewed as a sign of disrespect, the newspaper misspelled his name, referring to the GBBA president as "Dennis Hays." More fundamentally, however, the *Budget*'s primary objection to the circular was that by failing to state straightforwardly that the Owens Automatic signaled the beginning of the end for the skilled union glass worker, Hayes and the GBBA were simply ignoring reality.[56]

What the *Budget* was doing here was to use Hayes and the GBBA as surrogates for some of the manufacturers. That is, by characterizing the Hayes/GBBA approach to the Owens machine as obstructionist, the newspaper could indirectly and gently criticize the manufacturers who were, in its opinion, excessively cautious in automating their factories. The newspaper knew it could assert that Hayes was the problem, but in so doing, it also implied that Hayes was not acting alone, that he was being subtly (and inadvertently) supported by overly fearful manufacturers. On the mechanization issue, then, the *Budget* could hammer away on some points but had to walk a fine line on others, and its rhetoric reflected this duality. The newspaper could say that union rules created a brainless factory environment or that Denis Hayes had to be goaded into seeing the Owens machine, and its readers would likely nod in agreement. When it talked about the costs and benefits of mechanization, however, the newspaper exercised much more restraint and employed a more "objective" style of discourse. Articles and editorials on mechanization issues sometimes simply listed the number of machines in use in a particular factory or sector or the rates of production or the cost savings for the manufacturers using those machines. Knowing that the cost of conversion was high and that it was dictated by sources outside the manufacturers' control, the newspaper tried to let the mere listing of advantages speak to the question of mechanization. Recognizing both the power of the union and the expense of modernization, the newspaper was generally careful in these articles to use rational, dispassionate language in its subtle attempt to persuade the manufacturers to modernize. It was a delicate rhetorical course to navigate and provides an excellent example of one of the systems of discourse that permeated the glass industry debates of the early twentieth century.

Hidden behind this carefully crafted pattern of discourse, however, were the owners of the Pittsburgh bottle plants who had evolved as a special pocket of resistance to mechanization. They had historically spurned automation and, more so than manufacturers in other areas of the country, continued to do so by spurning the Owens Automatic as well. It was observed that, even in the nineteenth century, the failure of the Pittsburgh glass men "to embrace technological advances in the bottle industry stands in sharp contrast to the use and development of machines in the city's pressed glass industry."[57] To keep the Owens Automatic out of Pittsburgh for as long as possible, the district's glass-bottle factory owners engaged in a tacit conspiracy with the GBBA. For both the manufacturers and the union, this unacknowledged agreement was something of a pact with the devil. For the manufacturers, it meant that they had to maintain a continuing relationship with their nemesis, the GBBA, a relationship consisting of continual battles over wage rates and work conditions in the glass houses. But the manufacturers saw this as an acceptable trade-off because, if they could keep production costs low, they could make a profit even if manufacturers in other parts of the country used the Owens Automatic. If, on the other hand, the relationship with the GBBA proved too difficult, the manufacturers (or at least some of them) felt they could switch to the Owens machine.

As discussed in greater detail in chapter 4, Hayes and the GBBA had fewer options. Hayes undoubtedly knew that the pact with the manufacturers to work together to keep the Owens Automatic out of Pittsburgh, while preserving glass worker jobs, also necessitated keeping handmade bottle costs as low as possible. These production economies meant operating the Pittsburgh glass houses day and night and reducing the historically high wages of Pittsburgh's union glass workers. The alternative, however, was large-scale unemployment for the union glass workers and the demise of the union. The production economies also meant that the Pittsburgh glass-bottle plants needed to maintain and, if possible, increase their reliance on the cheap labor of the glass house boys. This situation brought both the manufacturers and the GBBA into direct and bitter confrontation with the Progressive Era reformers. Thus, in contrast to virtually every other section of the industrial landscape, the Pittsburgh glass union and the Pittsburgh glass manufacturers, united in their opposition to the invasion of the Owens machine, were also united in their opposition to child labor reform.

The Glass Interests and Progressive Reform

The *National Glass Budget* provides evidence of the glass manufacturers' views on both the glass house boys and child labor reform efforts. Based on what appeared in the *Budget*, the manufacturers' view of the boys was largely self-serving while their view of the reforms and the reformers was unrelentingly and unapologetically negative. The *Budget* tried to portray the boys as mischievous children while at the same time acknowledging their importance to the glass-production process. The newspaper tried to counter reform proposals by arguing that child labor was good because the glass house boys needed to learn work habits, the boys needed to be allowed to contribute to their families' economic resources, and glass house work was safe and enjoyable. When, in spite of these assertions regarding the value of child labor, the demands for reform persisted, the *Budget* resorted to slander and ad hominem attacks directed at the progressive reformers themselves.

Both the newspaper and the manufacturers had vital economic interests in the child labor debate, but the issue also provided them with an opportunity to give voice to other, less savory social views. More than occasionally, as the *Budget* argued against child labor reform, it also reflected the racist, misogynistic, nativist, and what we might characterize today as homophobic perspectives of the glass manufacturers. On the principal issue of child labor, so long as there were some glass houses making hand-blown bottles, the newspaper viewed child labor and the need to have an adequate pool of glass house boys as an absolute business necessity. Under those circumstances, the manufacturers fought to preserve the continued availability of those child workers by nearly any means at their disposal.

While the *Budget* editorialized on the question of child labor quite frequently, it only rarely referred to the glass house boys directly. The newspaper provided very little sense of the glass house boys as people; it ran virtually no human interest stories about them, had no articles describing their family life, aired no stories depicting their habits of play. To the contrary, the *Budget* mentioned the children only if doing so would support its position on child labor reform or other issues important to the manufacturers, such as its advocacy of increased mechanization in the glass factories or its contempt for the activities of the glass blowers' unions.

Probably because the manufacturers did not want to acknowledge in any way the possible effectiveness of labor strikes, the *Budget* rarely mentioned any of the many such events orchestrated by the glass house boys. One of the few references to such job actions appeared in 1905. The newspaper reported that several boys at the Bryce-Higbee Company, near Pittsburgh, asked in the middle of a shift to be let off to see a baseball game. When the request was refused, according to the *Budget*, the boys "threw an assortment of scrap iron, bricks and bread into the glass pots." The plant had to close "when the mixture declined to fuse into glass" and the boys, without permission, "attended the ball game." All was not forgiven, however, and four of the boys were charged with malicious mischief by the plant owner and brought before a local judge. The judge "talked to the boys in a fatherly manner, and when they were in tears [he] turned them over to their parents."[58]

It is easy to imagine how this incident could have been reported so as to reinforce other contemporaneous notions of American boyhood. Many popular stories of the day extolled the pluck of enterprising youngsters who, like Huck Finn or Tom Sawyer or Ragged Dick, would express a bit of independence and amusing feistiness, with the expectation that they would then get it out of their systems, settle down, and "get on in life."[59] But the glass house owners did not see in the glass house boys an image of children who, through independent action and cunning, might pull themselves up by their bootstraps. To the contrary, in the eyes of their employers, the glass house boys needed to be willing to work long hours, at low pay, and in dangerous conditions. When the boys were no longer needed in the glass houses, the manufacturers wanted to be able to cut them off to fend for themselves in the industrial labor market. With this in mind, the *Budget* makes it clear that the boys' foolishness was costly and that it was not to be tolerated. The newspaper clearly implies that even if these boys got off rather lightly in this instance, with both a judicial and parental reprimand, they were lucky. In the future, such actions could have far more serious consequences.

The *Budget* also used its editorializing about the boys as a means of criticizing the glass workers' union. In 1896, for instance, the newspaper recounted how boys at the Hogan, Evans & Company chimney glass factory struck for the right to continue to daub, which was the industry tradition of allowing boys to practice gathering and blowing glass, either freehand or using a mold, when there was a lull in the production process. Here the newspaper got double duty out of the boys' job action. First, the article made light of the walkout, thereby downplaying the potential power of the boys to disrupt the industrial process; they were after all "merely" boys. Playing on a familiar "idle hands are the devil's plaything" theme, the article reported that after the boys walked off the job, they "went either to the balls or such other places of vice or amusement as their fancy, sweet will and perhaps not over-nice tastes dictate." Daubing was a longstanding practice in the bottle industry, and this incident provided the opportunity for the newspaper to chide the glass workers' union for contributing to the problem by restricting apprenticeship opportunities, a matter closely tied to daubing. This issue was a continuing bone of contention between the union and the owners, with the owners wanting to expand apprenticeship opportunities. The newspaper commented that the "boys could see that in their daubs lay their only possible means of advancement [in the industry], and unless they could get back that right, they would be deprived of the chance of acquiring the trade of the blowers." The managers settled the strike by giving the boys the right to daub. A few years later, still concerned with the GBBA's restriction on apprenticeships, the *Budget*, in an editorial critical of GBBA president Denis A. Hayes, commented that there "is not a single union factory in which the number of American boys who wish to learn the art of blowing glass, is not arbitrarily restricted."[60]

References to the glass house boys figured prominently in a number of other *Budget* stories, such as those dealing with proposed child labor regulations. While the newspaper would nearly always oppose any such proffered reforms, when the proposals affected a geographic area that traditionally experienced a chronic shortage of boy help, these reforms also provided an opportunity for the *Budget* to link its support of continued employment of the glass house boys with other barely veiled nativist and racist sentiments. The newspaper readily acknowledged that the American glass industry had originally been built on the skills of foreign-born glassmakers. But these were men coming from solidly middle-class Nordic origins, largely from Germany and other northern European countries.[61] By the dawn of the twentieth century, however, the importance of these foreign-born glass artisans had diminished, and the skilled glass blowers in most American glass houses were predominantly American born. Further, because of tight union control over the supply of skilled glass men, there was little opportunity for a glass blower who was a recent immigrant to work in an American glass house.

The manufacturers were wary, however, of the more recent influx of various other immigrant groups into the country, in particular Asians on the West Coast and southern and eastern Europeans on the East Coast. These new immigrants produced concerns as well as benefits for the glass producers, and the pages of the *Budget* reflected this Janus-faced situation. On the positive side, in areas like Pittsburgh, the great influx of immigrant, working-class adults to labor in its steel and iron works included large numbers of young boys who might seek work in the glass houses. The manufacturers did not hesitate to employ these foreign-born boys. The manufacturers knew that the boys would work cheaply, but they also believed that the boys were malleable and might be Americanized through the process of industrial labor. If the supply of potential glass house boys was low, then the *Budget* would point out that immigration policies were too restrictive.

A *Budget* article dealing with the Illinois Glass Company highlighted such a problem. The company always had trouble finding a sufficient number of glass house boys to enable it to operate at full capacity. This situation was made worse, from the manufacturers' perspective, by the fact that Illinois had some of the most progressive child labor and compulsory education laws in the country. The newspaper announced in 1907 that, to address the "boy" shortage created by these state laws, the Illinois Glass Company would have to begin to employ "a large batch of Japanese workmen from the Pacific coast" because they would "work for less wages than other foreigners, and could be utilized at the company's factory in doing boy jobs."[62]

The obvious disrespect for immigrant workers is evident in both the title of the article, which disparagingly referred to the replacement workers as "Japs," and by saying that these men were willing to work for even lower wages than "other foreigners."

Greater anxiety was registered, however, in response to the controversial move made a few years earlier by the Obear-Nestor Glass Works in East St. Louis, Illinois, when it hired "negro women in place of the boys usually to be found in glass factories." The *Budget* was quick to point out that this solution to the shortage of glass house boys "is worrying the families who depend upon servants to do their work" because the women employed in the glass houses presumably would otherwise have worked as domestics. Sounding a note of alarm, the newspaper warned that the company was required to request "aid from the police in keeping order when the workmen and the negresses leave the plant at night."[63]

In the economic logic of the industry, immigrants and blacks were treated as the rough equivalent of, although less desirable than, child laborers. Hiring the black women also represented a potential disruption of the social order, and in the East St. Louis glass works case, the move was doubly alarming. The black women were taken from domestic work in the homes of the wealthy to do the work of the (primarily white) glass house boys. This situation went against custom and practice on several levels and, in the view of the *Budget*, was likely to lead to trouble. In playing on nativist and racist fears, the *Budget* was also able to use these stories to reinforce several of its other positions: its advocacy of increasing the number of apprenticeships, its long-term support of automation, and its stance against child labor reform. According to this logic, owners would not have to hire immigrants and black women if they could keep glass house boys at work in the factories. The best way to keep these boys in the glass houses, according to the *Budget*, was by defeating child labor reform legislation and providing incentives to the boys through apprenticeships.

Because any regulation of the supply of child labor was unwelcome, anyone who advocated such regulation was worthy of nothing but scorn. When the proposed regulations attacked a core child labor need of the glass houses, the owners intensified their response. However, because they were core child labor issues, they also attracted the particular attention of the reformers. Night work by children was just such a core issue in the

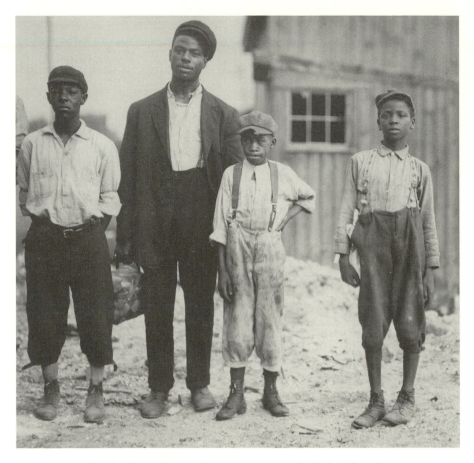

"In the Alexandria glass factories, negroes work side by side with
the white workers. Also in Richmond. There are some of those
working in Alexandria (Va.) Glass Factory." June 1911

Pittsburgh glass houses, and thus it was of great importance not only to
the factory owners but also to the progressives. Repeatedly, from 1905 until
1915, the Pennsylvania legislature considered the question of night work by
the western Pennsylvania glass house boys, and each consideration provided an opportunity for the Pittsburgh glass manufacturers and their or-
gan, the *Budget*, to rally in opposition.

The night work issue focused on Pennsylvania's glass house exception, which the state legislature created in 1905 as it considered a far-reaching child labor law. (A complete legislative analysis of this and the other important child labor laws is presented in chapter 6.) It is important to note here that the *Budget*'s response to some of these legislative proposals is a good indicator of the manufacturers' views of reform and the reformers. Just weeks before the 1905 session of the Pennsylvania legislature began, for example, the *Budget* reviewed the proposed child labor bill. The bill contained a wide range of proposed restrictions, including a general ban on night work for children under sixteen years of age. The article in the *Budget* addressed several other provisions in the bill and then focused on the night work section.

The newspaper first criticized the proposed legislation because it would "impose a great deal of recordings, description and senseless detail before children of a certain age can be employed." The bill would also have raised the minimum work age from thirteen to fourteen. With dripping sarcasm, the newspaper stated that "[n]o serious objection can be urged against" this part of the proposed law. Indeed, the *Budget* continued, the proposal should be extended, and parents encouraged "to send [their children] to school till 14, or even longer, . . . that they should [all] attend High School or College . . . and then be sent abroad for several years to see the world, come in contact with divers people, study foreign institutions, broaden their minds and enlarge their sympathies, and then come back . . . better Americans than ever." To make sure its point was not lost, the *Budget* added, "Of course, this would make it somewhat late in life to learn a trade, but that does not seem to concern" the reformers. Dropping the sarcasm, the newspaper concluded that no "child labor law, setting any age limit, can be made generally applicable without in many cases doing more harm than good." It added that, simply put, "[a]ll such laws are foolish."[64]

The principal feature of the 1905 Pennsylvania child labor bill was the proposed ban on night work. Not surprisingly, this provision generated substantial support among progressive reformers, and, also not surprisingly, this support made them the object of ridicule in the *Budget*. In March of that year, the Civic Club of Pittsburgh organized a public meeting to rally support for the legislation, especially the proposed night work ban. In its review of this particular meeting, the *Budget* could barely contain itself. First, it dismissed those who spoke at the meeting, including Owen

R. Lovejoy, a principal with the National Child Labor Committee, as only "various third and fourth magnitude stars of local and national glimmer." The newspaper reported that neither the legislation nor the reformers who were there to endorse it appear "to have any widespread roots [of support] among the working classes, whose children are most concerned, they being conspicuous by their absence, while the orators, without a single exception, were society ladies, club women, officials of consumers league[s]," and the like. The *Budget* then listed some of its specific criticisms. It noted that one of the speakers (i.e., Owen Lovejoy, whom the newspaper chose not to name) asserted at the meeting that a glass factory "not far from Pittsburgh" had been found to employ some "26 boys" under the legal age. The newspaper complained that, typical of such reformers, the speaker had made it impossible to either confirm or refute the charge because he failed to name the factory, identify the children, or give any meaningful specifics of the alleged offense. Rather, with some degree of accuracy as it would later turn out, the newspaper predicted that the whole child labor reform effort was pointless as far as the glass industry was concerned because the boys "will be dispensed with as machines are introduced, whether the child labor bill is passed or not." The *Budget* further discounted some of the reformers' primary arguments in support of the legislation by stating that, "whether [the law] will improve the displaced boys morally or otherwise, keep them out of devilment on the streets or out of danger of drowning in our unguarded rivers while bathing, put them into the school rooms, and make them pure and good, is quite another matter."[65] By suggesting that the boys were better off at work than not, the *Budget* was repeating a familiar argument of the glass factory owners.

The *National Glass Budget* often had to dance lightly between the twin, and potentially conflicting, goals of resisting child labor reform because it would disrupt the handmade glass operations and advocating modernization of those same factories. When the New Jersey legislature considered a ban on night work by children in 1906, the *Budget* found a way to speak in favor of the ban so that it could shame the few remaining New Jersey firms producing hand-blown glass into automating their production. Because most New Jersey glass factories, perhaps heeding previous admonitions appearing in the *Budget*, had already modernized, the state's glass manufacturers did not need a large pool of child workers. This fact was reinforced by Owen R. Lovejoy, who told an audience in Newark, New Jersey, that while the legislation was "aimed directly at the glass manufacturers in the southern part of the state," it had not met with much opposition from them because "they themselves had undergone a change of heart." Lovejoy confirmed that many of these manufacturers had already installed "the most modern methods of glass making [and] no longer required the work of boys."[66]

In this instance, the newspaper made no attempt to ridicule Lovejoy, as it had when he spoke in Pittsburgh the year before. Lovejoy was now a convenient tool the newspaper used to advance its goal of pushing the few remaining owners of unautomated glass factories in New Jersey toward the Owens machine. Several years later, however, when the same state legislature proposed raising the age limit for child workers from fourteen to sixteen and the "South Jersey bottle manufacturers" let it be known that they were "at present agitated over the prospect of the passage of [the] child labor bill," the *Budget* supported their position, arguing that the bill should be scuttled because the glass houses "are seriously handicapped by reason of not being able to secure an adequate supply of juvenile help and the passage of the proposed legislation would add materially to their troubles."[67]

When addressing the situation in western Pennsylvania, where the bottle manufacturers were less willing to modernize than in most other glass-producing regions, the *Budget* emphasized the negative aspects of any proposed child labor regulation rather than the benefits of the machine. When the Pennsylvania legislature revisited the night work ban in 1907, 1909, and 1911, the newspaper adamantly opposed any effort to revoke the glass house exception. The *Budget* charged that with the 1907 reform proposal, "the legislators will be requested to lend their support to a movement which if successful will drive out of our state the industries which have lifted her up to the proud position of first place in the galaxy of states, and at the same time turn the faces of many of our worthy poor towards alms houses and penal institutions which are now more than comfortably crowded." In its editorial that same day, the newspaper stepped up the rhetoric, characterizing the proponents of reform in Pennsylvania as "child labor freaks," who purposefully engaged in "outrageously false and wicked misrepresentation[s] of [working] conditions in Pennsylvania." In a series of disparaging remarks that hinged on gender caricatures, the *Budget* referred to the reformers as "motherless mothers and fatherless fathers who are agitating for the throwing of children into idleness." And then, as if to make sure the point would not be missed, the editorial complained that "we are being treated to so much driveling nonsense as regarding the torturing of youths in our factories, by wealthy spinsters, second hand wives of hen-pecked husbands, and men who earn their living through child labor agitation."[68]

When the Pennsylvania legislature in 1909 again considered eliminating the glass house exception, the *Budget* responded that the legislation was being pushed "at the instigation of freak reformers" and that it was unnecessary because "without exception the [glass] factories are well lighted and ventilated, both day and night, and . . . the juvenile help . . . are contented and happy." A few weeks later when the forces of reform seemed to be gaining momentum, the newspaper reminded its readers that, if this bill became law, "it would most seriously affect the glass industry of this state," that it was being championed by an "association of motherless wives and old maids," and, finally, that "this great industry would have to undergo a complete and expensive reorganization."[69]

In 1913, the advocates of reform again tried to revise the Pennsylvania child labor law to eliminate night work for the Pittsburgh glass house boys, and again the *Budget* rose to meet the challenge. In February, the newspaper began with a general announcement to its readers that the "tentative draft" of the proposed child labor bill included the "visionary ideas of well-meaning but mistaken and impractical people identified with the child labor movement." The state's glass manufacturers were then urged to "take an active interest" in the legislation because "final passage of a law [like this] would add to their troubles materially, while at the same time legislating into idleness many boys and girls whose earnings are a Godsend to poor and helpless parents."[70] Repeating these same charges several times over the next few months, the newspaper contended that the bill was "harmful to the industrial, mercantile and other pursuits in the state that require the service of minor help" and would be "an injustice to growing boys and girls whose earnings are an absolute necessity for family maintenance." The proponents were characterized as "humanitarians and theorists" who were at best "impracticable."[71]

Evidence for these last claims appeared when the *Budget* reprinted a letter from the state's recently fired chief factory inspector, J. C. Delaney. Delaney attacked one of the principal supporters of the bill, Charles Chute, formerly with the National Child Labor Committee and now the secretary for the Pennsylvania Child Labor Association and author of the 1911 NCLC investigative report highly critical of the child labor practices in Pennsylvania's glass factories. Delaney, speaking specifically about Chute, wrote to "protest against the too oft-repeated slanders against our commonwealth by the secretary of the child labor organization," whom Delaney thought was nothing more than a "carpetbagger from New York." Delaney characterized Chute as "a beardless youth" who was engaging in "venomous malice" against Pennsylvania glass manufacturers and "grossly misrepresenting [the] child labor conditions" in the industry.[72]

Later, the *Budget* was pleased to report that the night work ban was once again defeated and the "scheme of labor fakirs to prevent boys from acquiring a trade" had been "checkmated."[73] The checkmating, discussed at greater length in chapter 6, was the direct result of back-room pressure brought to bear on the legislature by the Pittsburgh glass manufacturers who could still wield significant political power. These industry representatives met secretly with high-placed state and federal politicians and brokered a deal to have the bill killed. The *Budget*, of course, chose not to provide elaboration on this point. The *Budget* did, however, indicate that the Pittsburgh glass workers were also very involved in the effort to thwart reform, and it is to the glass workers' part of the story that we now turn.

4

The Pittsburgh
Glass Workers and the
Glass Bottle Union

If any labor organization had ever stopped the introduction of ma-chinery, or if we knew of any way to stop the [Owens] automatic, I would feel much happier than I do today. We have the history and experience of other trade unions to learn from, and if in spite of the lessons which their history teaches, we butt our heads off against a stone wall, we will, later on, when our trade is taken from us, have remorse added to our misfortune for not having made some great and progressive effort to adjust our trade to the introduction of this formidable rival.

Denis A. Hayes, president of the glass
workers' union, May 27, 1909

GLASSMAKING, along with the related crafts of ceramics and metal work, were once known as the "black arts" because of the soot associated with the wood or coal fire that produced the intense heat required to create the end product and because many elements of the production processes were shrouded in mystery.[1] The secrets of glassmaking lay in the precise mixture of ingredients, the requisite heating, reheating, and cooling, and especially the skill needed to blow and shape the molten glass into desired shapes. The person who had this knowledge and skill was the master glass blower, and the position of power that he occupied in the American glass factories of the late nineteenth century was intimately intertwined with the history of glass. The contours of that history further reveal why the glass houses of Pittsburgh were such a challenging environment for the early-twentieth-century progressives trying to reform child labor laws.

For some insight into the importance of secrecy and mystery, one should look to Venice, which, by the Middle Ages, had become the center for European glass production. To maintain their preeminence, Venice's artisans depended on secrecy to control access to information about the production processes. One example of a proprietary secret dealt with color. Because of impurities in the typical admixture of ingredients, early glass bottles usually had a greenish color.[2] The Venetians, however, were among the first to find a way to produce commercial quantities of clear glass, making their bottles and flasks very desirable. Cognizant of the economic value of such knowledge, they imposed a high degree of state-sanctioned secrecy and control over production techniques.[3]

The Venetian government tried to isolate the glass artisans, and it made their industry a matter of special state concern. By the fifteenth century, the government had moved all of the glass factories out of Venice proper and onto the adjacent island of Murano. While this was ostensibly done to protect the city from the ever-present threat of fire associated with glassmaking operations, it also had the effect of confining the glassmakers and making it more difficult for them to pass their technical knowledge on to others. The glass workers were virtually imprisoned on the island so that the secrets of the manufacturing process would not become known to the outside world. If a glass worker left Murano without permission, he could be killed; if he managed to obtain permission to leave, the long arm of Venetian law still followed him.[4] A law passed in Venice in 1474 reinforced this point by mandating that, "[i]f any [glass] workman conveys his art to a strange country to the detriment of the Republic, he shall be sent an order to return to Venice. Failing to obey, his nearest relation shall be imprisoned. If he shall persist in remaining abroad and plying his art, an emissary shall be charged to kill him."[5]

Venice was clearly very serious about maintaining its economic advantages in glassmaking. To compensate for these rather significant limitations on free speech and travel, the Venetian authorities also rewarded the glassmakers certain privileges. They had the right "of coining a certain number of medals on the day of the blessing of the waters by the Doge. If one of their daughters married a noble the latter did not forfeit his nobility, and the children were noble."[6] To further underscore the element of control, however, Venice had by 1490 established several glass guilds so that the different branches of the glass-making process would be further separated from one another and, again, so that technical secrecy could be more easily preserved.[7]

The American glass blowers of the nineteenth century were heirs to this tradition of skill and secrecy. The secrecy was reinforced because the glass blowers' knowledge was rarely committed to writing and usually passed on from one generation of artisans to the next. Largely because they possessed such unique and valuable knowledge and were relatively few in number, the American glass blowers were able to organize into craft-based unions by the middle of the nineteenth century. By the end of the century, the Glass Bottle Blowers' Association of the United States and Canada had emerged as the principal union for the nation's glass blowers, and Denis A. Hayes reigned as its dynamic and virtually unchallenged leader for nearly the entire period under study here. The GBBA presence became particularly strong in western Pennsylvania, and the glass blowers in this district benefited greatly. By the start of the twentieth century, skilled Pittsburgh glass workers had been unionized for nearly forty years, they were among the best paid workers in America, and they and their union exercised tremendous control over nearly every operation on the furnace room floor.[8]

The Glass Bottle Blowers' Association

The GBBA can trace its roots to 1842, when a group of glass blowers met in Philadelphia. They prepared a union constitution, adopted a wage scale, and elected John Samuels as their president. A few years later, they were joined by several other nascent glass blower unions, and they named themselves the Glass Blowers' League.[9] This initial effort at trade union organization faltered but was rekindled shortly after the Civil War when, in 1867, another group of glass blowers again met in convention in Philadelphia. This group re-ratified the 1842 constitution of the Glass Blowers' League and renamed themselves the Druggist Ware Glass Blowers' League. The Druggist League was largely centered in Pennsylvania, with its eastern district, known as the Green Bottle Blowers, located in Philadelphia and its western district, the Green Glass Blowers, located in Pittsburgh. The two districts were semi-independent, and, in 1886, they each joined the Knights of Labor as District Assembly #143 (western district) and #149 (eastern district). By the early 1890s, the two districts had formally merged to form the Green Glass Workers' Association.[10]

The Green Glass Workers' Association's affiliation with the Knights of Labor lasted a little less than a decade. It began as a very logical association. The Knights had a growing national presence that could enhance the strength of the glass workers' association, and each group had a strong Pennsylvania connection. The Knights of Labor had been founded in 1869 "by a handful of Philadelphia garment cutters," and at their first national meeting in 1878, "two-thirds of the delegates [to the General Assembly] were from Pennsylvania."[11] Further, the longtime leader of the Knights, Terence V. Powderly, was a Pennsylvanian. But the ideological differences between the Green Glass Workers' Association and the Knights proved problematic. The Knights of Labor tended to "embrace broad, class-based programs of reform and redistribution" of wealth. They advocated a strong political action program that included a host of legislative reform proposals, from workplace hour and wage regulations to nationalization of monopolies and abolition of private banks.[12] Further, the Knights were not a strictly craft-based union but followed a broad and very inclusive membership program. They also tended to challenge the wage system directly rather than seek to improve the employment conditions of its members through such actions as collective bargaining.[13]

These programs did not mesh well with the needs and circumstances of the glass blowers. With their valuable trade skills and knowledge, they occupied an enviable and rare position of power among laboring people in the late nineteenth century. Unlike many other workers, especially the unskilled, the collective bargaining experiences of the glass blowers' union had already produced substantial material benefits for its members. Because the glass blowers had been able to leverage the capitalist system to work in their favor, the more socialist-leaning platform of the Knights of Labor was not entirely consistent with or supportive of the more conservative economic and political interests of the largely middle-class glass workers. By 1895, the Green Glass Workers' Association had left the Knights of Labor and, following the lead of Denis A. Hayes (then a national union delegate), changed its name to the Glass Bottle Blowers' Association of the United States and Canada. The next year Hayes was elected president of the GBBA, and in 1899, he led the move to affiliate with the American Federation of Labor (AFL), headed by Samuel Gompers.[14] Hayes remained president of the GBBA until his death in 1917, a period of nearly three decades that witnessed almost revolutionary change in the American glass industry.

The AFL proved to be a much more congenial home for the GBBA than the Knights of Labor had been. The AFL grew out of the Federation of Organized Trades and Labor Unions, which had its beginnings in Pittsburgh in November 1881.[15] The AFL initially supported programs similar to those advocated by the Knights of Labor, but as the Knights began to fade in power and effectiveness following the Haymarket riot in Chicago in 1886, Samuel Gompers and the AFL grew less interested in political activism and slowly distanced themselves from the Knights. Gompers grew wary of inclusive unionism and broad-based union actions when, as he saw it, the power of government was increasingly used to bludgeon unions in one major strike after another.[16]

After the turn of the century, Gompers and the AFL came to exemplify American "exceptionalism" or "voluntarism" in the trade union movement. This stance centered on a belief that industrial relations between workers and owners should be ordered through private union-management negotiations rather than through public political action or legislation. Gompers saw collective bargaining, rather than a class-based confrontation with the wage system, as the way to improve workers' employment conditions. This approach suited the GBBA very well, as it had already been very successful in using wage bargaining for the benefit of its members. Although Gompers proclaimed that the "best thing the State can do for Labor is to leave Labor alone," he did not eschew all forms of political assistance.[17] This view also fit comfortably within the history of western Pennsylvania glass interests because many government actions had benefited both manufacturers and glass workers alike. In particular, the AFL supported several governmental programs, including protective regulations for women, tariff and immigration restrictions, and, significantly for the purposes of this study, child labor reform. But in each case, not surprisingly, the underlying motivation for the AFL's position was as much economic self-interest as altruism. The AFL wanted "to put a floor under wage competition, to keep 'cheap labor' out of the labor markets in which its unions would then rely on voluntaristic means, on contract and collective action, to work out their fortunes."[18]

The skilled glass blowers, as well-paid, middle-class workers, generally supported the more conservative economic and collective-bargaining goals of the AFL, in particular those specific programs that would advance their own interests. The positions of the skilled glass workers and the GBBA regarding the programs and policies of the AFL were reflected in the pages of the glass workers' weekly newspaper, the *Commoner*. For example, the newspaper agreed with the AFL's advocacy of federal protective tariff legislation.[19] This type of legislation had greatly benefited the glass industry in the early part of the nineteenth century, and the glass workers fully supported it at the turn of the twentieth century. The glass workers also agreed with the AFL on the matter of increasing restrictions on foreign immigration.[20] The *Commoner*, in numerous articles and editorials supporting anti-immigration policies, reflected a less appealing side of the glass workers in that it expressed unapologetically nativist and racist views. On this issue, the workers shared some of the same concerns as the glass house owners. In one article in 1909, echoing a concern expressed two years earlier by the manufacturers' newspaper, the *National Glass Budget*, the *Commoner* complained about the chronic shortage of boy labor in the Illinois glass factories. The *Commoner* noted that, in addition to being forced to "import Greeks" because glass house boys were in short supply, the factories were "compelled to employ colored women to the exclusion of whites."[21]

The GBBA's position on the issue of child labor in the glass industry was a little more conflicted with that of its parent union, the AFL. On the one hand, because the AFL strongly supported progressive efforts to eliminate child workers from American factories, the GBBA was careful not to come out publicly in opposition to this stance. On the other hand, because many of the GBBA's members worked in hand-blown glass shops that depended upon the work of glass house boys, the union was also loath to speak out publicly in favor of child labor reform. Some of the correspondence between Denis A. Hayes and the governing board of the GBBA regarding the child labor issue offers evidence of how they tried to negotiate these opposing pressures. In 1908, for example, the New Jersey legislature was considering a child labor bill that was clearly directed at the state's glass factories. The bill called for a ban on night work by boys, and several members of the GBBA spoke out publicly against it. Most of the New Jersey glass houses were automated by then, so the number of GBBA glass blowers employed there who needed to have glass house boys working at night was relatively small. Perhaps taking this situation into account, Hayes, in a memorandum to the GBBA's executive committee, complained about the actions of these union members, stating that they had "place[d] themselves at the disposal of the glass manufacturers ... to oppose child labor legislation which is one of the fundamental principles of the labor movement." He said these glass men did not "represent the glass workers" and, worse, that their actions placed the GBBA "in a false position before the trade unions of the country."[22]

Hayes's scolding of the New Jersey glass workers was very consistent with, and could therefore be seen as an attempt to underscore GBBA support for, the AFL policy in favor of child labor reform. Yet, considering that the New Jersey glass men violated such a "fundamental" principle of unionism, the restraint of Hayes's condemnation indicated that the GBBA support of the AFL policy was circumscribed. Hayes could not come out too strongly in favor of child labor reform because to do so would be contrary to the union members whose jobs depended on the continued employability of the glass house boys. He could support the New Jersey law because it would directly impact only New Jersey glass workers, and, because they represented such a small proportion of the GBBA membership, the risk of a serious negative reaction was similarly small. On the other hand, a more strongly worded, broader-based statement in support of child labor reform would go against the interests of the Pittsburgh glass-bottle workers, whose activity required the nighttime employment of glass house boys. These considerations would explain why Hayes chose to criticize the New Jersey glass workers in the form of an internal GBBA memorandum rather than, for example, in a public statement issued to the *Commoner*. This way he could claim to be offering support for the AFL position on child labor and yet minimize the risk of angering the Pittsburgh glass workers, who represented a large and influential portion of his membership.

Hayes's deference to the Pittsburgh glass workers is evidenced by his failure to respond when they engaged in actions similar to those of the New Jersey glass men. In 1911, for example, when members of the Pittsburgh local of the GBBA engaged in very direct and very public lobbying efforts against child labor reform, Hayes never once issued a public or private rebuke. As discussed in detail in chapter 6, the actions of the Pittsburgh glass workers were instrumental in killing Pennsylvania's child labor reform legislation that year, yet neither Hayes nor anyone else in the GBBA is on record as offering any objection at all. As these events illustrate, the differences between the GBBA and the AFL on the issue of child labor were closely tied to the issue of mechanization in the union-controlled glass houses. The prospect of mechanization also caused conflicts within the union itself and between it and the manufacturers.

Glass Workers and Mechanization in the Glass Industry

As described in chapter 3, the nation's glass-bottle industry was beginning to turn to new forms of automated production processes in the late nineteenth century. The *Commoner* reported on the early developments in glass-blowing machines without much alarm. In 1888, for example, noting that a semi-automatic bottle blowing machine had been developed in England, the newspaper did not predict that it would have a great impact on American bottle makers.[23] Later that year, a report appeared on the test of a steam-powered bottle-making machine in Steubenville, Ohio, and the *Commoner* stated almost approvingly that this machine could, "with [just] one boy at five dollars a week, do one-third more work than a man at thirty-five dollars a week."[24] In 1897, when Michael J. Owens invented the paste mold machine described earlier, a writer for the *Commoner* conservatively estimated that it could make upwards of three thousand tumblers per day and opined that it was "the greatest piece of mechanism" it had "ever seen in the glass trade." The newspaper predicted that it "will revolutionize the trade by changing the system of working," with the result that "[b]lowers will become gatherers, instead of gatherers[,] blowers."[25]

The *Commoner* was not worried about these inventions because virtually all of them assisted rather than replaced the skilled labor of the glass blowers. To the extent that they allowed more glass to be made to meet the nation's rising demand, they actually worked to increase the jobs available for skilled glass men. To be sure, these technological innovations had some effect on the structure of labor in the glass-making process, but at first the new technology seemed primarily directed at eliminating some of the boy jobs, not the adults' jobs. As such, the editors of the *Commoner* did not feel these machines posed serious challenges to the economic livelihood of the skilled glass blowers.

In 1905, however, when the Owens Automatic first entered commercial production, the position of the glass workers regarding both mechanization in the glass houses and the use of the glass house boys became more complicated. This particular glass-making device posed the biggest single threat to the continued existence of the skilled glass workers, the GBBA, and the glass house boys. Hayes and the GBBA also realized, however, that they were not powerful enough to block the use of the Owens machine entirely. Hayes knew that his members could not compete with the Owens Automatic if one considered only the simple costs of production. If the Owens machine could make a gross of bottles for as little as ten cents and his glass workers required nearly a dollar and a half, then his glass workers were doomed.

But two factors related to the use of the Owens machine gave Hayes some hope. The first was cost and the other, reluctance. As noted in chapter 3, the Owens Bottle Machine Company had the exclusive right to license the Owens Automatic, and it had decided to set the licensing fee relatively high. While the company did this in part to slow the initial introduction of the machine so as not to cause a collapse in the glass-bottle market, this strategy also worked, perhaps inadvertently, to the advantage of the GBBA and its members by ensuring continued employment, at least in the short term. As discussed in chapter 2, the Pittsburgh district bottle manufacturers were reluctant to adopt the Owens Automatic, which was a significant help to the GBBA because the Pittsburgh glass houses were, collectively, the largest employers of union glass blowers.

Prior to the introduction of the Owens machine, the glass workers had tried several strategies to forestall the adverse effects of mechanization. In the late nineteenth century, for example, the American Flint Glass Workers Union called a strike in the chimney lamp factories under its control in an attempt to bar the introduction of a newly patented mechanical "crimper." This job action proved unsuccessful. A few years later, when Michael J. Owens introduced his automatic paste mold machine for making chimney lamps, the flint glass workers tried a different approach. They proposed the highly unusual strategy of purchasing the exclusive licensing rights to the device themselves in order to simply sit on the invention. Although the union leaders actually began negotiating for a price with Owens, they could not persuade their members to endorse this novel undertaking, and the proposal was dropped. Then, when the Macbeth-Evans Company in Pittsburgh purchased the rights to use the Owens chimney machine, the flint glass workers' union threatened to strike. Macbeth-Evans objected, and when no agreement could be reached with the union, the company simply broke its union contract and took the unusual step of becoming an open shop, but one that was fully mechanized. The loss of the Macbeth-Evans glass works greatly reduced the power, prestige, and financial viability of the American Flint Glass Workers Union.[26]

Denis A. Hayes and the GBBA were mindful of the actions of the flint glass union as they tested several other "antimechanization" strategies themselves. Prior to the invention of the Owens Automatic, the GBBA tried to prohibit its members from actively assisting in the development or use of certain mechanical innovations. In the 1890s, for example, when Charles Leng invented a bottle-finishing machine, the GBBA tried to impose a fifty-dollar fine on any of its members who would blow bottles for the Leng finisher. This strategy, however, proved unworkable.[27] When the Owens Automatic was first unveiled, the GBBA publicly questioned whether the machine was in violation of several existing patents, but this challenge, too, proved fruitless. The Owens company dismissed these allegations out of hand, and, as reported in the *Budget,* it "guaranteed to defend its patents against all infringement suits," charging that "no factory operating Owens machines could be stopped" because of such legal actions. There was, according to the newspaper, only a "string of dead patents from which interference is impossible."[28]

After these failures, Hayes and the GBBA tried to navigate past the shoals of mechanization with a more complex strategy of resistance and accommodation. Especially after traveling to Toledo to watch the Owens Automatic in operation, Hayes fully recognized the dramatic impact this particular invention would have on his members. But he also believed (or hoped) that they could meet the challenge with as little loss as possible. In a lengthy report to his membership in 1905, which was reported in full in the *Commoner,* Hayes talked about the "great machine problem, and especially the [Owens A]utomatic machine, which now confronts the bottle trade." He laid out the general GBBA position: "Intelligent, progressive labor organizations no longer antagonize the introduction of labor saving machinery. Instead of restricting production or limiting output, the object is now to reduce the hours of labor, thus enabling all workers to find employment, and through organization share in the social and industrial advancement of these times." He warned, however, that the "trade must go on adapting itself to the invasion of machinery."[29] In 1906, he suggested a more detailed strategy, arguing that the union must: (1) "agitate for further and gradual reduction" in the work day so that the available work could be spread out among as many union members as possible; (2) bring under GBBA jurisdiction "all bottle makers, whether employed as blowers or machine operators"; (3) reduce "the number of apprentices on a basis of one to thirty" journeyman blowers; and (4) get the manufacturers to agree to add a "union-made" label to all GBBA-produced glassware.[30] As the licenses to the Owens machine were sold to more and more manufacturers, however, the primary challenge for Hayes and the GBBA became to make sure the operators of these machines were union men, even if their particular level of glass-making skill was not needed to run the Owens Automatic.

It was a great benefit to Hayes and the GBBA that the Pittsburgh glass house owners were inclined to resist the introduction of the Owens Automatic. Because the owners' reluctance necessitated continued reliance on union glass blowers, the owners could count on the support of the GBBA in this regard. This support was no trivial matter. By the early twentieth century, the Pittsburgh glass workers, the vast majority of whom were union members, accounted for as much as 40 percent of the GBBA's total membership.[31] This meant both that the Pittsburgh local was very influential within the GBBA and that the GBBA could exercise considerable influence within Pittsburgh glass-bottle factories. By combining forces, the GBBA and the western Pennsylvania glass house owners effectively slowed the introduction of the Owens Automatic in the Pittsburgh district. But this alliance also spelled trouble for the GBBA, in the form of lower wages for glass workers and an increased reliance on child labor. These troubles were embedded in Hayes's dual strategy of resistance and accommodation regarding mechanization. Mechanization in any part of the glass-bottle industry put pressure on any remaining hand-blown factories to become more efficient, and efficiency meant both cutting wage rates for skilled glass workers and hiring more glass house boys. One of the great challenges for the GBBA from 1905 onward was to resist the seemingly relentless pressure from the factory owners, and particularly the western Pennsylvania glass houses, to reduce union pay rates. Considering the magnitude of the challenge, the GBBA was surprisingly successful at resisting this pressure, at least for a while.

The Wage Conferences between Labor and Management

The glass workers' unions and the glass factory owners had met annually to agree on wage rates at least since the 1880s. During these meetings, interactions between the union and the manufacturers were generally amicable, with very few disruptions in the negotiations, but the culture of cooperation was not flawless. The inherently competing interests of labor versus management would occasionally surface to disrupt this tenuous harmony.[32] When disturbances did arise, the pages of the *Commoner* (more so than the *National Glass Budget*) recorded these conflicts in some detail. In November 1887, for example, the *Commoner* reported on recent statements made by a Mr. Ripley, a Pittsburgh glass factory owner and the president of the Lime Glass Manufacturers' Association, an early trust in the glass-bottle trade. Ripley, criticizing the lime glass workers' union, a predecessorin-interest to the GBBA, complained bitterly that "the glass industry was controlled by the employees, [and] that the union was trying to do what the almighty did not see fit to do—prevent one man from making more than another man." The *Commoner* could not let these words stand unchallenged and commented that "capital should not get alarmed because labor is at last awakening. Labor only claims the same rights as are now granted to capital."[33] Here, the use of the rhetoric of class-based labor struggle is striking. At this time, many of the newspaper's readers, glass men and other workers alike, would have been affiliated with or at least sympathetic to the Knights of Labor, and such language would have been very consistent with the Knights' positions.

At the end of 1887, the *Commoner* used a much more cooperative tone as it reported on new factories being opened in the Ohio, Indiana, and Illinois gas belt. The newspaper stated that the glass manufacturers in other regions were concerned "because there is some cutting in prices being done" by these new glass factories that operated "outside of the manufacturers association." Because one of the main purposes of the glass trust was to control prices, the manufacturers' association was understandably worried. The *Commoner* went on to say that one "prominent manufacturer stated that he would like to see the blowers and the manufacturers make some arrangement that would put a stop to it." The solution suggested was a type of mutual back scratching. The manufacturer stated that the blowers' union should agree not to allow any of its members to work for a shop that "does not belong to the manufacturers association." And if the union agreed to this rule, then the "manufacturers should see that such [association] members ... should employ none but union men."[34] The *Commoner* does not say whether the manufacturers responded to this offer.

While it was not unusual for industrialists such as glass manufacturers to want all producers to toe the line on pricing, it was more unusual in late-nineteenth-century America for manufacturers to try to enlist the help of unions to accomplish this goal. Such cooperation had developed as an unusual characteristic of the glass industry and was evident in the handling of the annual wage conferences. After the GBBA became the principal glass blowers' union, the wage conferences were structured to maximize the possibility of mutually acceptable results and to minimize the chances of labor disruptions. Representatives of both the union and the manufac-

"A Blower With Foot Mold. question: 'Why cannot mold boys
[be] done away with?' Seneca Glass Works." Morgantown,
West Virginia, October 1908

turers' association instituted the process of meeting informally with each other in the spring, well before the official wage meeting. This preliminary conference allowed each side to talk more freely since they were not formally negotiating anything. They could use this preliminary meeting to float proposals or air concerns and then take time to work out differences well before the start of the new glass season in the fall. In early July, the union held its own official annual meeting to establish its formal positions on wages and other matters. Finally, in late July or August, the manufacturers and the union met in formal session to hammer out a new wage agreement. This process worked well most of the time, and wage agreements were nearly always concluded.

Occasionally, however, uncertain economic conditions or unsettling technological innovations disrupted the process. In 1896, for example, the glass industry was still feeling the effects of the disastrous economic recession of 1893, and wage discussions proved particularly difficult. The *Commoner* reported that the "bottle manufacturers and workers ... met at Cresson Springs to discuss a wage scale for the coming season. It was not expected that an agreement would be reached." At that meeting, the manufacturers refused union demands for a rate increase because of the expansion of non-union shops in the gas belt states and "the unsettled [economic] conditions of the country," both of which strongly argued against an increase in wages.[35] But, although no formal agreement was signed, most factories fired up their furnaces later in the fall and made glass anyway, with a de facto understanding to continue the previous year's wage scale. It was a pattern that would repeat itself often.

Maintaining wages in the face of adversity was not always possible, however. In 1898, for example, after the Ball Brothers factory began using the modified version of the Arbogast bottle machine to make fruit jars, the owners of competing hand-blown plants in Indiana demanded a 50 percent wage reduction from the GBBA. Although the reduction would affect only a small portion of the glass-bottle industry—and only a small number of his union members—Hayes initially resisted. In a move foreshadowing what would become a more common practice, however, he then agreed to a 45 percent cut.[36]

The greatest stress on the historic culture of labor-management cooperation in the glass industry came from the Owens Automatic. While

Denis A. Hayes's rhetoric of accommodation and adaptation to the Owens machine represented the long-term view of the GBBA, over the short term the prospect that the Owens Automatic would depress the glass workers' income had to be dealt with at the annual wage conferences. The Owens machine had an impact on not only wages but other glass house practices as well, such as the traditional summer stop rule. By custom, the glass workers took off for the months of July and August, the so-called summer stop, not only because the heat of those summer months made the furnace rooms particularly unbearable but also because in western Pennsylvania— the historic center of the industry—the lack of summer rain often made the rivers unnavigable. Even after the construction of canals and railroads, the practice of closing in the summer was standard in Pittsburgh, and the fact that it also became a national, industry-wide glass workers' rule again shows the power of the Pittsburgh glass blowers within the GBBA.

After the introduction of the Owens Automatic, however, nonautomated glass houses felt the economic pressure to produce glass twelve months a year (as well as around the clock) in order to compete. At several annual wage meetings after 1904, the manufacturers pressured the GBBA to end or at least ease the summer stop rule. In 1909, for example, Hayes told the glass workers that "the matter of a summer stop caused a prolonged discussion" at that year's preliminary wage conference, and the manufacturers "insisted upon working, in order, as they stated, to protect their trade from the competition of automatic machinery."[37] By 1911, as automation was cutting into wages and job security, pressure to end the summer stop was coming from the GBBA members themselves. Branch 106 in Columbus, Ohio, in an open letter to the general membership of the GBBA, requested that the summer stop be discontinued because "the machine operates continually day and night throughout the year," and the glass workers "therefore see our trade slipping away from us as we are idly walking the streets [during the summer stop]."[38] In the face of machine-driven economics, the summer stop rule proved to be a luxury the glass blowers could not afford. At the 1911 wage conference, Hayes agreed to cut the summer stop in half, from two months to one.[39]

Wages were, to be sure, the dominant feature of the annual conferences, and the Owens Automatic cast a long shadow there as well. The first wage conference held after the Owens machine was introduced occurred in the summer of 1905, and it proved unsettling. Although the Owens machine was still very new, its potential impact was of significant concern to the GBBA and its members. Even in limited use, the Owens machine was putting downward pressure on wages. At the preliminary wage meeting that year, held in Pittsburgh, the manufacturers let it be known that they wanted substantial wage concessions by the GBBA. In response, the *Commoner* tried to establish a positive tone and praised "the liberal policies of President Hayes and his associates in meeting the machine problem." The newspaper tried to reassure its readers that the "sessions held in Pittsburg [*sic*] were conducted in a most harmonious manner and there was an evident intention on the part of both sides to be fair in handling the question." Here, the newspaper's rhetoric was almost soothing and deferential, showing no hint of class-based labor strife or the union saber rattling that had marked some of its rhetoric in the 1880s.[40] The newspaper reflected the unspoken understanding that, to fight the Owens Automatic, the workers and their union were joining forces with, rather than fighting against, the manufacturers.

It was immediately after these preliminary wage meetings that Hayes was first permitted to visit the Libbey factory in Toledo and observe the Owens Automatic in action. The *Commoner* briefly reported on Hayes's visit in May.[41] In June, it ran a longer piece praising Hayes for venturing to Toledo and warning its readers of the seriousness of the challenge. In that article, the *Commoner* portrayed the workers' situation using the rhetoric of a military confrontation. Sounding very similar to the *National Glass Budget* seven years earlier, when that newspaper described an earlier period of mechanization, the *Commoner* stated in 1905 that the Hayes/Owens meeting represented "the first time in the history of the glass trade in this country that an official trip was made by the representative of a labor organization to see a machine in operation that was expected to *invade* their trade." The newspaper then counseled that it was in "the best interests of the workmen and all concerned that a clear conception of the machine's merits are known" and that "President Hayes shows wisdom in preparing in advance for the invasion of [the Owens] machinery."[42]

The Toledo experience solidified the union's fears about the long-term impact of this machine on the glass houses. Hayes and the GBBA understood that once the Owens machine was in widespread use, the likelihood of a rise in glass worker wages was slim but that the likelihood of a rise in glass worker unemployment was great. They adopted a defensive strategy, deciding to hold fast to the existing scale and resist the reductions demanded by the owners. Considering both the probable expense of converting to the new technology and the fact that the Owens machine still had only limited availability, Hayes thought that the owners' wage-reduction position was largely posturing and thus vulnerable. As the conference began in Atlantic City in August, the *Commoner* voiced both concern about the outcome and support for Hayes. In understated rhetoric, the newspaper stated that the prospect "of a reduction in wages to meet the competition of machine-made bottles and jars has caused uneasiness in the conference between members of the wage committee of the bottle manufacturers and the G.B.B.A." But, the newspaper continued, President Hayes had resolved "that his men are firm and will make every effort to avoid lowering the [wage] scale."[43]

As the 1905 meeting opened, the manufacturers demanded a 15 percent rollback in wages, but the GBBA stood firm. As the conference ended, the impact of the Owens Automatic became evident; for the first time since 1896, the parties remained at loggerheads and no wage agreement was reached. The *Commoner*, not allowing the obvious to go unstated, told its readers that "[t]he machine question was ... an important factor in the [failure of the] negotiations." Then, evidencing a far greater appreciation for the position of "capital" in this particular wage-price dilemma than it had shown some eight years earlier, the newspaper cautioned that all "sides appear to realize the danger of involving the trade in a prolonged lockout." Finally, not forgetting who its primary readers were, the *Commoner* praised the workers and their union by stating that it was to their credit that they had "always transacted business with the manufacturers in a spirit which has made their relations of a most friendly character and nothing in the way of bitterness will crop out to delay a settlement."[44]

Again, just as in 1896, even though the parties were unable to agree on wages, no strike or lockout resulted. In September, at the end of the traditional summer stop, the *Commoner* reported that, despite the lack of a formal agreement, the prior year's wages were being paid in the large number of factories "which are starting, or about to resume" glass production.[45] Later, the newspaper announced that "more bottle factories [will be] in operation by the end of this week than were running at the same period last season . . . and this practically concedes last year's wages to the blowers."[46] Hayes and the GBBA, it seemed, had played their hand well. They calculated correctly that, while the owners would have liked a 15 percent wage reduction, they would rather pay last year's wages on a de facto basis than risk either not producing any glass that season and losing market share to the machine-equipped shops or undertaking the expense and uncertainty of being forced to convert to automatic processes. For the moment, wages and jobs were preserved.

In succeeding years, the issue of mechanization influenced the agenda and outcome of all of the wage conferences between the GBBA and the manufacturers, and the question was not whether owners would seek a reduction but how much of a reduction they wanted.[47] In August 1906, at the conclusion of that year's wage conference, Hayes reported to his membership, in a manner typical of the interchanges between the parties on the subject, that the "manufacturers obstinately contended for . . . a reduction in wages of thirty-three and one-third per cent, . . . to meet competition from . . . machine made ware." Hayes told his members that he had responded that the strong demand for glass at the time made the machine-produced ware argument illusory. But the manufacturers held firm, and once again "the annual wage conference of 1906 adjourned without a [wage] scale being agreed to."[48] As before, however, most hand-blown glass plants remained open, and the previous wage scale was generally honored.

This pattern continued in 1907. In May, just before the preliminary wage conference, Hayes told his members that he expected "repeated demands for a reduction of wages" because the "difference in the cost of production between the machine and hand made bottles is so great." But again, he was able to forestall any giveback in wages.[49] Although the wage agreement the parties finally reached did not contain any reductions, the GBBA did agree to a 50 percent increase in the number of apprentices, a move they had strongly resisted in the past.[50] In 1908, however, the situation was made worse by a general economic downturn, which had resulted in the closure of many glass factories. In the spring, Hayes informed his membership that the situation "leaves us with about thirteen hundred idle members." Compounding these layoffs, the American Bottle Company in Newark, New Jersey, decided not only to leave its furnaces for handmade glass idle but also to keep all twenty-seven of its Owens Automatic machines operating at full speed. Hayes confided to his fellow union members that while he was trying to "come out of every [annual wage] contest with more gains than losses," it was becoming increasingly difficult. Recognizing that the upper hand in wage negotiations had shifted to the other side as a result of mechanization and using rhetoric that reflected accommodation rather than confrontation, he concluded that the way to accomplish the union's wage goals was "not to make too many demands, or insist upon things that may antagonize the manufacturers."[51] Yet, that year, Hayes was somehow once again able to hold off reductions and keep the 1907 agreement intact.[52]

The turning point came in the 1909 wage conference for the hand-blown wares sector. Just prior to the formal negotiating meeting, the *Commoner* informed its readers that, because of the Owens machine, the union was then paying benefits to "over 3,000 idle members."[53] Then, at the joint meeting, although the *Commoner* described the parties as "cordial" and that they worked "conscientiously and patiently," there was in fact no wage agreement until October, and in the end, Hayes agreed to reductions of 20 percent for workers in many lines of glassware.[54] After the conference, Hayes tried to put the best possible face on the loss when he reported to his membership that "the manufacturers [had] insisted upon obtaining a reduction of twenty-five per cent in wages" because of competition from the Owens machine, thus suggesting that the 20 percent reduction was more a victory than a defeat.[55] The GBBA had started down the slippery slope of concessions, and the slope was made all the more slippery by the rising number of licenses granted for the Owens Automatic. By the end of the first decade of the century, there were at least one hundred machines licensed for operation, permitting the manufacture of more than 4 million gross of bottles. In 1910, the GBBA agreed to an additional 10 percent wage cut for workers in many glass lines, and in 1911, as noted earlier, it agreed to further reductions in the summer stop.[56] In 1913, in the face of continuing pressure, the union agreed to reduce apprentice pay by 25 percent and to further reduce the wages for glass blowers by 25 percent as well.[57]

Glass blower employment and union membership were probably declining after 1909 as well, but the numbers are difficult to determine. Membership in all of the nation's glass-related unions had shown a steady increase from the 1890s, when it stood at about ten thousand, through 1910, when it reached nearly thirty thousand. The GBBA accounted for nearly ten thousand of these 1910 glass union members. Following 1910, however, the GBBA simply reported constant membership for the next several years, although the number of employed glass workers, and very probably union members, was undoubtedly declining.[58] Membership figures notwithstanding, by 1913, the glass workers and the GBBA may have realized that their wage battles were effectively lost. Coverage of the annual wage conferences, which had taken up as much as half of the *Commoner*'s front page in 1905 and 1906, had dwindled by 1913 to no more than a few column inches. Also in 1913, as the Pennsylvania legislature debated a reform proposal respecting the hand-blown glass-bottle plants in Pittsburgh, Senator Charles A. Snyder, a friend of the Pittsburgh glass manufacturers, told his legislative colleagues that within a year or two, all of the glass houses of western Pennsylvania would have fully automated production.[59]

Glass Workers and the Glass House Boys

The views of the adult glass workers and the GBBA toward child labor reform and the glass house boys were inextricably tied to the relative importance of those boys to the glass production process. For glass houses that adopted automated technologies, the importance of the boys diminished, but for those glass plants that retained hand-blown methods of production, their importance rose. During the time period under study here, the views of the glass workers and their union regarding the boys can be clearly seen in their responses to two separate but related problems. The first was directly related to the actions taken by the boys and the second, to the actions taken by the Progressive Era child labor reformers. The reactions of the glass workers and their union to both of these sets of events can be tracked in the pages of the *Commoner*.

The actions of the glass house boys that caused the greatest concern among the adult workers and the GBBA during this time period were their periodic acts of resistance in the glass factories and their troubling (at least to the *Commoner*) assertions of power through demonstrations of independent agency. These acts of resistance and independence usually took the form of occasional job actions: walkouts, work stoppages, and strikes. The *Commoner* uniformly tried to downplay the impact of these actions by infantilizing the boys, and in this sense they shared the approach of the manufacturers. Rather than focus on the economic impact that a strike by the glass house boys nearly always had, the newspaper typically characterized such strikes as attributable to a boy's need to play or watch a baseball game as the weather warmed up in the spring. For example, in the late nineteenth century, the *Commoner* reported that at the Hemmingway Glass Company plant in Muncie, Indiana, "[i]nstead of eating [lunch], an army of small boys began to sneak away from the factory," shutting it down for the rest of that warm summer day. In the same issue, the newspaper reported that "a small army of boys employed at Ball Bros. quit work to go swimming and as a result a big portion of the factory was [laid] off."[60] A few years later, the newspaper noted that boys had walked out of the Cunningham glass works in Pittsburgh "when the pleasant weather appeared last week," and the "shops lost several turns" of work.[61] Similarly, the *Commoner* reported in 1907 that both the "snappers at the Haines bottle plant" in Smethport, Pennsylvania, and the "small help" at Tibby Brothers glass works in Sharpsburg, Pennsylvania, went on strike and, at least in the latter case, had "caused the management and men considerable annoyance and loss."[62]

The argument that the glass house boy strikes were merely the result of spring fever, however, is not entirely consistent with other evidence surrounding these job actions. In many of these strikes, the glass house boys, some no older than fourteen, behaved very much like seasoned adult union organizers rather than carefree youths. It is not altogether surprising that these "boys," who worked like adults and in many instances drank and cursed like adults, should also conduct their strikes like adults. In many cases, the strikes were over the very traditional union concerns of wages and working conditions. In one instance, well before the turn of the century, the *Commoner* reported that the "crimping boys at the Excelsior [glass works] have gone out on strike for an advance of five cents on the turn." The boys did so because "the chimney business was booming" and they wanted part of the action. Although their demand would have raised their daily wage by only a nickel, the company refused, and "37 of the boys quit work."[63] A few years later, the newspaper reported that a number of the boys at the Heinz glass-bottle factory in Sharpsburg, Pennsylvania, "went on strike for an increase of 10 cents a day." When the management refused the demand, the strikers tried to broaden their base and "went to Tibby Bros. glass factory," also in Sharpsburg, "and asked the boys there to strike, but were unsuccessful in their efforts." The *Commoner*, not surprisingly, dismissed the action as merely "an outbreak of spring fever" rather than as an attempt by the boys to organize similarly situated "small help" at multiple locations, in the same way that adult glass workers might have tried to organize themselves.[64]

Other strikes produced better results for the boys. In 1907, the boys at the Indiana Bottle & Glass Company, in Cicero, Indiana, struck for higher wages. The *Commoner* reported that the boys "were out that week closing the factory down completely, but . . . the firm met them and settled the strike by granting them [an] increase in wages."[65] Similarly, the "small help at Beaver Falls Co-operative Flint Glass Co.," northwest of Pittsburgh, threatened a strike and were promised fifty cents more per week to keep the shops at work. In the same issue, the *Commoner* announced that the Whitall Tatum glass works in Millville, New Jersey, had come up with a creative way to try to head off wildcat strikes by the glass house boys. The management announced that it would give six-dollar bonuses to any boy who worked continuously from then until the end of June, five dollars to any boy with only one absence, and three dollars to any boy with only two absences.[66]

Although the glass house boys were without any form of formal labor organization and often had, at most, only minimal schooling, with few possessing more than rudimentary literacy, they nonetheless understood their importance in the production process, and they successfully organized repeated job actions in an industry otherwise noted for its harmonious labor-management relations. Possibly because the boys were not unionized and because many of their families dearly needed their income, these strikes were typically spontaneous, short lived, and, in any long-term economic sense, unsuccessful. But, given all that, they were surprisingly numerous and not without some degree of accomplishment. The approach of the *Commoner* in reporting on the job actions was usually to note the occurrence as briefly as possible, to make light of it, and then to emphasize that, while the strike may have resulted in a work stoppage, and therefore cost the adult workers some wages, it was easily resolved. These stories conveyed multiple, layered messages, sometimes working at cross purposes. They were probably intended to signal to the newspaper's adult glass worker readers that the

"Some of the youngsters on day shift (next week on night shift) at Old Dominion Glass Co., Alexandria, Va. I counted 7 white boys and several colored boys that seemed to be under 14 years old. The youngest ones would not give names, but the following are a few: Frank Elmore, 913 Gibbon St., apparently ten or eleven. Been there three months. Dannie Powell, 307 Columbus St. Henry O'Donnell, 1925[?] Duke St. Leslie Mason, 912 Wilke St." June 1911

boys were really not very powerful and that their strikes were more of a humorous inconvenience than a serious threat to the economic well-being of the glass houses. Even though the boys used union tactics, real union members, the newspaper implied, need not be overly concerned. But the same stories also announced quite the opposite message. It was probably clear to the *Commoner*'s readers that, by engaging in even these brief and occasional job actions, the boys could in fact bring a factory to a complete stop. The glass house boys, who, by staying on the job, enabled the adult glass worker to be among the best paid of American workers, could also, by walking out, turn that adult worker's wages to naught.

The complexity of the relationship between the GBBA and the glass house boys is further illustrated in other conflicts that took place on the factory floor. One such conflict involved the glass house boys and their ability to "daub." Daubing represented a potential challenge to the union and its members because, as noted earlier, by engaging in this practice, the boys could acquire skills that otherwise distinguished the unionized glass blowers and gatherers. Hayes and the GBBA, therefore, were understandably concerned. Historically, the GBBA sought strict control of the number of skilled glass workers. By doing so, it could maintain both the workers' wages and its own power on the factory floor by restricting the number of formal apprentice slots in the factories. Toward the same end, the union also tried to restrict the practice of daubing. Daubing, however, had risen to a type of informal, almost common-law right among the boys, and they demanded the right to continue the practice. Further, all parties realized that having a well-practiced boy on a production team could be very useful to the factory should a skilled adult blower or gatherer become ill, and daubing helped create a well-practiced boy. The GBBA was in a bit of a bind. It wanted the boys to have some glass-making knowledge so that they could operate with maximum effectiveness in the furnace rooms yet not so much as to be a threat to the union glass men.

Correspondence surrounding a GBBA executive resolution in 1902 shows how the union tried to navigate between these potentially conflicting positions. On July 15, 1902, the GBBA's executive board decided that, although it "has been in past years a custom in the trade for boys to fill moulds [a practice related to daubing], and to a greater or less extent they take advantage of such privileges, . . . we also believe this custom, if persisted in, will have a tendency to cause boys to go to nonunion [glass] houses to get the trade." Based on this concern, the board then resolved that "all locals are hereby instructed to stop boys from filling moulds and the tendency of boys daubing in the glass."[67] Almost immediately, the large GBBA branch in Streator, Illinois, which had a great many "boy" positions and an equally great difficulty in filling them, requested an exemption from the resolution. The board and Hayes, not wanting to exacerbate the boy shortage in Streator, reconsidered and said that they only meant to prevent the boys from filling molds and that boys could otherwise continue to daub. After further back-and-forth with the Streator branch, Hayes announced to all members that, because "a majority [of the board was] against the law being enforced as it now reads . . . it is therefore, set aside."[68]

These incidents illustrate the complex relationship between the glass house boys and the adult glass workers. In order to downplay the boys' potential to disrupt the production process through job actions, the glass workers, through the *Commoner*, sought to infantilize their actions. To reduce potential competition from these same boys for an ever-shrinking pool of adult jobs, the adult workers, through the GBBA, sought to restrict any access the boys might have to the "adult" skills of the profession. Yet, as mechanization increased, those same boys became indispensable to the hand-blown glass-bottle shops, and in order to keep them returning to the factory floor, the men realized they had to hold out to the boys the possibility of learning the more valuable adult glass-blowing skills. The "boys" were thus, once again, sometimes figured as children and sometimes as adults; they were both the saviors of the hand-blown bottle plants and their Achilles' heel as well.

Glass Workers and Progressive Era Reforms

Throughout the late nineteenth and early twentieth centuries, the Progressive Era child labor reformers were constantly trying to regulate the conditions of employment for the glass house boys in the Pennsylvania glass industry. For the GBBA and the glass workers, the issue of how to respond to the proposed child labor reforms proved to be complex, and their position evolved over time, reflecting the changing economic circumstances of the adult glass workers. Even toward the end of the nineteenth century, the glass workers, their unions, and the *Commoner* generally supported the idea of increased regulation of child labor. As we have seen, some of the early inventions in glassmaking reduced the need for glass house boys but continued to require the skills of the master glass blower. Thus, the adult glass workers could support mechanization, support child labor reform, and, at the same time, be secure in their own jobs. By the end of the first decade of the twentieth century, however, as the Owens Automatic began to invade the glass houses, the pressure on the hand-blown bottle factories increased substantially and so did the importance of the glass house boys. Responding to these changing conditions, the *Commoner*, the glass workers, and at least the Pittsburgh local of the GBBA shifted their stance from being supportive of to adamantly opposing any progressive reforms that might curtail the ability of the glass house boys to work, especially at night.

Early on, the glass workers and their newspaper displayed a more liberal attitude toward child labor. It was evident in 1889, when the Ohio state legislature considered raising from twelve to fourteen the minimum age that boys could work in factories. The glass factory owners, not surprisingly, opposed the proposed law, but the *Commoner* strongly supported it, warning its readers not to be taken in by the arguments advanced by the manufacturers. The manufacturers reportedly protested against the bill's passage by declaring that the boys "are better off in the factory making 50 to 75 cents a day than loafing around the streets" and that the boys should be allowed to work because they might be "the only support for [their] widowed mothers." But the *Commoner* cautioned that these arguments were nothing but subterfuge and that the "[m]anufacturers care nothing about the moral side of the question." Therefore, the newspaper concluded, "the bill spoken of ought to pass."[69] After receiving negative comments on this position from some readers to the effect that the proposed Ohio law might make it hard to find enough boys for glass factories in rural areas and thus might make it hard to keep the adult glass workers employed, the *Commoner* eased up, but only slightly. It asserted that "exceptions [to the law] may be made in this particular case, yet child labor under 14 years of age should be prohibited."[70]

That same year saw the passage of one of the most significant pieces of child labor legislation in Pennsylvania history: the Factory Inspection Act of 1889. This law, discussed in more detail in chapter 5 (and similar to the Illinois law championed by Florence Kelley a few years earlier), established the position of factory inspector. The Factory Inspection Act was the first major attempt to add serious legislative teeth to the Pennsylvania child labor laws. Again, the law was supported by the *Commoner*, without reservation. The newspaper noted with approval that the legislative committee of the Knights of Labor had endorsed the proposed legislation and that the leader of the Knights, Terence V. Powderly, had called it a model bill. Further, the newspaper stated approvingly that the bill had been "drawn by Mrs. Leonora Barry, Investigator of Women's Work in the Knights of

Labor," but that unfortunately it had been "fearfully mutilated [in the legis-lature] before it became a law." Thus, although the newspaper characterized the final law as "fairly good," the *Commoner* clearly would have preferred an even stronger reform statement.[71]

In one of the rare references to the boys themselves, the *Commoner* ran a long article in 1895 on the British parliament's recent efforts to raise the minimum working age for boys from fourteen to sixteen years. After men-tioning the English glass manufacturers' concern that any such law would unduly disrupt their production processes, the newspaper reminded its readers of the "raw faces," the "burnt fingers," and the glass cuts suffered by the glass house boys as they "walk a distance back and forth [in the factory] equal to about 20 miles" during a typical day's work. In language echoing reformers' concerns, the newspaper concluded, "We doubt that there is any kind of child labor that is more painful or exhaustive [*sic*] than that of the glass house boy, and he is deserving of more sympathy and better treat-ment than the average blower bestows upon him."[72]

As early as 1896, an article on glass industry mechanization in the *Na-tional Glass Budget* showed that while the glass workers were clearly con-cerned about preserving their own jobs in the face of automation in the glass industry, they were also happy to have the jobs of the glass house boys eliminated. The *Budget* stated that one particular machine, the "end-less chain ware conveyer," had largely replaced "the labor of the carrying-in boys at the Edward H. Everett Glass Works" located in Newark, Ohio. The *Commoner*, as quoted by the *Budget*, spoke favorably on the use of this particular machine to the extent that it only replaced the labor of the boys, reasoning that (in part because of the 1896 economic depression) there were more than enough skilled blowers on hand at the time. Thus, more apprentices were not needed and the boy jobs could be cut back. Although welcoming this support for continued glass house mechanization, the *Bud-get* could not resist needling the *Commoner*. While pleased that the work-ers' newspaper favored this particular form of automation and was look-ing out for the welfare of the glass house boys, the *Budget* predicted that machines would eventually take over all aspects of the trade and replace all laborers.[73] As the accuracy of this prediction became apparent, the views of the glass workers, the GBBA, and the *Commoner* on the need to maintain child labor changed considerably.

Although the *Commoner* showed a high level of concern with issues such as mechanization and child labor legislation, it, like the *National Glass Budget*, spent surprisingly little time (apart from the few stories on their job actions) discussing the boys themselves. However, what it did say about them is telling on several counts. In the late years of the nineteenth century, there were occasional stories about some accident or injury suffered by a boy worker. In 1888, for example, there was a brief account of a boy named Preston Potter who had "a hot mold handle" fall on him. In the two-sentence story, there is the note that the boy "may lose an arm."[74] In 1896, the *Commoner* reported on a fight that took place between two boys at a Charleroi, Pennsylvania, chimney glass shop over daubing rights. Apparently, one boy was caught daubing out of the furnace reserved for the other boy, a fight ensued, and one boy died.[75] Because the GBBA, as noted earlier, generally opposed the practice of daubing by boys, it is hardly surprising to find that the newspaper used this story as a type of morality tale to show the harm that could result when boys did engage in the practice.

As the economics of the industry began to change, however, so did the position of the *Commoner* on the question of the glass house boys and child labor reform. After 1905, virtually no stories that mention the background of the boys or the hardships of their work appear in the pages of the *Commoner*. Publishing such stories might have made the glass house boys appear more like actual children toiling day and night in front of searing hot furnaces and might thereby have provided ammunition for reformers in their fight to end industrial child labor. As the job security of the skilled glass men in the industry became increasingly tenuous, thanks first to the growth of nonunion shops in the gas belt states and then through the use of the Owens Automatic, the *Commoner* became more concerned with the job security of its adult glass worker readers than with the health and safety issues relating to the small help. Increasingly, the glass house boys lost whatever personal or individual attributes they might have been granted in the pages of the *Commoner*. Nearly all of the articles regarding the boys that appeared in the newspaper after 1905 treated them in terms of their economic impact on the factories. The boys became merely another interchangeable part of the process of industrial glass production.

One example of the *Commoner*'s dehumanization of the glass house boys centered on the availability of the boys for work in the glass houses.

When the *Commoner* reported on the problem of the scarcity of boys in the glass works in Zanesville, Ohio, Terre Haute, Indiana, Wheeling, West Virginia, Alton, Illinois, and Medford, New Jersey, it complained that the real problem with the shortage of boys was that it kept the glass workers' wages low.[76] The *Commoner* approvingly reported that, to counteract these "boy" shortages, the Salem Glass Works in New Jersey had "completed barracks near Salem creek for some of their New York boy help," the building being "fitted with a living room and 48 bunks."[77] These stories appeared after the introduction of the Owens Automatic and in light of the increased importance of the glass house boys in the hand-blown glass factories. The *Commoner* did not address the hardships such "barrack" living arrangements may have placed on the boys themselves. Rather, the stories emphasized that, if glass house boys were not available to work in the factory, the blowers could not work, and if the blowers did not work, they earned nothing.

These stories in the *Commoner* on the shortage of glass house boys are in contrast to a report on the same subject by the preeminent child labor reformer of the day, Florence Kelley. In the late nineteenth century in Illinois, where there was a chronic shortage of boys to work in the factories, Florence Kelley, then the state factory inspector, noted that many glass houses used orphaned or "adopted" boys to work the shifts. Often these boys were forced to live on barges or river rafts near the glass factories, and they rotated through the sleeping quarters much as they rotated through the alternating day and night shifts in the factory. Kelley, stressing the horror of such an arrangement and emphasizing the "child" nature of these particular glass house boys, used this as evidence to support the need for tougher child labor laws in Illinois.

The *Commoner*, reflecting the evolving position of the union and especially the Pittsburgh-based skilled workers on the issue of child labor, began to distance itself from reformers like Kelley and to align itself with the glass manufacturers. Whereas in earlier times the newspaper reprinted the manufacturers' complaints about child labor regulations and then immediately offered corrective, countervailing, or qualifying comments in order to distance itself from these management positions, in the early years of the twentieth century the newspaper began printing the complaints of the manufacturers without further comment. For example, in April 1905,

"Two young carrying-in boys in Alexandria (Va.) Glass Factory. Frank (on left) 702 N. Patrick St. could neither read nor write, having been to school only a few weeks in his life. Two older brothers work in the glass factory, and his father is a candy maker. Frank is working on night shift this week. Ashby Corbin (on right), 413 N. St. Asaph St. Has had only four terms of schooling." June 1911

the newspaper noted without comment that an Ohio bottle factory boss complained that a "new school law has played havoc with the glass plants here."[78] Similarly, the newspaper reported in 1907 that a proposed Indiana child labor bill would raise the minimum working age to sixteen, adding only that "glass men have found several objectionable features in the bill . . . [t]he principal contention [being] that the bill will prevent boys under 16 years of age from working in the glass factories at night."[79] The use of the ambiguous phrase "glass men," rather than the more definite "glass man-ufacturer" or "glass worker," while subtle, signaled a merging of interests among formerly opposed parties. Further, by not commenting on or overtly spinning the story, the newspaper could say that it was letting its readers come to their own conclusions on the matter. Yet, given that by 1907 the hand-blown glass-bottle plants could not function without the night work done by boys and that these plants needed a "virtual army" of small help, the conclusion that those readers would draw was fairly certain. However painful or exhausting the boys' labor might still be, the newspaper no longer urged sympathy or better treatment of them from the glass blowers but began to demand that glass house boys needed to be available for work at all hours.

After 1905, when the Pennsylvania legislature created the glass house exception to the general ban on night work for children under sixteen, the *Commoner* came to support this exception in the strongest possible terms. In 1907, the newspaper signaled the beginnings of this support when the Pennsylvania legislature again debated the night work issue. When it appeared that the legislature might actually erase the glass house exception, the *Commoner* objected, at first subtly and then with force. In the spring, the newspaper reported on a meeting the Civic Club of Allegheny County organized in support of the bill. This was the meeting headlined by Owen Lovejoy and, as noted earlier, reviewed disparagingly by the *National Glass Budget*. The *Commoner*, rather than distance itself from the *Budget*'s editorial position, reinforced it by calling the club's description of current Pennsylvania child labor practices "rather caustic."[80] Legislative proposals that the *Commoner* supported only several years earlier it now began to question. Two weeks later, when the Committee on Manufactures in the Pennsylvania House of Representatives conducted a hearing in Harrisburg regarding the child labor bill, glass industry representatives spoke in favor of several important amendments. Following this hearing, the *Commoner* reported quite positively that the "impression made on the committee [by the manufacturers] was apparently a satisfactory one and it was the general opinion that a bill will be reported that will be satisfactory to the glass interests of the state."[81] While the use of the term "caustic" in the first story was hardly inflammatory and the reference to "glass interests" (rather than "glass manufacturers") in the second was hardly decisive, both provide evidence of the use of subtle rhetorical shadings to announce that the *Commoner* was changing direction. It could no longer afford to support progressive child labor programs because to do so would mean economic death to many of its subscribers—the skilled adult glass-bottle blowers.

When the *Commoner* began to address Pennsylvania's 1907 child labor bill on its editorial page, the evolution was complete. Sounding more like an apologist for the manufacturers' association than a publication for workers, the *Commoner* stated that while there was "widespread agitation throughout the United States about the child labor question," much of that agitation "is based upon misunderstanding or lack of information as to the facts governing the employment of minors [in] . . . glass factories." The *Commoner*, glossing over volumes of evidence to the contrary, asserted that the glass industry had "for years been leading every effort toward bettering the conditions that obtain in their plants and especially with reference to small help." The "glass manufacturer of today," it argued, is "keep[ing] pace with the progressive spirit." But, it continued, while the "present agitation" for reform was being spearheaded by such groups as "the [Pennsylvania] Child Labor League and other civic bodies," these reformers, while no doubt mostly "honest," seriously misunderstood the "actual conditions" of the industry. This was very unusual rhetoric for a major industrial union in the early twentieth century.[82]

As if this were not sufficient, the *Commoner* gave further evidence of its opposition to reform by recounting a secondhand story "related by a leading flint glass manufacturer." According to this story, an artist hired by the Pennsylvania child labor association, an affiliate of the National Child Labor Committee, was instructed to prepare drawings of glass house boys. The artist was instructed to show only those boys who had a "wan, worn-out, hollow-cheeked and sunken-eyed appearance." The artist, so the story went, decided to visit a glass factory to see the boys in person. After touring the factory, the *Commoner* recounted, the artist complained to his guide that all of the boys he observed at work were "as sturdy, healthy and happy a lot" as he had ever seen. The article concluded that the artist's pictures of the glass house boys, based on his firsthand observations and reflecting his positive impression, were rejected by the child labor association because they were deemed unsuitable for its cause. This story, contended the *Commoner*, "shows to what extremes some of these philanthropists are resorting to in order to manufacture public sentiment in favor of radical legislation." The newspaper argued that the reformers' claims obscured the "truth" that the glass manufacturers "are as humane as any set of men in the industrial world." It concluded that the child labor problem will "doubtless soon be solved, but not through the hysterical efforts of parties who endeavor to mislead the public by giving out grossly exaggerated reports."[83]

In 1909, as the Pennsylvania legislature again considered child labor reform legislation, the progressives again mounted an attack on the child labor practices of the state's glass industry. The *Commoner* countered with a searing, gender-based attack on the proponents of reform: "If the supporters of the [child labor] bill don't know enough to gag their bitter-tongued, indiscreet female associates who could serve their country better by attending to their children (if they have any) they are entitled to and should receive very scant courtesy at the hands of the committee. This thing of a lot of fussy, hysterical, impractical and sentimental women sticking their noses into everybody's business is becoming a serious nuisance."[84]

In 1911, when yet another assault on the glass house exception was mounted in the Pennsylvania legislature, an editorial in the *Commoner* echoed yet again the rhetoric of the *Budget*. The *Commoner* called the progressives "half-baked reformers" who would do everyone a favor if they would "use a little common sense and investigate the practical side of a question before seeking to enact detrimental legislation."[85] By the end of the first decade of the twentieth century then, the glass workers and the GBBA, as shown in the pages of the *Commoner*, had little interest in child labor reform and were working diligently to thwart any such reform efforts in Pennsylvania.

Because of the actions of the GBBA, the western Pennsylvania glass industry presented a unique challenge for Pennsylvania's progressive reformers as the union repeatedly and successfully joined in the efforts to resist rather than embrace child labor reforms. The inability of the social progressives to forge an effective coalition with the GBBA was a key factor in their inability to secure child labor reforms in Pennsylvania that would affect the Pittsburgh glass house boys. To keep the boys at work in the factories, the Pittsburgh local of the GBBA, with the silent support of the national office, actively lobbied *against* Progressive Era child reform legislation. This was a highly unusual if not unique circumstance in the labor movement of the day, and it placed Hayes and the GBBA in an unusual position. The Pittsburgh glass workers were openly lobbying the Pennsylvania legislature against child labor reform at the same time the tacit position of the national GBBA and the official position of the AFL lent support to such reform. Because the Pittsburgh union members helped provide the critical mass to Pennsylvania's anti-reform efforts, the union helped stymie progressive efforts to overturn the glass house exception until 1915, when, as Senator Snyder predicted, automation had fully taken over the Pittsburgh bottle plants and night work by the boys was no longer economically necessary for the industry or the union.

School Law and Compulsory Education in Pennsylvania

*I am a warm champion of school education, [but] I fail to see the
connection between the "three R's" and the necessity for [children]
seeking employment and the ability to do the work.*

J. C. Delaney, Pennsylvania factory inspector

ANY SOCIAL PROGRESSIVES, in Pennsylvania and elsewhere, valued formal, public school–based education for the
children of the working classes. They worried that a child who
received only work-based training might be relegated to a lifetime of low
wages, menial labor, and poverty, and the reformers wanted to provide educational alternatives for these children. The educational programs that the
progressives envisioned specifically for the children of working-class families were intended to provide them with opportunities for socialization, to
train them to be good citizens, and, for the children of recent immigrants,
to "Americanize" them. In Pennsylvania, the curriculum advanced by the
progressives typically included the "common English branches," which
stressed a practical, nonclassical education. The goal was to enable the children to begin to mirror the values of the middle class.[1] The progressives
believed that a combination of school reform, together with child labor
laws, could best serve as a vehicle for extending the concept of sheltered
childhood from the middle class to all children.

The progressives were entering into a longstanding conversation concerning the relative value of school and work as venues for learning, and
they were trying to change the nature of that conversation. Many of the
historical arguments advanced in support of allowing young children to
work—arguments that the progressives began to challenge—centered on
the educational aspects of the employment experience: children could learn
a trade, they could learn the value of money, they could learn responsibility,
and they could learn how to avoid becoming a financial burden on society. Especially for workers who were recent immigrants, and perhaps even
more so for their children, work was understood to be a crucial form of ac-
culturation. Having a job could teach the worker what it meant to be a citizen; it was part of the process of becoming an American. Progressive Era
reformers did not argue that the educational aspects of the work environment were unimportant but rather that they should not supplant school-
based learning. As schools became more available, the progressive ideal of
making those schools available to all children generated friction over the
relative importance of those schools versus the workplace as educational
sites. State legislatures became important places for trying to resolve these
conflicts, and the programs and policies adopted by state lawmakers to

balance school-work tension were informed by conceptions of social class, traditional views of workplace education, and by the developing ideals of sheltered childhood. An analysis of how Pennsylvania school law developed during the late nineteenth and early twentieth centuries, and how it affected the lives of the Pittsburgh glass house boys, provides evidence of how legislators, and by extension the public at large, viewed these children and the education they should receive.

The development of schools in Pennsylvania during this period was part of the vast expansion in free, public education taking place throughout most of the country. In the nineteenth century, public schools spread from the urban, industrializing Northeast, through the Midwest and West, and eventually, in the twentieth century, to the South.[2] This expanding system of "common schools" was initially directed to meet the needs of the children of middle-class families, and the theories behind this expansion of public education were consistent with the ideals of sheltered childhood being adopted in these middle-class households.[3] Attendance at these schools, at least initially, was entirely voluntary. However, as the reformers strove to ensure that the common schools could be used by all children, especially those of the working class, they came to realize that a policy of strictly voluntary attendance was not sufficient. The progressives knew that the families of working-class children would find the lure of their child's employment very hard to resist, and therefore the law would have to require the child's attendance at school if the societal value of the common school system were to be realized. Thus, compulsory education laws came to be seen as a necessary element of Progressive Era school law reforms.

Analysis of the development of school law in Pennsylvania reveals that the reforms that actually materialized, although based on progressive notions of making educational opportunities available for everyone, were the result of legislative reinterpretation. In school reform, as with other Progressive Era legislative programs, state legislators brought a wide variety of political perspectives to bear on the problems under consideration. While there were some strong progressive voices in the Pennsylvania legislature during this period, other voices favored the state's industrial interests and the immediate economic needs of its citizens. Because of the breadth of views represented, when the legislature dealt with problems such as school reform, it was often conflicted over the proper scope and content of such

"Carrying-in Boy at the Lehr (15 years old), Glass Works, Grafton, W.Va. Has worked for several years. Works nine hours. Day shift one week, night shift next week. Gets $1.25 per day." October 1908

reform. These conflicts were especially evident when state lawmakers tried to balance the relative importance, for the children of the state, of industrial work and school attendance.

We have already seen the importance of this balancing in the prominent role that questions of schooling played in Elizabeth Beardsley Butler's study of the Pittsburgh-area glass house boys in *The Pittsburgh Survey*. The National Child Labor Committee also often linked its investigations supporting and legislative proposals regarding child labor reforms with reform proposals for education laws. The investigative studies of the Pittsburgh glass house boys that Charles Chute and Herschel Jones conducted as "special agents" of the NCLC, for example, sought to demonstrate that work in the glass factories, and especially night work, had a deleterious effect on the boys' ability to go to school. The studies by Chute and Jones showed that many of the parents of the glass house boys believed that their employment, even at very low "boy" wages, was an economic necessity for the family. These and other reports underscored for the reformers that if the children of the working class were going to be able to go to school, there needed to be an effective set of compulsory attendance laws. The Pennsylvania legislature, on the other hand, approached school reform with a focus on the more immediate economic needs of working-class families. When it came to the education of working-class children then, the legislature, much like the families of the glass house boys and much to the chagrin of the progressive reformers, often favored the factory over the school. Reform was never an easy matter in Pennsylvania.

Schools and Work in Nineteenth-Century Pennsylvania

The Pennsylvania General Assembly began to investigate the proper boundary between work and schooling for the state's children as early as the third decade of the nineteenth century. While few of these early investigations resulted in legislation, when the legislature later in the century actually did pass school laws, especially those related to compulsory education, they were important not only for what they attempted to regulate but for what they excluded from regulation. While the laws generally set minimum standards respecting the terms and conditions for the education (and employment) of children in the state, they also created systems of exemption whereby whole classes of children were excluded from the general educational requirements. Even for those children included within the scope of the laws, however, the laws were unevenly applied, and their effectiveness was compromised by ambiguity, poor drafting, and inconsistencies. As with child labor regulations, the standards established were often vague, the proofs required were often illusory, and the people designated to enforce the laws were often less than enthusiastic in fulfilling their duties.

In Pennsylvania, as in other northern states during the nineteenth century, laws related to education took up a considerable amount of the legislature's time and energy. Initial concerns focused on creating a network of common schools, that is, a system of tax-supported institutions, principally elementary schools, that would be free and open to all children.[4] Later, states focused on related issues, including compulsory attendance at those common schools. Before the Civil War, the basic concept of the common school was hotly debated, with Pennsylvania in the thick of the debate.[5] While it was understood by some at the time that an effective system of public schools required public financing and that a smoothly functioning school system could enhance the economic well-being of the commonwealth and its communities, not all legislators, indeed not all citizens, concurred. Many people in Pennsylvania believed that there simply was no direct economic return on public investment in schools and thus considered the investment ill advised. In 1826, Thaddeus Stevens, who would later go on to national political fame as a staunch abolitionist, was a young elected official from Pennsylvania fighting for tax-supported common schools. In the face of mounting resistance to the idea that the public should pay for education, Stevens stated that he hoped Pennsylvanians would one day "learn to dread ignorance more than taxation."[6]

While the relationship between work and school that developed during the Progressive Era was a bitterly contested borderland, the contest was not reducible to a simple binary of school versus work, especially for the young boys who worked in the Pittsburgh glass factories. Some held the view that children, *all* children, should receive, almost as part of their republican birthright, a common education. Others saw what they believed to be the economic and social reality, also buttressed by well-developed ideological scaffolding, that even young children should work, not only to support the family economy but also to learn a useful trade. Others argued that in order to work effectively, especially at the growing number of white-collar jobs (e.g., in law, accounting, and management), the child needed more formal educational training. Still others argued that with the vast number of industrial and mill jobs available, young persons stood to gain more from on-the-job, rather than school-based, education.

In 1824, Pennsylvania lawmakers appointed a committee to "inquire into the expediency of requiring the proprietors of manufacturing establishments who may employ children under the age of 12 years, to provide for them the means of instruction, at least two hours each day in the rudiments of an English education."[7] Although the committee recommended legislation regarding the educational instruction of working children, the recommendation was never enacted into law.[8] Two legislative sessions later, another bill was considered by the Pennsylvania House of Representatives to make it unlawful for any manufacturing concern to employ a child between the ages of twelve and eighteen who did not have a certificate of schooling. The bill also would have made it illegal for a manufacturer not to make certain provisions for the child's educational instruction at work. This time the bill passed in the House chamber but died in the Senate.[9] Although no law resulted from either of these bills, they indicate that while the state was concerned about the education of its children, there was a preference within the state legislature to have the education of working-class children taken care of by their employers.

There is some evidence that the legislature came under pressure from members of the working class itself to have the state, rather than the employer, provide for the educational needs of working-class children. As early as 1829, a workingmen's society in Philadelphia resolved that "[n]o system of education, which a freeman can accept, has yet been established for the poor; whilst thousands of dollars of the public money has been appropriated for building colleges and academies for the rich." Each member of the state legislature was asked to support the concept of an "equal and general system of education," and the group, demanding better schools for all, declared that there could be "no real liberty in a republic without a wide diffusion of real intelligence."[10] But little progress was made. In 1838, a bill was introduced into the state Senate stating that if a child worker could not read, write, or "keep an account," that child would need to attend school for three months per year before being allowed to work. But, as with the previous legislative efforts, no law resulted.

It is not unusual that the early-nineteenth-century Pennsylvania legislature investigated employer-provided education for child workers rather than seeking to fund common schools out of the public treasury. Some members of the reform movement at the time stressed that the need for manual and vocational education for working class and orphaned children should be provided by the private sector; workplace education was thus an idea they championed. In its history of child labor legislation in Pennsylvania published in 1934, the Pennsylvania Department of Labor and Industry's Bureau of Women and Children refers to the "Dyottville System" as an instance of factory-sponsored education for working children. Quoting from an 1833 report entitled "An Exposition of the System of Moral and Mental Labor Established at the Glass Factory of Dyottville, in the County of Philadelphia," the bureau history notes that the Dyottville System was intended to lessen the "mass of human ignorance" by "shedding light on the benighted understanding . . . and reforming the evil passions of the vicious heart."[11] These were rather strong terms when one realizes that some of the children who were to be the pupils were as young as six years old.

As the bureau history reports, the daily routine planned for these young children was "a disillusioning revelation." The glass house employed the children, probably as part of an apprenticeship agreement with their families, and provided them with living quarters as well as instruction in the craft of glassmaking. In addition, the glass company agreed to provide other "opportunities for recreation and education." The company agreed to employ a "competent teacher" and two assistants who were expected to instruct the children in "Reading, Writing and Arithmetic," with grammar classes for those children who wanted additional study. That the children had any time or energy for study was amazing. They were up at first daylight, with prayers before breakfast, and at work in the glass house by 7:00 A.M. They then worked ten hours, not including lunch or breaks, and then had supper. Their school instruction was limited to an hour after supper. In the words of the bureau history, "one cannot imagine that many of the children would be able materially to improve their minds in the one hour allotted for education" after putting in their standard work day. These were obviously not the ideal conditions under which to teach small children, but the company was offering more than what was required by law.[12]

However Dickensian the scenario, employer-provided education for working children had the potential to address at least two recurring legislative concerns in Pennsylvania regarding the common school movement. First was the concern over cost, as had been noted earlier by Thaddeus Stevens. To the extent that employers provided even rudimentary educational opportunities for working-class children, the financial burden could be shifted from the commonwealth's taxpayers to the business sector. Second, there was a concern, as would be expressed later by several of the state's governors when considering compulsory education legislation, that the individual liberty of the citizens was improperly compromised if the state compelled the attendance of its children in the commonwealth's common schools. That is, to the extent that the state required children to go to school, it infringed on the innate prerogatives of families to decide not only how but whether to educate their children or not and also to decide whether those children belonged in school or at work. The factory school, on the other hand, had the potential to dissipate these tensions. The child could be sent "willingly" to work, economic compulsion aside, and if educational opportunities were also part of the employment contract, the issue of state compunction was eliminated.

As the bureau history suggests, however, such schemes as the Dyottville System did not so "favorably impress the legislators" that they became state policy. Rather, substantial forces continued to lobby the state to make some more direct "public" provision for the education of all of its children, including those of the working class.[13] The legislature eventually responded by establishing a system of publicly supported common schools.[14] However, because the reformers realized that simply making schooling available to the children of the working class would not ensure their attendance, compulsory education laws were also proposed. The resulting legislation became an important link between the common school movement and Progressive Era child labor regulations.

Compulsory Education Legislation

In April 1874, the lower house of the Pennsylvania General Assembly debated one of the state's first compulsory education bills but rejected it with a 50-to-34 vote on the third reading.[15] In 1889, at least two similar bills were under consideration in the Pennsylvania House of Representatives. Both, however, were reported out of committee "with a negative recommendation," and both died in the House.[16] In 1891, a compulsory education bill passed both houses of the General Assembly but met with a gubernatorial veto. In his message back to the legislature explaining the reasons for his disapproval, Governor Robert E. Patterson described the bill as violating key principles of freedom of choice:

[S]erious political, educational and social problems . . . have not yet been definitely or satisfactorily solved, by the experience of other states. . . . This state has provided with increasing liberality for the education of all the children of all its citizens. While it has furnished the opportunity to all, it has imposed the obligation of attendance on none. Free attendance upon free schools seems to most benefit a free people. I am well aware of the necessity claimed to exist for compelling certain classes of the people to aveil [sic] themselves of the opportunities afforded them, but compulsory education is such an invasion upon existing systems in our commonwealth, that if it is to be inaugurated it should be done [only] under the most favorable circumstances.[17]

The movement, however, was not thwarted.

Two years later, in the next legislative session, Governor Patterson was afforded a second opportunity to provide for the compulsory education of Pennsylvania's children. This education bill was passed by the House of Representatives on April 4, 1893, by a vote of 120 to 48, and by the Senate, with virtually no vocal opposition and only a handful of minor amendments, by a vote of 33 to 10.[18] The House then approved the Senate's changes, voting 106 to 22, and sent the bill on to the governor.[19] Despite these very substantial majorities in both legislative chambers and the absence of any significant negative comments or discussion in either the House or the Senate, Governor Patterson again vetoed the bill. In his May 31, 1893, veto message, he reiterated the concerns he had expressed in 1891 and added a series of further objections. He said he had vetoed the bill because

the subjection of homes and families to the espionage which it provides, the investiture the secretary of the school board with the authority of a prosecuting officer, the erection of every magistrate's office into a court wherein parents and guardians may be arraigned for an offense, against which [only] their poverty is to be a competent plea, the imposition of a fine without any provisions for its collection in case payment is refused, and the ambiguous provisions that "satisfactory excuse," to comply with the requirements of this act shall acquit offenders under it, all tend to make the law highly objectionable, if not utterly futile.[20]

The proponents of compulsory education achieved success two years later, but only with the election of a new governor, Daniel H. Hastings, and increased resolve within the General Assembly.[21]

The 1895 compulsory education bill easily passed the House and was sent to the Senate, where it was approved on a 38-to-3 vote after the requisite three readings, with virtually no comment or amendment to the House's language.[22] Governor Hastings signed it on May 16, albeit with some reservations. In a rare postscript added to the end of the bill, he noted that although the "General Assembly [had] in the sessions of 1891 and 1893 passed a compulsory education act somewhat similar to the present measure, each . . . met with Executive disapproval." While he had not issued either of those vetoes, he clearly shared similar concerns about the bill then on his desk and its potential intrusions into the private affairs of the state's citizens. He explained his decision to sign the bill as follows:

There appears to be throughout the Commonwealth a general desire for such a law. I have not received a single protest from any citizen against this bill as far as I recall. The unanimity with which it was passed by the Legislature as well as the large number of requests made upon me to sign it, clearly indicate the general desire on the part of the people for a compulsory education law. Under these circumstances I am convinced that I should not obtrude any individual judgment which I may have on the question of public policy. The measure provides for compulsory education in perhaps the least objectionable form . . . and offends as little against the personal rights of the citizens as possible.[23]

The 1895 law could be seen as less obtrusive in part because it was relatively short and simple. It required parents to send children between the ages of eight and thirteen to a "school in which the common English branches are taught . . . during at least sixteen weeks each year." There were only a few exceptions to this attendance requirement, including an exemption for children who were deemed to be either physically or mentally unfit and one for those children for whom no school was available "within two miles of the nearest traveled road." The new law also allowed, but did not require, school districts to hire an "attendance" officer to aid in enforcing the law. Finally, although these newly minted, if optional, attendance officers were directed "to look after, [and] apprehend [truants] and place [them] in such schools as the person in parental authority may designate," the officer was granted no special police power or other authority to do so.

It is interesting, considering the legislature's historic interest in the educational needs of working children (a history that stretched some seventy years into the past), that the 1895 law contained no reference at all to the special circumstances of children between eight and thirteen years of age who might have jobs that would interfere with their ability to attend school. At this time, there were nearly 2 million children under the age of fourteen employed throughout the country; Pennsylvania, as one of the leading industrial centers of the nation, undoubtedly had more than its fair share of them. But the potential conflict between school and work was minimized to the extent that the official minimum age for most industrial, manufacturing, and related employments in the state in 1895 was thirteen years, the same as the upper limit of the school attendance requirement.[24] There was, however, at least a slight facial inconsistency between the 1895 attendance requirement and the state's mining laws; the minimum age for boys employed to work in mines was twelve.[25] Such an inconsistency in the state's education and child labor laws was not unusual. During this period, when there was an inconsistency like this, the school laws in Pennsylvania tended to set the more stringent standard and, at least legally if not in actual practice, trump the more lenient labor regulations. The inconsistencies, however, rarely led to material difficulties because one of the hallmarks of almost every area of legislation affecting working children in Pennsylvania was, as stated earlier, lax enforcement.

Just two years after passing its first compulsory education law, the Pennsylvania legislature amended it.[26] If the legislative record surrounding these amendments is any indication, the compulsory attendance law of 1895, despite its rather tepid reception at the desk of the governor, had been well received by the people of the commonwealth. The 1897 bill originated in the Senate, where the record reveals not a single negative comment or amendment prior to its final approval on May 10, 1897.[27] Similarly, in the House of Representatives, although a handful of changes were proposed by the Committee on Education to which the bill had been committed and a few amendments were added on the House floor, none appeared to be controversial, and the final passage of the bill on June 28 was by a vote of 118 to 4.[28]

Signed by Governor Hastings on July 12, 1897, the law now required children from eight to sixteen years of age to attend school for "at least seventy per centum of the time in which school in their respective districts shall be in session." This was a substantial strengthening of the law and, on its face, it represented a more serious conflict with the state's then extant child labor laws, since there were literally thousands of Pennsylvania's children under the age of sixteen who were otherwise lawfully employed, not only in the mines but also in factories and businesses. To resolve this conflict, the 1897 law provided the first of what would become a standard working-child exemption, stating simply that the compulsory attendance requirements would "not apply to any child between the ages of thirteen and sixteen years that [sic] is regularly engaged in any useful employment or service." The new law also expanded the scope of the attendance officer provisions, establishing a requirement for such officials in all city school districts (but still discretionary in nonurban areas) and giving them the nominal ability, without any further elaboration or clarification, to "arrest" suspected truants.[29]

Other discrepancies existed between the school law and the child labor regulations in place in 1897, but there is no evidence that they led to problems in enforcement. The mining laws still allowed boys between twelve and thirteen years of age to work in both bituminous and anthracite coal mines. The school law, on the other hand, continued to require any child under thirteen years of age to attend school, since the newly created working-child exemption did not take effect until the child was thirteen. Further, the working-child exemption was silent as to what evidence was needed, by way of letter, affidavit, or certificate, to prove the child's age or that the child had employment. The general child labor law of 1897, on the other hand, required that if any child under sixteen wanted to work, he or she had to produce "an affidavit made by the parent or guardian, stating the age . . . of said child." Interestingly, this particular labor law also stated that any child under the age of sixteen who was otherwise employable was prohibited from working if he or she "cannot read and write in the English language, unless he presents a certificate of having attended during the preceding year, an evening or day school for a period of sixteen weeks."[30] This inconsistency led to the curious situation in which the compulsory education law of the state would allow any child over thirteen to work, whether he or she could read and write or not; whereas the child labor law required not only that the child be of proper age but also that, if under sixteen, he or she needed to be able to read and write (or attend school for sixteen weeks).

The working-child exemption in the school law is significant. It was a blanket exemption contingent only on the age of the child. The direct implication was that any formal schooling beyond the age of twelve was not as important for this child as working and that whatever the child might need to learn could be learned in the factory. The legislature was saying that for these children, work was more important than school. Even when superimposed on the 1897 child labor law, the requirements for leaving school for work were minimal. First, all that was needed to certify the child's age was the word of his or her parent (or if no parent were alive, the word of the child). Second, while the "literacy" certificate needed to be signed by "the teacher or teachers of the school," it needed only attest to the child's attendance, not his or her English-language competency. Thus, in Pennsylvania, a functionally illiterate child could, quite legally, leave school after age twelve to work so long as he or she had attended school for sixteen weeks.

It is also telling that the labor law and the school law were each signed by the governor within less than seventy-five days of each other: the labor law on April 29, 1897, and the school law on July 12. One might have expected greater consistency between two laws enacted in such proximity. The discrepancies, however, show a casualness, a lack of concern for detail, and a tolerance for inconsistency that, as will be seen in the detailed discussion of the child labor laws in chapter 6, seems to typify the work of the General Assembly during this period.

This approach to satisfying the educational needs of working children by using a combination of both school and child labor law provisions was continued in 1901 when the Pennsylvania legislature made two changes to the state's school law. The first change was made on May 11, 1901, when Governor William A. Stone signed a brief, two-sentence law into effect. This act provided that "whenever school directors . . . shall be requested by fifty or more taxpayers, they shall establish . . . night schools for the manual training of children above the age of twelve years."[31] Attendance at these manual training schools was entirely voluntary, and there was no specific curricular requirement that they teach the "common English branches." Thus, attendance at an evening manual training school was not intended to supersede the basic schooling requirements contained in the regular compulsory education law. Further, the school officials could close these schools if attendance should "fall below fifteen [students] nightly." This law was completely separate from the more substantial revisions to the compulsory education law signed two months later, on July 11, 1901.[32] The manual training schools were, as their name implies, intended to augment the education being received by the state's working-class children on the factory floor. Such schools had an industrial rather than a general education curriculum.

The more significant revision to the state's school laws was the compulsory education law signed in July. With the revision, the law continued to apply to all children between eight and sixteen years of age but now required that they attend school "continuously during the entire time in which [it] . . . shall be in session." For the child between thirteen and sixteen years of age who was "regularly engaged in any useful employment," the law now stated that the child must be able to "read and write the English language intelligently" in order to avoid the attendance requirements. Further, in what we might today see as a type of home-schooling provision, the law provided an additional attendance exemption, probably only available to the children of wealthier families, described as follows: "[T]his act shall not apply to any child that [sic] has been . . . instructed in English, in the common branches of learning for a like period of time, by any legally qualified governess or private tutor in a family."[33] The law, however, contained no legal qualifications for such governesses or tutors. Finally, the provisions respecting the attendance officer were also adjusted. While the officers were still required only in urban school districts, they now were granted "full police power without warrant . . . to look after, and arrest and apprehend truants."[34]

Although the 1901 school law echoed the child labor regulations in creating a literacy standard for its working-child exemption, it did not, unlike the child labor law in force at the time or even the school law from 1897, require any explicit means by which to certify that the literacy standard was in fact being met. The standard was stricter than the child labor law, however, in that it required the working child to be able to read and write the English language "intelligently," but even this key adverb was left undefined. The general child labor law's literacy provisions would not adopt the qualifying language, that is, the word *intelligently*, until 1909.[35]

Finally, similar to the prior legislation, the 1901 school law provided that it would be enforced by an attendance officer. However, while the attendance officer was now functioning more like a constable, he, unlike the factory inspector who enforced the child labor regulations, still did not have the express power to enter private property without a warrant. Under the school law, the attendance officer could apprehend and arrest the nonattending child. This authorization focused on the child and is in contrast to the language of authorization found in the Factory Inspection Act of 1889. The earlier law provided expressly that "said inspector shall be empowered to visit and inspect, at all reasonable hours and as often as practicable, the factories, workshops and other establishments in the State employing women and children" in order to enforce the law.[36] The differences in language are significant. Because the school law looked to the child and not the place of employment, the attendance officer had only limited ability to enforce the compulsory education law directly against children who were actually working and in violation of its provisions. He could not seek out those children in their places of employment but had to find them elsewhere. As we saw earlier in Elizabeth Beardsley Butler's description of the glass house boys in Sharpsburg, Pennsylvania, the school officials there effectively used these types of limitations to evade their responsibilities and limit their compulsory attendance enforcement activities to just those children who were already enrolled in their schools.

With the 1905 amendment of the 1901 law, a working child between the ages of thirteen and sixteen who wanted to be exempt from attending school needed a "certificate of age and ability to read and write the English language intelligently" that was to be issued by any of the types of public officials listed. Not surprisingly, perhaps, the attendance exemption afforded to students taught at home by "any legally qualified governess or private teacher in a family" did not require a similar certification to prove compliance.[37] The nearly universal acceptance and approval of this law is evidenced by the fact that on April 4, 1905, when the bill passed both the legislative chambers simultaneously, it did so with only a single legislator out of 178 voting against it.[38]

In 1907, the law was again revised, raising the base age for the working-child exemption to fourteen.[39] This change may have been an indication of the legislature's heightened concern for the educational attainment of the state's children, or it may have been done only to bring the school law into line with the current child labor laws in terms of age requirements. The record is silent as to the motivation of the legislature. Under the Mining Act of 1903 and the Anthracite Mining Act of 1905, for example, the minimum age for any boy working in or about any coal mine in the state had been raised to fourteen. The Factory Act of 1905, affecting child labor employment at virtually all of the state's other manufacturing, mercantile, and industrial establishments, also raised the minimum working age to fourteen. The school law underwent a more complete revision in 1911, but for the purposes of this study, the changes were slight.[40] The working-child exemption remained substantially the same as it was in 1907, and the exception for children taught privately in their own homes was adjusted only slightly.[41] The 1911 law initiated a requirement for at least a minimal certification system for private tutors and required that they furnish the appropriate school district with a "list of the names and residences of all children between eight and sixteen years of age ... taught by such private teacher" on an annual basis.[42]

The changes made to the school laws over time clearly highlight the two often conflicting elements of Pennsylvania's Progressive Era educational reforms. On the one hand, there was a steady increase in the general level of state regulatory concern for the education of its children, but, on the other hand, there was also a selective set of exemptions from those same education requirements. In terms of the increased "progressive" nature of the changes, the several laws and amendments tended to increase the ages of the children covered by the regulations, the amount of time those children spent in school, and the authority of the attendance officer, who, along with the factory inspector, remained the primary entity responsible for enforcing the law. In none of these areas is there any indication of substantial legislative backsliding.

However, the very fact that the school law contained a working-child exemption, as well as the exemption for students taught by private tutors or governesses, is instructive. These exemptions are evidence that class bias was built into the state's statutory system of public education. That is, the legislature established different standards for obtaining exemptions from compulsory school attendance, and the various standards largely corresponded to particular socioeconomic classes. The tutor/governess exemption, while technically open to all, was generally available only to the wealthy, who could afford to hire private tutors and/or governesses. Similarly, the working-child exemption, while not limited on its face to any one group of parents, was much more likely to be used by poor families who felt economically compelled to send their children to work. The regular public schools, then, were left largely for the children of the middle class. This was perfectly consistent with the credentialing function associated with a common school education at the time.

Prior to industrialization, few jobs were so technical in nature that a long education was needed to do most jobs effectively. This situation meant that there was some measure of social mobility available through workplace advancement. In other words, for those jobs that were more complex or technically demanding, apprenticeships were available, providing the young worker with a system of specific, job-related instruction and making it possible for someone to improve his or her social and economic standing through simple hard work. With increased industrialization, however, came increased specialization and an increased array of professional jobs. As the numbers and types of apprenticeships declined, there was a growing demand for more specific educational training to ensure one's entry into certain fields of employment.[43] Public schooling began to assume more and more of the credentialing and preparatory functions, especially for the newer, higher-paying, and more knowledge-based professional employments.

Those who could afford the relative economic luxury of keeping their children out of the workforce and in school helped ensure that those children would be credentialed for these professional jobs. By doing so, they could also ensure, to a substantial degree, the future economic well-being of those children. Middle-class parents were well aware of this scenario. They had begun to make special efforts both to shelter the early development of their children from external, worldly influences such as industrial work and to ensure that their children made full use of the formal schooling opportunities that were available.[44] Many families, however, like those of the Pittsburgh glass house boys, simply could not afford to keep their children in school. In such families, as we have seen, "[t]he demands of a market

"Two of the boys on night shift in the More-Jonas [Jones?] Glass Co." Bridgeton,
New Jersey, November 1909

economy made these children indispensable economic resources."[45] The
adult members of these families could not themselves secure the professional jobs that were becoming more common in the expanding economy,
and they were largely unable to make it possible for their children to do so
either. Thus, the ability to utilize the developing systems of public education became a mark of class difference, and the common school system
worked to reinforce, rather than provide an avenue of escape from, systems
of social stratification.

This is not to say that learning the official common school curriculum
was either necessary or sufficient for economic success. Indeed, as Harvey
Graff has shown, illiteracy as defined by school standards "did not consign
all men to poverty, and conversely, many literate workers were poor."[46] In

this regard, it is important to distinguish between the value of literacy derived from the common school curriculum (i.e., the knowledge base that came from learning the official curriculum, not just being able to read and write) and the value of learning other lessons taught in those schools. For many industrial workers in the late nineteenth century, literacy learned on the shop floor was not only often sufficient for job performance and advancement but also could be superior to literacy acquired in school. This, of course, is not to say that schooling had no value, but what was being credentialed by having a child complete his or her enrollment in the common school system was not simply the mastery of the content of the formal curriculum. Rather, it was also the learning of the "hidden" curriculum, the acquisition of the "non-cognitive personality traits stressed in schools, such as subordination and discipline," that, as Graff argues, often had "a more direct influence on worker earnings and productivity" than literacy per se.[47]

All of this made the situation for the glass house boys, in the eyes of progressive reformers, even more dismal. To be sure, notwithstanding their lack of formal schooling, some glass house boys went on to successful careers in and out of the glass houses. Several of the men who ran the Pittsburgh glass-bottle factories had started out as mold-holding or carrying-off boys. Michael J. Owens, the most important glass industry inventor of the century, had worked as a glass house boy, and several of the Pittsburgh legislators engaged in blocking child labor reform liked to remind their colleagues that they had themselves started out as glass house boys. But success for a few only underscores the loss for the many. These were children who were neither credentialed through formal schooling nor skilled through on-the-job training. If these children were to be able to take advantage of the benefits of the new public schools, the reformers believed they would need to be compelled to "choose" school over work in the glass houses. But the school law, especially with the working-child exemption, effectively removed the glass house boys from the scope of the state's compulsory education laws. The reformers could not, therefore, expect to use the state education laws as a tool for removing the Pittsburgh glass house boys from their workplaces. Thus, they focused their efforts on strengthening the child labor laws.

6

Child Labor Laws
in Pennsylvania

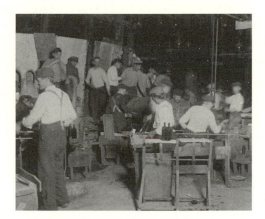

*No minor under sixteen shall be employed in any establishment
between the hours of nine post meridian and six ante meridian:
Provided, That where the material in process of manufacture requires the application of manual labor for an extended period . . . ,
to prevent waste or destruction of said material, male minors over
fourteen years of age . . . may be employed . . . after nine post meridian.*

Laws of Pennsylvania, Act no. 226, 1905

IN 1905, THE PENNSYLVANIA LEGISLATURE passed a child labor law that would have far-reaching consequences. This law contained a night employment provision that, together with an important qualification thereto, became both central to the continued existence of the Pittsburgh glass-bottle factories and the focus of nearly ten years of rancorous legislative debates and back-room deals. Section 5 of that 1905 statute contained the first night work prohibition in the history of Pennsylvania's child labor laws. It stated simply that "[n]o minor [under sixteen years of age] shall be employed in any establishment between the hours of nine post meridian and six ante meridian."[1] Although Pennsylvania was not the first industrial state to enact such a ban, by doing so it did join a small group of progressive leaders. In 1888, Massachusetts passed the nation's first law prohibiting children from working at night. In 1889, New York passed similar legislation, followed by Minnesota in 1895, Ohio in 1898, and Michigan and Wisconsin in 1899.[2] If the law had been applied just as described in the quoted passage, it would have represented a major victory for the progressive forces in the state. But the significance of this major progressive achievement was blunted for the glass house boys of Pittsburgh. The western Pennsylvania glass interests saved themselves from what they saw as a potential disaster by having their supporters in the state legislature add a qualification to the law. This qualification provided that the otherwise ubiquitous night work ban would not apply "where the material in process of manufacture requires the application of manual labor for an extended period after nine o'clock post meridian, to prevent waste or destruction of said material."[3] This was the infamous "glass house exception" that permitted night work by boys. Although the word "glass" is not mentioned, this qualification was inserted to benefit the glass industry and particularly the bottle plants of Pittsburgh. In subsequent sessions, legislators would change the phrasing, allowing for night work by minors where the process of manufacture was "continuous" rather than where "waste" might occur, but the effect was the same.[4]

The legislators had created a legal loophole for the benefit of one specific sector, of one particular industry, in one region of the state. Given that Pennsylvania had, at that time, a long history of enacting child labor regulations, the glass house exception might seem anomalous. But, despite the legislature's rather longstanding reform efforts, actual progress toward more restrictive child labor legislation had been uneven. Further, the particular circumstances at work in the early-twentieth-century glass houses of Pittsburgh—the influences of the manufacturers, the union and labor interests, mechanization, and the boys and their families—meant that any reforms directed at the glass house boys who worked there would be particularly slow in coming to fruition. Because of this, it would take years of fierce legislative struggle before the loophole that was the glass house exception was closed.

The road that led to the 1905 child labor law had its origin almost sixty years earlier, in 1848, when Pennsylvania enacted its first child labor law. On March 28, 1848, Pennsylvania became one of the first states in the nation to regulate the employment of child workers in its factories.[5] This law prohibited children under the age of twelve from working in any "cotton, woolen, silk or flax factory" in the state. This law represented an important initial regulatory step, even if it applied only to a relatively small portion of the state's employers.[6] Children over twelve who were employed in any of the listed industries, as well as in "paper" and "bagging" factories, could not work more than ten hours per day or sixty hours per week. Children over fourteen were allowed to waive the working-hour restrictions by contract if their parents or guardians agreed. Any other industry could hire children regardless of age, and those children could legally work for any length of time at all. Further, despite the fact that, as shown in chapter 5, the state legislature had demonstrated an earlier interest in the education of working-class children, this first child labor law was silent on any requirement regarding schooling or literacy standards for working children.

The penalty provision in the 1848 law was somewhat unusual. It stated that if any employer covered by the act violated any of its provisions, that employer would have to "pay a penalty of fifty dollars, one-half thereof to the party so employed, and the other half to the commonwealth."[7] This provision represented the combination of a traditional criminal penalty or fine, payable to the state, and a type of statutory tort recovery, payable to the "injured" party, here the child worker. Because under state law at the time the father had the right to his child's wages, this latter payment was effectively directed to the child's parents. This blended penalty clause was tinkered with in subsequent years before it was abandoned in 1887. In 1849, for example, Pennsylvania lawmakers amended the penalty provision so that the state's portion of the recovery would go to "the county in which the offense was committed."[8] Then, in 1855, the legislature decided that the state's share of the penalty should "be applied to the use of the public schools of the proper district."[9] Finally, in 1887, the legislature eliminated the parent-directed statutory tort recovery and sent the entire penalty for child labor violations to the state treasury.[10]

Another form of parental involvement in the regulatory scheme of the state's child labor laws was also inaugurated with the 1848 law and would continue into the early twentieth century. As noted above, although that law limited the hours of work for all children over the age of twelve, minors over fourteen were permitted to work for as long as they chose, with the approval of their parents. Allowing parents to effectively override a state regulation proved to be a common feature in other areas of Pennsylvania's child labor legislation, especially in terms of age certifications. As previously discussed, where the economic survival of working-class families often depended on the income of their children, parents frequently were willing to obtain the required certificates by any means necessary, including fraud, in order to enable their children to work. Needless to say, Progressive Era reformers found this penchant of Pennsylvania lawmakers to statutorily authorize parental evasion of child labor regulations particularly problematic.

In 1849, the General Assembly strengthened its initial child labor law with several amendments. First, the legislature increased the minimum age for employment from twelve to thirteen and then expanded slightly the list of industries covered to include "all cotton, woolen, silk, paper, bagging and flax factories."[11] In addition to redirecting part of the fine recovery, they also added an educational requirement for employment. The law now stated that no child between the ages of thirteen and sixteen "shall be employed in any of the factories aforesaid, for a longer period than nine calendar months in any one year . . . who shall not have attended school for at least three consecutive months within the same year."[12]

The legislative history surrounding the 1848 and 1849 child labor laws makes evident that the political importance of these regulations was growing. The legislators who were in support of such laws attempted to position themselves as responsible public servants, enacting regulations protecting the state's children at the direct request of their constituents. In 1848, for example, lawmakers made numerous references to petitions "signed by several thousand citizens" favoring such legislation.[13] In 1849, in support of strengthening the 1848 law, one lawmaker dramatically presented the Senate with "a petition twenty-one feet long, signed by female operatives in Philadelphia praying ... [that] all minors [should be] prevented from working in factories more than ten hours in one day."[14] Although the wording of the petitions themselves was not reproduced in the record, it is clear that the legislators felt it important to refer to them in open session to demonstrate popular support for their cause.

The child labor legislation eventually enacted in 1849, however, only slightly changed the prior year's law. Even so, some discord among the legislators began to surface in the record, especially in the Senate. After acknowledging the literally dozens of petitions they had received, the senators got down to business. Reference was made to numerous proposed amendments to the child labor bill, both on the floor of the Senate and in committee, with some accepted and others rejected, but the record is generally silent on the particular language of any of these various proposals. Two of the amendments that do appear in the record make visible the opposing factions developing within the Senate on the question of child labor. On the bill's second reading, a pair of senators offered two amendments to alter the law's introductory language. The introduction to a bill serves as a preamble that, while usually not technically part of the compulsory language of the law, may be inserted by the lawmakers to emphasize a particular point and may be used by the courts to determine the underlying legislative intent. The first amendment would have changed the introductory language to state, rather surprisingly, that the law was "calculated so to injure and embarrass the manufacturing interests within this Commonwealth, as to give foreign manufacturers a decided advantage over our own." The second amendment provided that "the prohibition of the employment of minors under twelve years of age, as workers in factories, is justifiable only, because they should not be deprived of the opportunity of obtaining suitable education in the schools provided by our laws."[15]

Pointedly ironic, these two amendments could each reasonably be read as supporting the manufacturing interests in the state and their opposition to any regulation of child employment. Containing language that reflected more than a little irritation, the first tried to expose what its sponsors saw as the serious competitive disadvantage Pennsylvania businesses would suffer if they were deprived of child workers under the age of twelve. The second alluded to the fact that, at the time, Pennsylvania lacked a compulsory school attendance law. The implied argument here was that if the *only* justification for removing children from the workplace was so that they could attend school, then *because* the state did not require the latter it *should not* restrict the employment of children. Although these amendments failed to win approval, the manufacturers' opposition to child labor regulation continued to play a role in these debates in subsequent legislative sessions. The glass manufacturers in particular proved especially adept at blocking reforms by appropriating some of the same arguments advanced in support of each of these amendments.

Approaching the 1849 child labor revisions from a different position, two other senators proposed to strengthen the existing law by substantially broadening the industries covered. Under this amendment the law would be extended to cover "any rolling mills, nail factories, printing offices, tanneries, farming and mining, black and white smithing, to all employed by carpenters, cabinet makers, book binders, stage drivers, railroad conductors, brakemen, and others, to raftmen, boatmen, . . . all engaged in packing beef, pork, and other provisions; and all engaged in building, constructing and repairing any railroad, canal or turnpike road; [and to all offices, storehouses, wood mills, lumber yards, furnaces, forges]."[16] This proposed change foreshadowed the view of many subsequent reformers that child labor regulations, if they were to be truly effective, should cover all of the state's industrial and manufacturing employers. While this amendment also failed to win the approval of the Senate, the reformers continued to try to expand the coverage of the state's child labor regulations.

The Pennsylvania child labor regulations enacted in 1848 and 1849 were repeatedly revised in subsequent years. Between 1848–1849 and the mid-1880s, for example, the General Assembly returned to the issue of child labor about five times but made few significant changes in the law. Beginning with the 1887 legislative session, however, coincident with the rise of progressivism generally, increased pressure was brought to bear on the Pennsylvania legislature to enact more substantial child labor regulations. As a result, from 1887 until 1915, no fewer than a dozen laws were passed by the state's General Assembly addressing the terms and conditions of child workers engaged in various forms of industrial employment. This was a substantial increase in legislative activity over the previous forty years. As we have seen, although the state's glass manufacturers did not welcome *any* child labor regulations, few of the changes enacted posed significant risks to their traditional systems of glass manufacture or production, until 1905.

Among the child labor regulations that had relatively minor impact on the glass industry were those dealing with the maximum number of hours that children were allowed to work, the minimum ages of employment, the enumeration of industries covered by the child labor laws or parts thereof, and, as discussed in chapter 5, the need for a certificate regarding the child worker's ability to read and write. Allowable work hours for children, for example, remained constant at ten hours per day and sixty per week, as set by the 1848–1849 laws, until 1893, when the legislature *raised* the daily maximum to twelve hours.[17] While this was hardly a "progressive" move, the twelve-hour maximum remained unchanged until 1909, when the hours for children working in both factories and mines were reduced to ten per day once again and the weekly total was set at fifty-eight hours.[18] The fluctuations in the maximum allowable hours of child labor, from ten, to twelve, and then back to ten, while a bit confusing, were not of great concern to the Pittsburgh glass-bottle manufacturers because union rules had long established the typical work day at between eight and nine hours, and the work of the glass house boys mirrored those union-rule hours of employment.

The minimum age for the employment of children was set at thirteen by the 1849 child labor law. Apart from the exceptions for mining and theatrical or entertainment work, this age limit remained the standard in the industries covered by the child labor laws until 1887, when the minimum age was actually lowered—also hardly a "progressive" change—to twelve, the age limit established in the 1848 child labor law.[19] In 1893, the minimum age was again raised to thirteen for general factory work and to fourteen for children working in or around elevators.[20] Then, in 1905, the General Assembly seemed to settle on fourteen as the earliest age at which children could be employed anywhere in the commonwealth in any nonmining, nonagricultural, or nondomestic service job.[21] As with the hours-of-work regulations, while the legislature demonstrated some uncertainty as to what the age limits should be, these fluctuations did not greatly concern the Pittsburgh glass houses because there was no scarcity of child workers in Pittsburgh and because enforcement of the age standard was often lax. On this last point it is important to note that lax enforcement had several variations. Not only did some officials simply ignore the law that they were charged to carry out but some also were co-conspirators with those who were evading it. One is reminded of Fred Hall's comment in 1910 as he tried to account for why J. C. Delaney, the Pennsylvania factory inspector, had reported virtually no underage children at work in the state's factories. Hall indicated that "hundreds of our 11, 12, and 13-year old children [must] have been recorded statistically by the Pennsylvania [factory] inspectors as being between 14 and 16."[22]

Several child labor laws required children to meet some basic educational standards as a condition for employment. The 1849 child labor law, for example, required a little more than three months of schooling per year for certain working children, and this remained the standard until 1889, when, in yet another move that is hard to characterize as "progressive," the legislature simply dropped all references to literacy or schooling requirements for working children.[23] As noted in chapter 5, beginning in 1897, the compulsory attendance laws required a reading/writing certification for working children, and in 1901, this same certification requirement was included in the child labor law. The child labor law allowed the certificate to be issued by any "person authorized to administer oaths," which at the time included notaries public as well as many minor elected officials.[24] The standard proved largely illusory, and thus of relatively little concern to the glass house managers, because the employer wanting child labor simply had to hire a notary who would issue the requisite certificates as a matter of course.

In 1905, the educational requirement under the child labor law remained the same, but the certification procedure was modestly strengthened. First, the form of all certificates was standardized across the state, and second, at least for the literacy requirement, the list of issuers was narrowed to include only the factory inspector, the deputies of the inspector, and various school officials.[25] In 1909, state lawmakers made the last adjustment to the child labor literacy requirements before it undertook a massive legislative overhaul in 1915; the 1909 law required that child workers be able to read and write "intelligently."[26] As we have seen, the factory inspector at that time, J. C. Delaney, who was one of the principal enforcement officers for the child labor laws, was also on record as questioning the very need for any literacy standard at all. Therefore, placing him in charge of issuing literacy certificates was something like putting the fox in charge of the henhouse. Under these circumstances, the certification requirements for reading and writing did not have a serious impact on the Pittsburgh glass manufacturers.

An additional area of regulatory concern that might have adversely affected the Pittsburgh glass industry involved the legislature's repeated attempts to identify which industries were to be covered by the child labor provisions. Between 1849 and 1874, employment of the glass house boys was not restricted at all since the factory-related child labor laws applied only to cotton, woolen, flax, silk, paper, and bag-making businesses. In 1887, however, the legislature vastly expanded the types of establishments that would be subject to the law. In this three-sentence statute, the legislature made it unlawful for anyone "to employ any child under the age of twelve years to do any work in or about *any mill, manufactory or mine* in the Commonwealth."[27] This legislation was breathtakingly simple, direct, and broad. The child labor law went from covering only six industrial categories to including virtually every industrial or factory employer in the state. This sweeping regulation conflicted slightly with the age standard the legislature had set in two mining acts passed two years earlier, in 1885, but this inconsistency was rather easily resolved a few years later.[28] The breadth of the 1887 law was compromised somewhat because it lacked any specific means of enforcement in the areas of factory and mercantile employment, but this defect was also addressed two years later by the Factory Inspection Act of 1889.[29] On its face, the 1887 child labor law, coupled with the 1889 factory inspection provisions, was a major piece of progressive legislation. While the precise language would be modified in subsequent legislative sessions, the coverage of the child labor regulations remained substantially the same until 1909.[30]

In 1909, the legislature undertook a somewhat different approach to establishing the scope of coverage of the child labor law. It went from a relatively brief but broad description of the employers who were subject to the law ("any mill, manufactory or mine in the Commonwealth") to a very

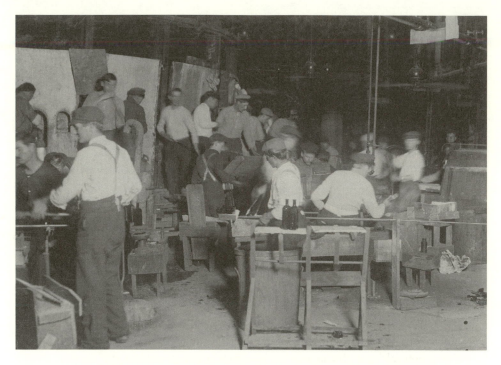

"Night scene in Cumberland Glass Works, Bridgeton, N.J. Small boy in middle distance of Photo." November 1909

specific enumeration. In a particularly confusing jumble of restrictions, the 1909 law prohibited all minors under the age of eighteen from working in or about any of a number of specifically identified dangerous employments, including any "sawmill, quarry, laundry, . . . bindery establishment; dock, wharf, vessel or boat, . . . railroad, . . . blast-furnaces, tanneries, . . . or . . . wherein nitroglycerine, dynamite, . . . or other high or dangerous explosive, is manufactured, compounded or stored."[31] Minors over sixteen years of age were allowed to be employed in some less dangerous activities, such as for "the manufacture or preparation of . . . paints, . . . matches, . . . or the manufacture . . . [of] cigars." Minors between fourteen and sixteen years of age could be employed in making these products if they could read and write English "intelligently" and if they could prove "to the satisfaction of the Factory Inspector that the danger or menace to the health and safety of [such] minor . . . has been removed."[32] Finally, minors over fourteen who satisfied the aforesaid literacy requirement could work in any of the less dangerous jobs from a specific list, including any "mercantile establishments, stores, . . . business offices; hotels . . . or in any factory . . . [where] power machinery is not used."[33] Because glass was not enumerated with any of the other "dangerous" employments, the minimum official age for glass house boys remained fourteen, and, in Pittsburgh at least, this age requirement posed no significant problem.

Therefore, while the changes made in the child labor laws after 1848 may have been fairly substantial in theory, in practice the glass industry in Pittsburgh was generally unaffected. It remained fully subject to the child labor law from 1887 forward, but the vast majority of the law's specific provisions, while unwelcome, were no more than an annoyance. Especially after the invention of the continuous tank system in the late nineteenth century and following the "invasion" of labor-saving machinery into the glass houses at the start of the twentieth century, the major child labor concern of the glass-bottle manufacturers in Pittsburgh was night work. They could live with age and reading/writing certificates, they were not seriously impacted by a ten-hour workday limit, and so long as their factories were not listed by the legislature as unusually dangerous, those restrictions were unimportant. The real issue was that they simply had to have the boys work at night, and none of these laws addressed that concern. The situation changed with the child labor law of 1905, when the progressive forces in Pennsylvania and their supporters in the state legislature placed night work for the glass house boys squarely on the legislative agenda.

The Glass House Exception

Progressive reformers considered night work as perhaps the most onerous aspect of child labor, and the Pennsylvania progressives had reason to be pleased when the 1905 legislature enacted the general night work ban. But, as noted above, it was at best a partial victory. The National Child Labor Committee and its affiliate, the Pennsylvania Child Labor Association, had lobbied very hard to have the ban extend to all children in the state, but they were unable to overcome the power of the western Pennsylvania glass interests. The legislative history surrounding the passage of the 1905 child labor law sheds light on the workings of the Pennsylvania legislature at the time and helps explain why the glass interests prevailed on the question of night work for the glass house boys of Pittsburgh.

The child labor bill was introduced in the Pennsylvania Senate by Senator John C. Crawford of Pittsburgh on March 20, 1905, and referred to the Committee on Judiciary Special. The bill received its first reading the next day.[34] On March 29, it was presented to the Senate on its second reading, and it was then that the full text of the bill appears in the record for the first time. This text contained several provisions specifically marked in the record for either deletion (lined through) or addition (underscored). These changes indicate that the committee acted on its own to rewrite parts of the bill and then presented these proposed revisions to the Senate for its approval. One of the committee-marked changes involved the hours when night work was prohibited. The committee had reduced those hours from 6:00 P.M. through 7:00 A.M. to 9:00 P.M. through 6:00 A.M., thus slightly weakening the prohibition. Section 3 of the bill, presented to the Senate on its second reading, contained both a general night work prohibition and the glass house exception, but neither of these was marked in any way, giving the impression that each had been in the bill from its inception.[35] Each section of the entire bill was then read to the Senate seriatim and fully approved, with no recorded comments or amendments.[36] The Senate received the child labor bill for its third reading the next day, March 30, 1905, and approved it by a final vote of 33 to 1.

Because the legislative process is never fully transparent, it is often difficult to determine from the official record of a bill exactly what happens to it and when. For the 1905 child labor bill, however, the available record makes clear that a Senate committee could, on its own, revise a bill's language and thus could exercise a fair amount of influence over the structure of proposed legislation. Also, when presented with committee-sponsored changes, the Senate was willing to accept revisions without significant comments or questions; in the case of the 1905 bill, they did so even though they had approved the unrevised language a little more than a week earlier. The record here does not, however, make clear what the original language of the bill was, whether changes were made to that language, and, if so, when they were made and by whom. The night work prohibition and the glass house exception illustrate this uncertainty. Both the prohibition and the exception appear in the bill presented for second reading, but neither was specifically marked as an addition. Two interpretations seem possible: either the bill contained both of these provisions in its original form, before it got to the committee, or the committee added one or both but wanted to obscure its actions. As will be discussed below, extrinsic evidence indicates that while the prohibitory language was part of the bill from its inception, the language concerning the glass house exception was not and was instead inserted by the committee. By making the glass house exception appear as though it were part of the original language of the bill, the Committee on Judiciary Special was resorting to deceit and subterfuge to facilitate the adoption of the glass house exception. If we assume that at least some of the senators who voted on this language during the second reading realized it was new, but unmarked, then by remaining silent on the matter they became partners in the deception. If that is the case, then the object of the intended deception was the public or, more specifically, those among the public who might try to rely on the legislative record to determine how this particular part of the bill became the law of the state. Here, the actions of the committee were successful in the sense that after the exception was added, the bill received a near-unanimous vote of approval in the Senate on March 30, and the Senate sent the bill over to the House of Representatives for action.[37]

In the lower house, Representative Bryan C. Osborne of Venango County introduced the child labor bill on April 3, 1905, and it was sent to the Committee on Judiciary General. Following its first reading the next day, the bill was presented to the House for second reading on April 5.[38] The full text of the House bill appears in the record then for the first time, and the language of section 3, containing both the night work prohibition and the glass house exception, is the same as in the Senate-approved version. During the bill's second reading, one amendment was accepted reducing the daily maximum hours of work from twelve to ten, and the amended bill was then approved. The House reviewed the child labor bill for its third reading on April 10, 1905, and approved it by a unanimous vote.[39]

Thus, the general prohibition on night work and the glass house exception were approved by both the Pennsylvania House and Senate with no significant chamber-sponsored amendments, virtually no legislative comments, and only one contrary vote. As later confirmed by the actions of the state's factory inspector, the legislature intended the exception to apply only to the glass industry, even though there is nothing in the broad language of the text that identified a specific industry. While battle lines were clearly drawn over the next few years, the births of both the night work prohibition and the glass house exception were, based on the official legislative record, apparently devoid of controversy and not sufficiently important to merit even casual comment within the legislature. But appearances in this case are misleading.

As we have seen, the glass interests in the state had a long history of very effective lobbying and were well positioned to thwart any significant reform efforts. This was confirmed later in 1905, when Dr. Samuel Mc-Cune Lindsay, the general secretary of the National Child Labor Committee, talked about the 1905 Pennsylvania child labor law in his opening address at the organization's second annual meeting. He prefaced his remarks by saying that "few laws are put in operation where there is not sufficient strength in the opposition to secure amendments and make the law inoperative in some respects."[40] The "opposition" Lindsay referred to was the western Pennsylvania glass interests, and the part of the law that they made "inoperative" was the night work provision as it applied to the glass house boys. Lindsay had strong praise for the bill as originally introduced in the Pennsylvania legislature. He noted that it was a commendable piece of progressive legislation that raised the minimum age of work to fourteen, required independent and reasonably reliable age certification procedures, and, of particular significance to the NCLC and for the purposes of this analysis, banned *all* night work by *all* children under sixteen in *all* occupations in the state.

Lindsay then laid bare the tactics used by the glass interests to derail the general night work ban. He explained that early in the process of legislative consideration, "industries came officially in a body with skilled lobbies, doing their best both openly and secretly to defeat the legislation." Lindsay then pointed specifically to one group, "men representing a very degraded industry, one where public sentiment is both among the employer and among the working men [and] it is still back in the middle age stage, and that is the glass industry." These remarks indicate that the bill as originally committed to the Senate Committee on Judiciary Special on March 20, 1905, included the general night work prohibition but not the glass house exception. The language of the glass house exception was thus in all likelihood added by the committee prior to the second reading of the bill on March 29, 1905.[41]

Lindsay recognized that the glass manufacturers were working diligently in the 1905 state legislature, "both openly and secretly," to make sure that the general ban on night work would not include their glass house boys. Because the manufacturers most in need of these boys were the glass-bottle plant owners of Pittsburgh and because these owners were so important in the industry, the western Pennsylvania bottle manufacturers were strongly represented in these efforts and were probably physically present. But of even greater significance is Lindsay's statement that the opponents of child labor reform in Pennsylvania included "the working men ... [in] the glass industry." This places the adult glass workers and their union, the Glass Bottle Blowers' Association of the United States and Canada, in league with the manufacturers and sharing the same "degraded" view of child labor. It also places them in the thick of the anti-reform lobbying efforts to water down the 1905 child labor law. Lindsay reported that the combined effort of the glass interests succeeded in forcing a legislative change that was solely for their own benefit, and thus, "a compromise was effected by which the glass industry was exempt" from the night work prohibitions.[42]

The glass interests were successful in having the glass house exception inserted into the 1905 law in large measure because they had cultivated important friends in high places. As Lindsay observed, "the chairman of the Senate Committee, the State Senator of Pennsylvania before whose committee this [1905] bill came[,] happened to be a local representative who represented the glass manufacturer's interests, and he practically served notice upon all parties concerned, that if the glass interests were taken care of that the bill might possibly go through, and if they were not it could under no circumstances ever get beyond his committee."[43] The committee Lindsay referred to was the Senate Committee on Judiciary Special, which almost always asserted jurisdiction over any child labor legislation within the Senate in the early years of the twentieth century. The chair of that committee in 1905, also referred to but not named by Lindsay, was John E. Fox of Dauphin County, in east-central Pennsylvania. Fox was not a legislator to be ignored when it came to questions involving glass and child labor. Between 1905 and 1912, when he left the legislature, Fox was a member of virtually every Senate committee to which any of the child labor bills acted on during that period were entrusted. He was virtually alone in this distinction, and, because of his length of service in the Senate, he was one of the most senior senators on each of these committees and thus one of the most influential. He played a hand, often the controlling one, in virtually every successful attempt to protect the glass interests from the night work prohibition. Together with allies such as Arthur G. Dewalt of Lehigh County and John Crawford, Elliot Roberts, and Joseph A. Longfitt of Pittsburgh, Fox, as a strategically placed, powerful politician, represented a form of early-twentieth-century political corruption. The power of this corruption became particularly evident in the 1909 legislative session.

Short Tempers and Legislative Frustration

No child labor legislation affecting the glass house boys emerged from the 1907 Pennsylvania legislature. In 1909, the progressive forces made a strong bid to bring the glass house boys within the scope of the night work ban, but, as the record makes clear, the glass interests could still count on powerful legislative support. The 1909 child labor bill was introduced in the Pennsylvania House of Representatives, and on March 2, 1909, it received a positive vote on its first reading. On March 20 it received its second reading, and the full text of the bill appeared in the record for the first time.[44] Section 5 of the bill contained a prophylactic, unqualified prohibition on night work, stating simply that "[n]o minor under the age of sixteen shall be employed between the hours of nine post meridian and six ante meridian." There was no glass house exception. The House approved this particular language and the entire bill without comment. The next day, on its third reading, the House gave final approval to the bill and sent it to the Senate.[45]

In the Senate, the bill was referred to the Committee on Judiciary Special on April 1, 1909, and it received its first reading on April 6. The *Legislative Journal* for that day states that the bill was read in full and approved, but it does not print the actual text. The next day it was brought to the floor for the second reading. The Committee on Judiciary Special added section 6, which contained a new version of the glass house exception, stating that, "where the usual process of manufacture or the nature of the business . . . is

of a kind that customarily necessitates a continuous day and night employment, male minors not under the age of fourteen years may be employed
day and night." When exactly the committee did this is not clear, but that
it was the committee that authorized this change seems certain since the
record of actions taken by the Senate to this point makes no reference to
any Senate-sponsored amendments, changes, or additions and the glass
house exception was not in the bill sent over by the House. Regardless of
when the exception was added, the senators agreed to it without comment,
and following the complete presentation of the bill, they approved it on its
second reading.[46]

On April 8, 1909, the child labor bill was presented to the Senate for
what should have been its third and final reading.[47] The Senate approved
an initial amendment that further expanded the law's protection of female
minors by raising the age limit for the maximum hours provisions to eighteen. The remainder of the bill, including the glass house exception contained in section 6, was read section by section and similarly approved.
At this point, the Senate, having duly approved the bill on three readings,
would normally vote to send the bill to a conference committee to iron out
any differences between the Senate and House versions, but that did not
happen here. Instead, after the last section was voted on, the clerk asked the
senators if they would "agree to transcribe the bill for [its] third reading."
The Senate agreed without comment.[48] There is no recorded explanation
for why a second "third" reading was needed. Perhaps, as provided in the
rules of the Senate in force at the time, the third reading was suspended at
the request of one of the senators.[49] While no rationale is apparent in the
record, the work on the 1909 bill was not yet finished.

The child labor bill was returned to the Senate for its second "third"
reading on the afternoon of April 12, but interestingly, the legislative record
for that day contains no transcript of those particular proceedings. The
afternoon session is, however, referred to in the record of the Senate's deliberations from later that evening. In the afternoon session, Senator Willis James Hulings from Venango County offered an amendment to simply remove section 6 from the child labor bill. That is, Hulings moved to
completely delete the glass house exception from the general night work
prohibition.[50] This amendment passed and the remainder of the bill was
then approved. But, again, instead of concluding this second "third" reading

with a vote on final passage and sending the Senate bill to a House/Senate conference committee, the bill was once again recommitted to the Committee on Judiciary Special chaired by John E. Fox.

The committee reported back to the Senate later that same evening, and the Senate again resumed its consideration of the child labor bill. This is where the *Legislative Journal* picks up the record of proceedings for the day. According to this record, however, the bill brought back to the Senate by the committee was not the same bill that the senators had voted on only hours before. The committee had, on its own motion, simply voided Senator Hulings's amendment, which had been approved by the full Senate, and reinstated the glass house exception. Senator Fox, the stalwart supporter of the glass industry and the night work exception, moved for "reconsideration" of the bill. Reconsideration was the normal parliamentary procedure to have the legislative body resume its consideration of a bill, but here, because the language in the bill before the Senate had obviously been altered, exactly what was up for reconsideration was not perfectly clear. Senator Webster Grim, a strong advocate for child labor reform, asked for clarification. He suggested that if the committee's version of the bill was to stand, the full Senate needed to first reconsider (and reverse) its approval of the Hulings amendment. To his surprise, the Senate president told him that the amendment had already been eliminated and the "reconsideration" was for the bill in its committee-altered form. Grim was taken aback: "Mr. President, I do not see how that can be done. Do I understand that we have agreed to the bill on third reading [this afternoon] and the amendments are [now] stricken out of the bill as amended?" The president confirmed that that was correct; the amendments had indeed been stricken out.[51]

The president then recognized Senator Dewalt from Lehigh County, who tried to shed some light on the subject. Dewalt addressed the Senate: "Mr. President, as I understand, it is simply this, that the bill was amended [this afternoon] so as to exclude from employment in the glass works of this State, minors under a certain age at certain hours. That amendment was carried this afternoon. [The bill] was then recommitted to the committee and has now been reported out *as it originally was*. . . . Otherwise that provision in regard to the glass works or minors of glass works remains."[52] Senator Fox then confirmed to the Senate that, notwithstanding that body's earlier approval of the Hulings amendment eliminating the glass house exception, the bill was rewritten by his committee such that it now "permits [minor children] to be employed [at night]." The president of the Senate concurred in this understanding by stating that the question before the Senate "is upon the adoption of the original bill, exclusive of the [Hulings] amendment." Senator Dewalt then offered an additional explanation. In doing so he partly pulled back the veil of legislative secrecy to expose the power of special interests in the workings of Pennsylvania government in the first decade of the twentieth century. Dewalt explained, "I have been informed by the head of an establishment where there is the employment of [night child] labor, that they are willing to have the bill passed in its present form. . . . In other words, the bill stood no chance of passing at all in its original form [i.e., in the form submitted to the committee earlier in the afternoon with the Hulings amendment] and they are well satisfied to take it as it now exists."[53] Dewalt thus admitted that the head of a glass-bottle plant, most likely from the Pittsburgh region—virtually the only industry in the state that could employ children at night—or its representative had had direct access to the senators as they deliberated in committee and that this particular industrial representative had enough power to direct the committee to revise the bill.

Senator Hulings was incredulous. He realized that the glass interests and Fox's committee had used blunt political force to simply override his previously approved amendment, but he refused to accept this reality without comment. Addressing the Senate president, he said,

I understand the amendment is before the Senate. We have reconsidered the vote by which it passed but we have not determined to strike out the amendment. However, that may be, there may be parties outside of the Senate who have the authority or wisdom to come in here and tell the Senate what they must do. It may be true that there are some influences so powerful in the State of Pennsylvania, manufacturing establishments and the like, that can insist upon that which becomes the deliberate vote of the Senate, be thrown away or the bill shall fail. I understand that every friend of the Childs' [sic] Labor Movement is opposed to the young children of the State working at night. If that is the deliberate conviction of the Senate, why should the bill fail?

While not answering the specific question posed by Hulings, Senator Fox rose to say that "the people who represented the glass manufacturers . . . in the western part of the State" told the committee that "they would have to close down their business establishments as they could not employ sufficient labor to conduct them and because of that assertion and the prominence given to it, the Childs' Labor Association agreed to the exception."[54] The "sufficient labor" Fox mentioned was a specific reference to child labor.

The Senate committee, probably at the direction of Senators Fox and Dewalt, had engineered the resuscitation of the glass house exception in direct contradiction to the vote taken by the full Senate just hours earlier. Industrial interests had some form of access to the committee as it deliberated and persuaded that group of senators to reinsert the exception. The most troubling aspect, however, is Senator Fox's final comment that "the Childs' Labor Association agreed to the exception." Here Fox is referring to the Pennsylvania affiliate of the National Child Labor Committee. His comment suggests that members of the affiliate were also privy to the Senate committee deliberations and that they agreed to the position taken by the industrial interests. That is, this reform group made a decision to accept the glass house exception and compromise its stance against child labor. If Fox's assertion is correct, it would be difficult to reconcile this decision by the NCLC affiliate with the publications and public advocacy of both it and the National Child Labor Committee as a whole. Fox's claim, however, is not supported by extrinsic evidence.

In presenting the obviously rewritten bill to the full Senate and implying that without the inclusion of the glass house exception the bill would not pass, Senators Fox and Dewalt were in effect threatening to sabotage the entire child labor bill—telling the senators that if they did not pass the bill with the exception included, they (Fox and Dewalt) would make sure that there would be no child labor bill at all during that session. Although it is possible that the NCLC affiliate, recognizing this as a real trade-off, agreed to sacrifice the glass boys to achieve that end, such a scenario is unlikely. More probably, Senator Fox deployed the fabricated comment to win votes for final passage of the bill, and they succeeded.

Later accounts suggest that Fox either grossly mischaracterized the position of the Pennsylvania child labor reformers or he simply made the comment up out of whole cloth. In 1913, when Herschel H. Jones, as special agent of the NCLC, prepared his detailed investigation of the western

Pennsylvania glass houses, he included a brief description of the Pennsylvania child labor law then in effect, including the glass house exception. Jones explained that this exception, the sole exception of its kind in Pennsylvania state law to the night work prohibition,

was obtained through the power . . . of the [western Pennsylvania] glass manufacturers and is for their benefit expressly. In 1909 when a revision of the child labor laws was attempted, the prospects were very good for the elimination of the infamous "glass exception" until Mr. D. A. Ripley, according to his own statement in an interview with the writer [i.e., Jones] on January 21, 1913, who was at that time leading the fight for the glass manufacturers, went to Washington, D.C. and saw Oliver and Penrose, telling them "how things stood." Penrose gave him a letter to Boss McNichol. . . . Boss McNichol passed the word around the legislature and the bill was "killed" and the child labor people were unable to do anything.[55]

Jones's comments indicate that the glass industry in western Pennsylvania had powerful friends and that it was able to use them to their advantage. Ripley was a Pittsburgh-area glass man of long standing. George T. Oliver was a Republican, born in Pittsburgh, and the state's junior U.S. senator. Boies Penrose was Pennsylvania's senior U.S. senator at the time, also a Republican, who hailed from Philadelphia. Finally, James P. "Strawberry Jim" McNichol was the leader of the Pennsylvania Senate and the very powerful party machine boss. Based on the intervention of Oliver, Penrose, and McNichol, Jones reported, the Hulings amendment was eliminated and the glass house exception reinstated. Further, as compensation for their actions on behalf of the Pittsburgh glass interests, Jones said, the politicians were able to secure substantial campaign contributions from the western Pennsylvania glass manufacturers.[56] Jones's statement that the "child labor people were unable to do anything" suggests not that they concurred in retaining the glass house exception but rather that they were simply powerless to stop it. This is hardly evidence that they "agreed to the exception."

Whatever the underlying justifications, reasoning, or threats, the Senate complied with Fox's committee and voted *unanimously* (with only ten senators "absent or not voting") to approve the bill in the committee-altered form. On April 13, the House dutifully consented to the Senate's version and approved the child labor bill by a vote of 188 to 4, with 15 "absent or not voting."[57]

Although no child labor legislation emerged from the 1911 legislative session, a child labor bill was considered in 1913 and was once again actively contested. And again, just as in 1909, the legislative record is revelatory. The initial bill originated in the House of Representatives and contained no language whatsoever creating any exception to the general night work prohibition. The bill was introduced by Representative T. Henry Walnut, a friend of reform, who was born in New Jersey and raised in Philadelphia. He studied law at the University of Pennsylvania (the same school that had denied admission to Florence Kelley several years earlier) and was elected to the state legislature in 1910. The "Walnut bill" was approved on its first reading on March 17, 1913, and nine days later returned to the floor of the house for its second reading. At that point, Representative Oliver M. Letzkus offered the glass house exception as an amendment to section 8 of the legislation.[58] Letzkus, who represented Pittsburgh, was born and raised in that city. He attended a parochial school until the age of twelve, when he started a thirty-year career in the glass industry by working as a glass house boy with the McCully Window Glass Works on Pittsburgh's south side. He was elected to the House in 1910. Following the standard language prohibiting night work, the Letzkus proposal read:

Excepting that where the process of manufacture or the nature of the business is of a kind that necessitates a continuous day and night employment male minors not under fourteen years of age may be employed day or night or partly day and partly night. Provided however that the parent or guardian of a boy or boys over fourteen years of age furnish the employer with an affidavit that wages earned by said boy are necessary for the maintenance of said boy or the family of which he is a member and that said parent or guardian is unable in any other manner to provide said maintenance and provided further that said employment shall not exceed nine hours during any twenty-four hours for minors under the age of sixteen.[59]

The proposal sparked an emotional debate. Representative Walnut, the sponsor of the legislation, was adamant. Noting that this, or a similar amendment, "has been tacked on to the Child Labor Bill for a number of years in this State," he complained that the language of the amendment should be rejected because it was so clearly counter to "the intention of the legislation to prevent the working of boys at night between the ages of fourteen and sixteen." He further observed that the amendment would result in "a very curious [piece of] legislation" because, "if passed, [it] would nullify the whole bill." Letzkus responded, providing yet additional insight into the anti-reform forces at work both in the Pittsburgh glass factories and the legislature. Making clear the role played by the GBBA and the glass blowers, Letzkus explained that

this amendment has been introduced at the request of the glass workers in my district, all union glass factories. Last fall . . . the workers accepted a twenty per cent reduction in order to compete with the machine glass bottle plants. If this amendment is not attached to the bill, you will . . . be reducing their wages just one hour per day more than they had to accept last fall in the settlement of wages . . . [and no one] wants to reduce anybody's wages, and the Bill in its original form will reduce the wages in the glass houses. The work is not hard, and the boys between the ages of fourteen and sixteen do not work hard, and it is sometimes necessary for them to work in order to provide the necessities of life for the family.[60]

The "machine" Letzkus refers to was, of course, the Owens Automatic. The Pittsburgh local of the Glass Bottle Blowers' Association, which, as Letzkus noted, controlled virtually all of the Pittsburgh bottle-making factories, opposed the introduction of "the machine" into their factories and thus also opposed any child labor legislation that would prevent the glass house boys from working at night. The glass manufacturers were, of course, in accord.

One of his fellow representatives objected to the breadth of the language contained in the Letzkus amendment. This colleague was afraid "that by opening up the way for the glass workers of Pittsburgh, we are opening up the way for every other industry in the State of Pennsylvania" to employ children at night. He said that if he could be assured otherwise, then he would be "inclined to help this particular industry." Letzkus tried to reassure him by saying that it was up to the state's factory inspector to apply this exception and that the inspector had decided to apply it only to the glass works in Pittsburgh.[61]

Letzkus then sought to reemphasize both the importance and the relative ease of the work required by the boys. Perhaps drawing on his own experience, he asserted that although a "boy has to go into a glass house when he is young . . . [t]he work in a glass factory is not a hardship." In support of that assertion, he noted that even after the boys got off their night shift at about "three o'clock in the morning," many of them "stay around until daylight and will play a game of ball, so you can see that the work is not hard."[62] Here, like the glass workers and the glass manufacturers, Letzkus emphasized the boys' inclination to play in order to mute the hardships of their lives. As we have seen, the progressives offered a rather different explanation for why the boys might have stayed around the glass factories after their night shifts ended: there was no public transportation at that hour and some boys preferred not to walk home through dark streets.

Representative Walnut, a reform legislator, could not let Letzkus's comments go unchallenged. Walnut relied on, but did not directly reference, the reports that Herschel Jones and Charles Chute of the NCLC had recently prepared regarding the Pittsburgh glass houses:

A great deal of testimony has been secured after a careful investigation of the conditions in the very places that the gentleman [Letzkus] has referred to, and from a medical observation has been determined that not only for the children but the men as well but it is particularly injurious to the children, and this was so well recognized that every other industry in every other state engaged in this business has enacted this very proposition that we propose to enact here. . . . [T]his bill would merely put Pennsylvania in her proper place by recognizing the needs of the children of the State.[63]

Representative Walnut appeared to carry the day. The amendment to reinstate the glass house exception was defeated, and the entire bill then was approved on second reading. On April 15, the bill was approved on its third reading and was sent, with no glass house exception, to the Senate.[64] But the war was not yet over.

The Senate version received its first reading on June 9, 1913.[65] It is unclear if any changes had been made in the House bill because, as usual, the record of proceedings in the Senate does not include the exact language read and voted on. But for the second reading the next day, the changes became evident. By then, section 8 contained several amendments, added, in all likelihood, by the Senate committee, including an explicit glass house exception.[66] Immediately, Senator Samuel W. Salus moved to delete the committee-inserted glass house exception language. His proposal passed without debate, and the entire bill was approved on second reading.[67]

The bill's third reading was on June 18. Once again, however, the committee had, on its own motion, reinserted the glass house exception in section 8. The insertion was virtually identical to the language removed on the second reading.[68] Again, Senator Salus moved to strike the exception from the bill. He noted that the night work exception was used only by the glass factories, "where children under the age of sixteen years are allowed to work at night. I understand that those boys of any age are taken in those glass factories between fourteen and sixteen, mostly to work at night, and I understand it is the only industry in the State where this is allowed and it is one of the sections that the people interested in the bill are extremely anxious to have taken out of the bill." Senator Charles A. Snyder rose to the defense of the provision. The original language, he noted, was supported by the factory owners, who "had considerable money invested in their several plants and if this exemption was not to be granted," he claimed, they would have to close. He also noted that he had been "presented a petition signed by a majority of pretty nearly nine-tenths of all the glass workers in the State, the fathers of these boys, these minors, and then by the minors themselves, asking that they be permitted to continue to work."[69]

The petition referred to by Senator Snyder is critical. It refers not only to the glass workers' support of the glass house exception, discussed earlier, but also to support from the families of the boys and the boys themselves. The boys, silent in so much of the debate concerning child labor, are here made to speak out in favor of their desire to work at night in the glass houses. That they wanted to be able to continue to work in the glass houses at night is consistent with other evidence; even the NCLC reports from Jones and Chute allude to this. What Snyder did not address is that, given the likelihood that many of the boys' families were recent immigrants with limited English-language skills and that many of the boys themselves probably could not read, it is difficult to know what it means to claim that perhaps as many as nine-tenths of them signed a petition in support of the bill. Technicalities aside, the rhetorical effect of Senator Snyder's comment was powerful, making it appear that the glass house exception was supported by virtually everyone directly involved in the daily (or nightly) work of these factories.

Indeed, the glass blowers' union was doing more to support the glass house exception than just having its members sign petitions. Nearly three months earlier, on March 6, 7, and 13, 1913, members from the Pittsburgh local of the GBBA went to Harrisburg to lobby the legislature in favor of retaining the glass house exception in the child labor bill that was about to be considered. They met with John H. Maurer, president of the Pennsylvania Federation of Labor, "to urge the imperative necessity of an amendment [in favor of the glass house exception] to the Walnut child labor bill." Although Maurer assured them that he would advocate on their behalf, by April the GBBA members, worried that Maurer was not up to the task, wrote a letter directly to Governor John K. Tener arguing their case that "it is absolutely necessary for the boys" to work both day and night shifts. They assured the governor, as they had assured Maurer, that "the boy glass workers are not abused in any way" in their day and night employment and that "they are infinitely better off in our factories than on the streets." They concluded that "the glass workers in Pennsylvania, who constitute nearly 40 per cent of the glass workers of the entire United States, are almost unanimously and quite unalterably opposed to the Walnut bill" because it failed to provide a glass house exception.[70]

These, of course, are persuasive political arguments. While it was not unusual at this time for manufacturers to oppose child labor regulations, it was also almost unheard of for their anti-reform voices to be joined by both the adult workers in the industry affected by the child labor restrictions and their union. And, then, on the slim chance that this most unusual suite of support for the glass house exception might not be sufficient to persuade the rest of the legislators to vote in favor of the bill, Senator Snyder reasoned further that the exception, while very necessary at the moment, would not be needed much longer. He noted that only about 560 boys were working in the glass houses at that time and that the supporters of the glass house exception had assured the committee that "we thought it was no more than proper and just that the Committee should allow the exception … which permits the glass workers to continue as they have, because we believe that by the time the Senate meets again one-half of these five hundred and sixty boys will be out of the business because of the machinery that will be installed." The reform forces in Pennsylvania had grown stronger, however, and these combined arguments proved unsuccessful. The amendment failed and the full bill, without a glass house exception, was approved.[71]

Although the child labor bill had been read for the third time, there were differences between the House and Senate versions, so the battle had not yet been concluded. On June 23, the Senate sent its version of the 1913 child labor bill to the House for concurrence in the Senate changes.[72] The house refused to concur, and, as usual, a conference committee was established with members from both chambers. What was unusual, however, was that the conference committee could not reach a compromise agreement, and on June 27, the last day of the 1913 legislative session, the House conferees asked to be discharged from their responsibilities. The request was granted. In support of his discharge request, Representative Walnut, the leader of the House conference committee, noted,

We feel that the measure as it passed this body was proper and would not have put Pennsylvania insofar as legislation on this most important subject is concerned in a position wherein she would not need to feel ashamed at the protection granted to her children in industry. The vital principles of the bill are those pertained [sic] to the hours of employment and the working of children between fourteen and sixteen at night. . . . [E]very effort has been made to secure the enactment of such a [night employment] regulation. Two years ago a bill was introduced which passed this House but was amended as previous bills have been amended in the Senate by the insertion of a proviso that the prohibition should not apply to industries requiring continuous day and night operations, which made the bill little more than a mockery upon the statute books.

He went on to note that the only beneficiary of the night work exception was the glass industry and that, among all the glass-producing states, only Pennsylvania and West Virginia still allowed night work by children. Further, he noted that while the conference committees had agreed to a compromise on the allowable hours of employment, the committee could not reach an agreement on the night work issue. As such, he concluded, the "measure which once promised so much for the advancement of child labor legislation in Pennsylvania" had been changed so much by the glass house exception that it now "would accomplish so little that the principle which we advocate will ultimately be advanced far better by its rejection than its acceptance."[73]

A few moments later, after the House had voted on an unrelated matter, Representative Richard J. Baldwin of Delaware County asked the House to revisit the child labor bill and adopt the Senate version. He succeeded in having the House delegates to the conference committee reinstated, and Representative Walnut and the committee went back to the Senate for one last try.[74] This too was to no avail. The House members reported back late in the evening of June 27. In the closing hours of that final day of the session, the House members were tired and tempers were getting short. Again Walnut reported that the conference committee could not reach a compromise on the issue of the glass house exception. Baldwin then moved to allow for the House to reconsider its vote of nonconcurrence with the Senate amendments to the overall bill. Walnut, although he acknowledged that the "Child Labor [A]ssociation has not taken a position" on whether they would support the bill with the glass house exception included, stated that he still opposed it. When Baldwin arose in a last attempt to speak in the bill's favor, the legislative record notes in parentheses that "cries for [calling the] question all over the House interfered with the speaker continuing." Baldwin's efforts were rewarded, however, as the House voted to reconsider.[75]

Those efforts still were not enough. Upon reconsideration, although the full House voted 70 to 66 to concur in the Senate amendments and pass the bill, the motion failed because the state constitution required (as it still does) a majority "of all the elected members of the House to vote in the affirmative, not just a majority of those voting, even if a quorum be present."[76] Seventy votes did not constitute a sufficient majority. The 1913 law died, and the glass house exception from the 1911 law remained in effect. Representative John R. K. Scott laid the blame for failing to enact a 1913 child labor law squarely at the door of the Senate. He argued that the Senate, playing to the greed of the industrial interests, used strong-arm tactics in delaying consideration of the bill so that no time would be left for compromise or further amendment. He asserted that with the inclusion of "their cunning exceptions" regarding working hours and "their glass house exceptions, they attempt to give us by statute that which is worse than we have on our statute books today."[77] Within moments, the House voted with the Senate to adjourn for the year.

The End of the Exception

By any measure, the next child labor bill, in 1915, was a legislative cake walk. Introduced in the House on March 3, 1915, the proposed legislation included no glass house exception to the broad night work prohibition. The bill received its first reading on March 31, and by April 6 it was fully approved on its third reading by a vote of 179 to 6.[78] The only drama came during the second reading.[79] Section 4 of the bill—the night work prohibition—provided, inter alia, that no child under sixteen could work more than ten hours in any day, fifty-one hours in any week, or between the hours of eight o'clock in the evening and six o'clock in the morning.

Representative Baldwin moved to increase the maximum weekly hours to fifty-four and delete the night work prohibition altogether. There ensued a lengthy debate that focused entirely on the efficacy of the fifty-one- versus fifty-four-hour maximum. Late in the debate, Representative Edwin R. Cox of Philadelphia County, who had sponsored the original bill, noted that Baldwin's amendment would delete the night work language. Baldwin apologized and said he would not oppose its reinclusion. No change was offered, however, and the Baldwin amendment went down to defeat. The remainder of the bill, with its blanket night work prohibition and without a glass house exception, was read and approved.[80]

In the Senate, the bill sailed through even more smoothly. The bill was introduced on April 7 and received its first reading on April 27. Within a week, it was approved on third reading without any amendments whatsoever.[81] While Senator Charles A. Snyder, a longtime advocate of the manufacturing interests and a staunch opponent of child labor regulations, spoke at length, he never mentioned the glass industry or night work, and he offered no changes in the proposed law. And that was the anticlimactic end of the glass house exception. The Senate voted to approve the bill and thereby end the ten-year existence of the glass house exception.

Typical ways to account for legislative change simply do not work here. No single factor explains the rise or fall of the glass house exception. This exception was not created *simply* because the glass manufacturers wanted it, although their wishes carried substantial weight in the state legislature. It was not retained for ten years *simply* because the glass workers and their union supported it, although their support was very important. It was not eliminated in the end *simply* because the Owens Automatic finally asserted its technological dominance and made the work of the glass house boys obsolete, although this particular invention was revolutionary. Rather, the unique combination of forces opposed to reform—the manufacturers, the boys and their families, and most importantly, the glass workers and their union—continually stymied progressive attempts to remove these boys from the western Pennsylvania glass houses. And, until 1915, the progressives proved unable to address the concerns of the boys and their families or match the power of the glass interests. All of these factors coalesced in the halls of the General Assembly of Pennsylvania to prolong a legislative exception that was anomalous in the history of American labor law.

Notes

Note on Citations

For clarity, all references to laws of the Commonwealth of Pennsylvania appear with notations for act number, date of enactment, and the page in the printed *Laws of the General Assembly of Pennsylvania* (indicated by the abbreviation P.L.). References to Pennsylvania state legislative records are to the *House Journal, Senate Journal,* or *Legislative Journal,* with dates and page references. U.S. Supreme Court cases appear in the body of the text following *Bluebook* format, which gives the name of the case, volume, Reporter, page, and year.

Preface

1. This is legislative history in the fullest sense, not in the narrow, technical sense employed by lawyers and judges in the context of litigation, where the proper construction of specific statutory language is at issue. In court briefs and memoranda, legislative history typically refers only to the committee reports, floor debates, hearing testimony, and the like, generated by the legislature that enacted the subject statute. Under these circumstances, the historian's purpose is to determine what the lawmakers were thinking when they passed the legislation so that the court can apply the law in a manner consistent with the intent of the legislature. In this study, however, the purpose is broader. I am concerned with the operation of law in its social and cultural context.

2. Pennsylvania Constitution of 1874, Art. 2, sec. 12.

3. Ibid., Art. 3, sec. 4; Art. 3, sec. 5.

4. See, e.g., Dubofsky, *Industrialism and the American Worker, 1865–1920;* Foner, *History of the Labor Movement in the United States;* Harris, *Keystone of Democracy.*

5. Between 1882 and 1887, the *Commoner* was published under the name *Commoner and Labor Herald* and served as a general workers' weekly newspaper. While carrying regular columns for the several glass trades (flint glass, window glass, and green or bottle glass), the newspaper also covered news of interest to other trades, including railroads, building construction, and steel. Especially during the sessions of the Pennsylvania legislature, there would be articles (usually written by a member of the legislative committee of the Knights of Labor) concerning labor bills that might be of interest to the general workers who constituted much of the readership. With

a name change in 1887 to the *Commoner and American Glass Worker*, the newspaper began evolving into strictly a glass workers' journal. By the turn of the twentieth century, the transition was complete, and the publication's columns, articles, and features focused almost exclusively on glass issues. In 1911, apparently to avoid confusion with the *Commoner*, a newspaper published in William Jennings Bryan's home state of Nebraska, the name was changed yet again, to *Glassworker: America's Glass Trade Newspaper*, leaving no doubt of the narrower emphasis. From 1882 to 1915 the newspaper had no fewer than seven principal editors, with H. W. Gauding, a man with connections to the flint glass workers, enjoying the longest continuous tenure, from November 1902 until January 1914. Mirroring the more conservative leanings of the GBBA as it switched affiliations from the Knights of Labor to the AFL, its level of political coverage, especially in connection with the Pennsylvania legislature, decreased during the last decade of the nineteenth century and remained relatively low thereafter. Because the bottle trade was the largest segment of the glass industry and because the largest proportion of glass workers in the bottle sector worked in Pittsburgh, the interests and welfare of these workers were a central concern to the newspaper. Its editorial policy thus reflected a commitment to protecting the jobs and improving the wages, benefits, and working conditions of these unionized bottle blowers. For both convenience and consistency, this newspaper will be referred to herein as simply the *Commoner*.

6. Flanagan, *America Reformed*; Davis, *Spearheads for Reform*; Sklar, "Two Political Cultures in the Progressive Era."

7. *Commoner*, editorial, Mar. 27, 1909.

8. See "Restriction of Small Help," *National Glass Budget*, Mar. 18, 1905 (first quote); "The Proposed Child Labor Bill," *National Glass Budget*, Dec. 22, 1906 (second quote); *National Glass Budget*, editorial, Dec. 22, 1906 (third quote); "The 'Glass Exception,'" *National Glass Budget*, Mar. 20, 1909 (fourth quote).

9. See Mintz, *Huck's Raft*.

Chapter 1. Child Labor Reforms and the National Child Labor Committee

The epigraph is from Spargo, *Bitter Cry of the Children*, 155–56.

1. Scoville, *Revolution in Glassmaking*, 321.

2. Hindman, *Child Labor*, 45–46.

3. National Child Labor Committee, "Child Labor Laws in All States."

4. Zelizer, "From Child Labor to Child Work," 90; Catlin, *Labor Problem*, 336. While part of the reason for this decline may have been the enactment of two federal laws attempting to ban child labor, each of these statutes was later declared unconstitutional by the Supreme Court of the United States, so there must have been other factors involved. In 1916, Congress had enacted a sweeping child labor law based on its constitutionally derived power to regulate interstate commerce. Children under

fourteen were prohibited from all covered employments, and children between fourteen and sixteen could work no more than eight hours per day and no hours at night. The law was immediately challenged in federal court by a father, a Mr. Dagenhart, on behalf of his two sons, who worked in a North Carolina cotton mill. In reality, the case was being pushed by the National Manufacturers Association. When the case reached the U.S. Supreme Court in 1918, the Court ruled the first federal child labor law unconstitutional (*Hammer v. Dagenhart*, 247 U.S. 251 [1918]). Congress quickly passed a similar law, this time predicated on its taxing power. Again the National Manufacturers Association organized a challenge to the regulation, and again, in 1922, it was successful in overturning the law (*Bailey v. Drexel Furniture Co.*, 259 U.S. 34 [1922]).

5. Larner, "Glass House Boys," 355.

6. Weeks, *Report on the Statistics of Wages in Manufacturing Industries*, vii–viii, ix.

7. Ibid., xvii.

8. U.S. Senate, *Report on Conditions of Woman and Child Wage-Earners in the United States*, 155.

9. Davis, *Development of the American Glass Industry*, 142.

10. Ibid.

11. Link and McCormick, *Progressivism*, 2.

12. Ibid.

13. Hofstadter, *Age of Reform*, 148; Link and McCormick, *Progressivism*, 4; McGerr, *Fierce Discontent*, 4; Mowry, "Progressivism: Middle-Class Disillusionment," 196–97.

14. Dye, introduction to *Gender, Class, Race, and Reform in the Progressive Era*, 2.

15. Sklar, "Two Political Cultures in the Progressive Era," 40.

16. Davis, *Spearheads for Reform*, xiii; Dye, introduction to *Gender, Class, Race, and Reform in the Progressive Era*, 6. See also Davis and McCree, *Eighty Years at Hull House*.

17. Dye, introduction to *Gender, Class, Race, and Reform in the Progressive Era*, 1; Kett, "Juveniles and Progressive Children," 191.

18. Flanagan, "Gender and Urban Political Reform," 1034.

19. Ibid., 1035.

20. Ibid., 1040.

21. It may be important to note that there was no direct political action component to the programs generated by either of the two clubs, but that does not mean that they did not have access to channels of power. The men of the male City Club ran the businesses and industries that, in many cases, were the primary beneficiaries of that group's proposals, so indirect implementation was very likely. The Women's City Club, of course, had no such direct access to political power within the city.

22. Sklar, "Two Political Cultures in the Progressive Era," 44.

23. Ibid., 42–48.

24. Ibid., 51 (first three quotes), 53 (fourth quote).

25. Ibid., 53, 61.

26. Ibid., 53–55.

27. In July 1906, millionaire industrialist Russell Sage died, leaving $65 million to his wife, Olivia Sage, and his brothers. One of Olivia Sage's attorneys, Robert W. de Forest, a founding member of the nascent National Child Labor Committee, suggested what at the time was a relatively novel idea: that she use some of the capital to establish a philanthropic foundation. She agreed, and with $10 million, she formed the Russell Sage Foundation. For *The Pittsburgh Survey*, research was conducted between 1907 and 1908, and the results were published in six volumes between 1909 and 1914. Four of the volumes were in the form of individual monographs, and the last two comprised a series of smaller research reports prepared during the course of the *Survey*. Of these last two volumes, one focused on the public sector and the other, *Wage-Earning Pittsburgh*, focused on the private economy, social environment, and jobs within the district.

28. Greenwald and Anderson, *Pittsburgh Surveyed*, 7.

29. Cohen, "Failure of Fair Wages and the Death of Labor Republicanism," 50.

30. *Pittsburgh Gazette*, Mar. 7, 1909, 1.

31. Greenwald and Anderson, *Pittsburgh Surveyed*, 8–9.

32. Ibid., 11.

33. Blumberg, *Florence Kelley*, xi.

34. Ibid., 2–6.

35. Sklar, *Florence Kelley and the Nation's Work*, 3–49.

36. Ibid., 44 (first quote), 45–46 (subsequent quotes).

37. Blumberg, *Florence Kelley*, 18.

38. Sklar, *Florence Kelley and the Nation's Work*, 46.

39. Blumberg, *Florence Kelley*, 30; Sklar, *Florence Kelley and the Nation's Work*, 51–67 (quote from 67).

40. Sklar, *Florence Kelley and the Nation's Work*, 75 (quote), 100.

41. Ibid., 167.

42. Quoted in Davis and McCree, *Eighty Years at Hull House*, 37.

43. Ibid., 39.

44. Ibid., 40.

45. Sklar, *Florence Kelley and the Nation's Work*, 279 (first quote), 280 (second through fifth quotes).

46. Sklar, *Florence Kelley and the Nation's Work*, 281 (newspaper quote), 284–86.

47. Hindman, *Child Labor*, 49.

48. Ibid., 56–57.

49. Quoted in Trattner, *Crusade for the Children*, 58. Adler used the word *holocaust* to describe what he saw as the widespread destruction of childhood by, and its sacrifice to, child labor.

50. Quoted in National Child Labor Committee, "Proceedings of the Second Annual Meeting," 1.

51. Ibid., 5, 6.

52. Ibid., 7.

53. Addams, "National Protection for Children," 57.

54. *United States v. Darby Lumber Co.*, 312 U.S. 100 (1941).

55. Regarding the fact that federal action on the child labor issue was effectively unavailable throughout the Progressive Era, see note 4 to this chapter, above.

Chapter 2. Progressive Reform and Child Labor in the Pennsylvania Glass Industry

The epigraph is from Butler, "Sharpsburg," 279.

1. Butler, "Sharpsburg," 297.

2. During the period under study here, the glass house boys engaged in repeated strikes, which shut down the glass houses where they were employed. These acts of independence and resistance on the part of the boys provide substantial evidence that the boys themselves considered the working conditions of the nation's glass factories detrimental. Yet these strikes were never mentioned in the child labor reform speeches, articles, or reports of the progressives. The reason for this omission is probably that these types of job actions provided much stronger support for the idea that the glass house boys were actually more adult in their behaviors than childlike.

3. Mintz, *Huck's Raft*, 76.

4. Ibid.

5. Finkelstein, "Casting Networks of Good Influence," 123.

6. Zelizer, *Pricing the Priceless Child*, 3.

7. Mintz, *Huck's Raft*, 76.

8. Butler, "Sharpsburg."

9. Butler's rhetoric does not have the heart-on-the-sleeve passion of John Spargo describing night work in the glass houses or the sentimentality of the NCLC Child Labor Bulletin from 1914, in which one could read a story about a little medicine bottle that talks to a middle-class boy, bedridden with a slight cold, about the hardships of the children who made the bottle as they toiled in the heat of the glass factories.

10. Cohen, "Child-Saving and Progressivism, 1885–1915," 273–309. The negative consequences of industrialization on the lives of the working urban poor have been well documented. Ronald Cohen comments, "In Homestead, Pennsylvania, Margaret F. Byington discovered in 1909 the frightful results of uncontrolled [industrial] change: 'Summing up the results of indifference on one side and ignorance on the other, we find a high infant death-rate, a knowledge of evil among little children, intolerable sanitary conditions, a low standard of living, a failure of the community to assimilate this new race [of immigrants] in its midst.'" Ibid., 273.

11. Parton, "Pittsburg," 21.

12. Trollope, *North America*, 364–65.

13. Quoted in Butler, "Sharpsburg," 300.

14. U.S. Senate, *Report on Conditions of Woman and Child Wage-Earners in the United States*, 233–36.

15. Quoted in Butler, "Sharpsburg," 300.

16. U.S. Senate, *Report on Conditions of Woman and Child Wage-Earners in the United States*, 154.

17. Butler, "Sharpsburg," 300.

18. Laws of Pennsylvania, Act no. 98, Apr. 10, 1905, P.L. 131.

19. Butler, "Sharpsburg," 285.

20. Ibid., 297.

21. Quoted in ibid.

22. Hindman, *Child Labor*, 133 (quote); Lovejoy, *Children of the Glass Industry in Pennsylvania*, 1907.

23. Hindman, *Child Labor*, 132.

24. Butler, "Sharpsburg," 298.

25. Ibid., 299 (including interviewee quotes).

26. National Child Labor Committee, "Child Labor Laws in All States." States such as Nevada (ibid., 44), Tennessee (ibid., 65), and Texas (ibid., 66) required no certificates whatsoever, while other states such as Indiana required only an age affidavit, from the "parent or guardian, or by the minor himself." Ibid., 21.

27. Davis, "Difficulties of a Factory Inspector," 127.

28. Laws of Pennsylvania, Act no. 235, sec. 5, May 20, 1889, P.L. 243; Trattner, *Crusade for the Children*, 35. Pennsylvania was also not the first state to use the factory inspector model to address the child labor law enforcement problem. Massachusetts instituted the nation's first factory inspection program in 1867, and Connecticut followed two years later, thus marking the beginning of this avenue for enforcement for child labor protective legislation.

29. Harris, *Keystone of Democracy*, 97. These were probably excellent salaries for the time when one considers that, according to the Pennsylvania Bureau of Industrial Statistics, it was estimated that in the late nineteenth century, "a family of five required $600 to maintain a decent standard of living in urban areas." Ibid.

30. Laws of Pennsylvania, Act no. 235, sec. 5, May 20, 1889, P.L. 243.

31. Commonwealth of Pennsylvania, *Journal of the Senate* (1889), 155, 526, 586, 675.

32. Ibid., 403.

33. Commonwealth of Pennsylvania, *Journal of the House of Representatives* (1889), 701, 1136 (quote).

34. Commonwealth of Pennsylvania, *Legislative Journal* (1889), 1590.

35. Ibid., 2474; Commonwealth of Pennsylvania, *Journal of the House of Representatives* (1889), 1527.

36. Martins, *Report of the Factory Inspector*, 8–9.

37. See, e.g., Campbell, *Eleventh Annual Report of the Factory Inspector of the Commonwealth of Pennsylvania . . . 1900.*

38. See, e.g., Watchorn, *Fourth Annual Report of the Factory Inspector . . . 1893*; Watchorn, *Fifth Annual Report of the Factory Inspector . . . 1894*; Campbell, *Sixth Annual Report of the Factory Inspector . . . 1895*.

39. Watchorn, *Fourth Annual Report of the Factory Inspector . . . 1893*, 5.

40. Quoted in Campbell, *Twelfth Annual Report of the Factory Inspector . . . 1901*, 977.

41. Campbell, *Thirteenth Annual Report of the Factory Inspector . . . 1902*, 9.

42. Watchorn, *Fifth Annual Report of the Factory Inspector . . . 1894*, 9.

43. Campbell, *Thirteenth Annual Report of the Factory Inspector . . . 1902*, 10.

44. Martins, *Report of the Factory Inspector*, 8–9.

45. Campbell, *Seventh Annual Report of the Factory Inspector . . . 1896*, 5.

46. Delaney, *Seventeenth Annual Report of the Chief Factory Inspector . . . 1906*, 27.

47. Watchorn, *Fourth Annual Report of the Factory Inspector . . . 1893*, 55.

48. *Who's Who in Pennsylvania*, s.v. Delaney, J. C.

49. *National Glass Budget*, editorial, Dec. 17, 1904.

50. Kelley, "Child Labor Legislation and Enforcement in New England and the Middle States," 66–67.

51. As chapter 5 explains, Pennsylvania's approach to school and compulsory attendance laws at the time largely confirms Kelley's criticisms.

52. Kelley, "Child Labor Legislation and Enforcement in New England and the Middle States," 68–69.

53. Kelley, "Obstacles to the Enforcement of Child Labor Legislation," 52.

54. Delaney, *Fifteenth Annual Report of the Factory Inspector . . . 1904*, 5.

55. Delaney, *Sixteenth Annual Report of the Chief Factory Inspector . . . 1905*, 8.

56. Quoted in Kelley, "Factory Inspection in Pittsburgh," 208 fn.

57. Hall, "Child Labor Statistics," 115–16.

58. Hall, "Pennsylvania Child Labor Association," 184–85.

59. Kelley, "Factory Inspection in Pittsburgh," 189–91 (quote from 189).

60. Ibid., 192–95.

61. Quoted in ibid., 208, 208 fn.

62. Chute, "Enforcement of Child Labor Laws," 108, 109, 110.

63. Ibid., 112.

64. *National Glass Budget*, editorial, Jan. 11, 1913.

65. Lovejoy, *Children of the Glass Industry in Pennsylvania*, 4.

66. Ibid., 9.

67. Russell Freedman notes in *Kids at Work* that photographer Lewis Hine also had to disguise himself in order "to gain access to factories, mines, sweatshops, and mills," sometimes posing as a fire inspector, an insurance salesman, or even an industrial photographer in order to get pictures of children at work. Freedman, *Kids at Work*, 26.

68. Chute, " Glass Industry and Child Labor Legislation," 2.

69. Ibid., 1.

70. Ibid., 7–8.

71. Ibid., 10.

72. Ibid., 14–16.

73. Ibid., 22.

74. Ibid., 28–29, 30–32.

75. Ibid., 27, 30–31.

76. Ibid., 34–36.

77. Hindman, *Child Labor*, 135.

78. Chute, "Glass Industry and Child Labor Legislation," 41–42.

79. Jones, "Investigation of Glass Factories of Western Pennsylvania," 1.

80. Ibid., 9.

81. Ibid., 12–13 (emphasis in original).

82. Chute, "Glass Industry and Child Labor Legislation," 32 (emphasis added).

83. "Glass Company Not at Fault," *National Glass Budget*, Dec. 22, 1900. These circumstances were not unique to Pittsburgh. Louis Arrington, the state factory inspector for Illinois, commented on it after visiting the Illinois Glass Works in Alton in 1900. He later said he had found "about 60 boys ranging from 13 to 10 years of age" working in the factory when the minimum age set by state law was fourteen. He found that each of these boys had given the company an affidavit, signed by a parent or guardian, certifying that the child in question was at least fourteen years of age. Arrington said that he learned from this inspection "that the parents of the children have been committing perjury in order to secure work for their boys in the glass works." Ibid.

84. Dye, introduction to *Gender, Class, Race, and Reform in the Progressive Era*, 6.

85. Kett, "Juveniles and Progressive Children," 192.

86. Dye, introduction to *Gender, Class, Race, and Reform in the Progressive Era*, 6.

Chapter 3. Glass House Owners and the Politics of Glass

The epigraph is from *National Glass Budget*, editorial, Mar. 13, 1909.

1. Rogers and Beard, *5000 Years of Glass*, 2.

2. Moore, *Old Glass*, 3; Perry, *Glass Industry*, 14.

3. Perry, *Glass Industry*, 5.

4. Binning, "Glass Industry of Western Pennsylvania, 1797–1860," 29–30.

5. McKearin and McKearin, *Two Hundred Years of American Blown Glass*, 26.

6. Scoville, *Revolution in Glassmaking*, 23–24.

7. Innes, *Pittsburgh Glass, 1797–1891*, 7–8; Perry, *Glass Industry*, 73.

8. McKearin and McKearin, *Two Hundred Years of American Blown Glass*, 47.

9. Ibid., 138, 334; Scoville, *Revolution in Glassmaking*, 18 n53.

10. McKearin and McKearin, *Two Hundred Years of American Blown Glass*, 71.

11. Steinfeld, *Invention of Free Labor*, 4.

12. Ibid., 9.

13. Ibid.

14. Because the children were legal minors, there were limits on the enforceability of any contract they entered into. But the nature of these "contracts" was that a cash wage would be paid at the end of the contract period (usually the end of a day or a week). Therefore, enforcement of such short "contracts" on the part of the employer was rarely if ever a problem.

15. There were an estimated five glass factories in Pittsburgh in 1813, eight in 1826, and thirty-three in 1857, with nine of these being flint glass houses and twenty-four being window glass and bottle plants. Moore, *Old Glass*, 379.

16. Scoville, *Revolution in Glassmaking*, 7. Warren Scoville notes that some of these figures may well be underestimates because of the inadequate returns for several of the early Census reports.

17. McKearin and McKearin, *Two Hundred Years of American Blown Glass*, 133–35.

18. Binning, "Glass Industry of Western Pennsylvania, 1797–1860," 51–53 (quote from 53, emphasis added).

19. McKearin and McKearin, *Two Hundred Years of American Blown Glass*, 134; Binning, "Glass Industry of Western Pennsylvania, 1797–1860," 70.

20. Binning, "Glass Industry of Western Pennsylvania, 1797–1860," 70–71.

21. Ibid., 75–79.

22. Ibid., 103–5.

23. Ibid., 107, 124.

24. Ibid., 124.

25. Scoville, *Revolution in Glassmaking*, 44–45.

26. Davis, *Development of the American Glass Industry*, 143.

27. Ibid., 142.

28. Weeks, *Report on the Statistics of Wages in Manufacturing Industries*, 80–95.

29. Zembala, "Machines in the Glasshouse," 307.

30. Ibid., 258.

31. Ibid., 262.

32. Ibid., 268–70, 339.

33. Ibid., 342.

34. There were other types of machines being invented as well. They included the McKee tumbler finisher, the Cleveland tableware finisher, the Chambers-Blair machine for chimneys and globes, the McKee-Schmunk mold press and the Beatty-Brady press for tableware production, and the Arduser-O'Neil white liner machine. "Glass Working Machinery," *National Glass Budget*, Sept. 24, 1898.

35. "An Up-to-Date Glass Plant," *National Glass Budget*, June 25, 1898.

36. "Glass Working Machinery," *National Glass Budget*, Sept. 24, 1898.

37. "The Owens Machine at St. Helens," *National Glass Budget*, Oct. 21, 1899.

38. "Inventors of Machinery," *National Glass Budget*, June 25, 1898.

39. Ibid.

40. Walbridge, *American Bottles Old & New*, 68.

41. "The Era of the Machine," *National Glass Budget*, Aug. 19, 1899.

42. "Machine Invasion," *National Glass Budget*, Mar. 28, 1903.

43. *National Glass Budget*, editorial, May 23, 1903.

44. "The Owens Bottle Machine," *National Glass Budget*, Aug. 15, 1903.

45. Zembala, "Machines in the Glasshouse," 342.

46. Annual Stockholder Report, Owens Bottle Machine Company, Sept. 1908, GBBA Papers, Kheel Center for Labor-Management Documentation and Archives, Cornell University, Ithaca, NY.

47. Walbridge, *American Bottles Old & New*, 89, 95–99.

48. Zembala, "Machines in the Glasshouse," 103, 344.

49. *National Glass Budget*, editorial, Mar. 4, 1905.

50. Ibid.

51. Ibid., July 18, 1903.

52. Ibid.

53. Ibid., Mar. 25, 1905.

54. Ibid., Apr. 8, 1905.

55. "Hayes on the Owens Machine," *National Glass Budget*, Apr. 29, 1905.

56. *National Glass Budget*, editorial, Apr. 29, 1905.

57. Wilson, *American Glass, 1760–1930*, 269.

58. "Shut Glass Factory Down," *National Glass Budget*, June 17, 1905.

59. Avery, *Behold the Child*, 184–89.

60. "Another Strike Settled," *National Glass Budget*, Apr. 18, 1896; *National Glass Budget*, editorial, Oct. 11, 1902.

61. See, e.g., "Started by Foreigners," *National Glass Budget*, Apr. 7, 1900.

62. "Japs to Replace Child Labor," *National Glass Budget*, Jan. 12, 1907.

63. "Negro Women Supplant Boys," *National Glass Budget*, Oct. 20, 1906.

64. "More Child Labor Laws," *National Glass Budget*, Dec. 31, 1904.

65. "Restriction of Small Help," *National Glass Budget*, Mar. 18, 1905.

66. "Machinery Displacing Child Labor," *National Glass Budget*, Feb. 17, 1906.

67. "Jersey Child Labor Legislation," *National Glass Budget*, Jan. 25, 1913.

68. "The Proposed Child Labor Bill," and "A Merry Christmas to All" (editorial), both in *National Glass Budget*, Dec. 22, 1906.

69. *National Glass Budget*, editorial, Mar. 13, 1909; "The 'Glass Exception,'" *National Glass Budget*, Mar. 20, 1909.

70. "Proposed Child Labor Law," *National Glass Budget*, Feb. 1, 1913.

71. *National Glass Budget*, editorials, Feb. 8, Feb. 22, 1913.

72. Quoted in *National Glass Budget*, editorial, Mar. 8, 1913.

73. "At Harrisburg Last Wednesday," *National Glass Budget*, June 17, 1913.

Chapter 4. The Pittsburgh Glass Workers
and the Glass Bottle Union

The epigraph is from Denis A. Hayes to J. E. Daily, Evansville Branch of the GBBA, May 27, 1909, quoted in *Commoner*, editorial, Mar. 27, 1909.

1. Rogers and Beard, *5000 Years of Glass*, 21; Frank, *Glass and Archaeology*, 17; Phillips, *Glass*, 7; Moore, *Old Glass*, 3.

2. Even into the early twentieth century, glass-bottle production was often referred to as the "green glass" sector.

3. Perry, *Glass Industry*, 16–18.

4. Moore, *Old Glass*, 31.

5. Biser, *Elements of Glass and Glassmaking*, 8.

6. Moore, *Old Glass*, 31.

7. Perry, *Glass Industry*, 26.

8. Binning, "Glass Industry of Western Pennsylvania, 1797–1860," ii.

9. Minton, *Flame and Heart*, 7.

10. Hoffman, *Contemporary Analysis of a Labor Union*, 4.

11. Harris, *Keystone of Democracy*, 98–99.

12. Forbath, *Law and the Shaping of the American Labor Movement*, 1 (quote), 13.

13. Harris, *Keystone of Democracy*, 100.

14. Golden Anniversary Convention Brochure, July 1927, GBBA Papers.

15. Harris, *Keystone of Democracy*, 100.

16. Forbath, *Law and the Shaping of the American Labor Movement*, 15.

17. Quoted in ibid., 1 n2.

18. Forbath, *Law and the Shaping of the American Labor Movement*, 17.

19. "Framing a New Tariff Bill," *Commoner*, Dec. 19, 1896.

20. "Views of a Manufacturer," *Commoner*, Apr. 17, 1909.

21. Ibid. Later that year (1909), the newspaper provided further evidence of the racist tendencies of the glass workers when it reviewed the Pittsburgh Alvin Theater's production of *The Clansman*. Theatrical reviews were unusual in the pages of the *Commoner*, which normally limited its entertainment coverage to baseball and other sporting pursuits. This review was, therefore, all the more interesting because of its rarity. The play, based on the book of the same name by Thomas F. Dixon Jr., later inspired D. W. Griffith's landmark movie, *The Birth of a Nation*. The *Commoner* effusively praised the theatrical production's enviable "qualities of loyal heroism" portrayed through the figures of "brave" Confederate soldiers who after the Civil War "valiantly" opposed "carpetbagger government and the menace of negro supremacy." The review concluded with the rather chilling statement that "no more thrilling picture has ever been devised by the dramatist than that of the Ku Klux Klan in 'The Clansman.'" "'The Clansman' at the Alvin," *Commoner*, May 1, 1909.

22. Denis A. Hayes, memo to GBBA Executive Board, Apr. 13, 1908, GBBA Papers.

23. "Blowing by Machinery," *Commoner*, Jan. 21, 1888.

24. "The Glass Worker," *Commoner*, Mar. 10, 1888.

25. "Toledo's Blowing Machine," *Commoner*, Apr. 17, 1897.

26. Zembala, "Machines in the Glasshouse," 345–47.

27. "Finishing a Bottle," *National Glass Budget*, Feb. 20, 1904.

28. "Owens Bottle Blowing Machine," *National Glass Budget*, Apr. 30, 1904.

29. "Report," *Commoner*, July 15, 1905.

30. "Invasion of Bottle Machines," *National Glass Budget*, Nov. 10, 1906.

31. "Labor Fakir Deceived Labor," *National Glass Budget*, Apr. 12, 1913.

32. In 1880, for example, the U.S. Census report issued by Joseph Weeks noted that there were at least 762 labor disturbances (strikes and lockouts) in the country and that Pennsylvania, as the country's leading industrial state, accounted for a substantial portion of these. The report also showed that very few of these disturbances were in the glass industry. Of the labor disputes reported, the greatest number, 236, or about 31 percent, were in the iron and steel industries, and of these disputes, 142 were in Pennsylvania. The next largest number of strikes and lockouts involved coal miners, 158 job actions in all (about 21 percent of the total), with 60 of these in Pennsylvania. At the bottom of the list came the nation's glass industry, with only 27 recorded labor disputes, of which only 15 took place in Pennsylvania. Weeks, *Report on Strikes and Lockouts, 1880*, 14–16. As unions, especially the GBBA, became more important in the glass industry, the level of strike activity dropped even further.

33. Quoted in "The Glass Worker," *Commoner*, Nov. 13, 1887.

34. "Bottle Men Cutting Prices," *Commoner*, Dec. 31, 1887.

35. "Bottle Men's Conference," *Commoner*, Aug. 15, 1896.

36. Denis A. Hayes to Officers and Members of GBBA, circular, Oct. 20, 1898, GBBA Papers.

37. Hayes to Officers and Members, May 24, 1909, GBBA Papers.

38. Branch No. 106 to Officers and Members, Mar. 27, 1911, GBBA Papers. See also "Bottle Conference Held," *Commoner*, Mar. 4, 1911.

39. "Atlantic City Conference[:] Last Year's Rules and Wages," *Commoner*, Aug. 12, 1911.

40. "Bottle Conference Concluded," *Commoner*, May 20, 1905.

41. "The GBBA Inspects the Owens Machine," *Commoner*, May 6, 1905.

42. "Modern Methods in Vogue in Bottle Trade," *Commoner*, June 3, 1905 (emphasis added).

43. "With the Bottle Blowers," *Commoner*, Aug. 5, 1905.

44. "A Report of the GBBA-Manufacturers Conference in Atlantic City," *Commoner*, Aug. 12, 1905.

45. "Many Plants Have Started in the Glass Bottle Trade," *Commoner*, Sept. 9, 1905.

46. "Last Year's Scale Will Obtain This Season in Bottle Trade," *Commoner*, Oct. 21, 1905.

47. "Bottle Men Hold Conference," *Commoner*, May 18, 1907.

48. Hayes to Officers and Members, Aug. 7, 1906, GBBA Papers.

49. Ibid., May 6, 1907.

50. "Scale Has Been Signed," *Commoner*, Aug. 10, 1907.

51. Hayes to Officers and Members, circular, May 6, 1908, GBBA Papers.

52. "Last Year's List and Rules Adopted," *Commoner*, Aug. 15, 1908.

53. *Commoner*, editorial, July 10, 1909.

54. "No Agreement Was Reached at Atlantic City Conference," *Commoner*, Aug. 7, 1909; "Bottle Blowers Settlement Made Last Week," *Commoner*, Oct. 1, 1909.

55. Hayes to Officers and Members, Aug. 20, 1909, GBBA Papers.

56. "The Glass Bottle Blowers' Wage Scale Is Settled," *Commoner*, Aug. 13, 1910; "Atlantic City Conference[:] Last Year's Rules and Wages," *Commoner*, Aug. 12, 1911.

57. "Settlement Was Made," *Commoner*, Sept. 6, 1913; "Settlement Was Made in the Glass Bottle Trade," *Commoner*, Sept. 5, 1914.

58. Wolman, *Growth of American Trade Unions, 1880–1923*, 57.

59. Commonwealth of Pennsylvania, *Legislative Journal* (1913), 4451.

60. "Pranks of Boys," *Commoner*, June 15, 1895.

61. "Pith of the Week's News," *Commoner*, Apr. 8, 1905.

62. Ibid., Apr. 20, 1907.

63. "Strike of Glassmen," *Commoner*, Oct. 30, 1887.

64. "Pith of the Week's News," *Commoner*, Apr. 29, 1905.

65. "Small Help Strike at Cicero," *Commoner*, Apr. 20, 1907.

66. "Pith of the Week's News," *Commoner*, May 11, 1907. See also ibid., May 18, 1907.

67. Denis A. Hayes, memorandum to GBBA Executive Board, Sept. 27, 1902, GBBA Papers.

68. Denis A. Hayes to GBBA Officers & Members, circular, Oct. 30, 1902, GBBA Papers.

69. "Glass House Boys," *Commoner*, Jan. 26, 1889.

70. Ibid., Feb. 9, 1889.

71. "State Legislative Work," *Commoner*, May 18, 1889.

72. "Glass House Boys," *Commoner*, May 25, 1895.

73. "Knocking Out the Boys," *National Glass Budget*, Mar. 28, 1896.

74. "The Glass Worker," *Commoner*, Mar. 3, 1888.

75. "Fatal Ending to a Boys' Fight," *Commoner*, Apr. 25, 1896.

76. "Pith of the Week's News," *Commoner*, Jan. 19, 1907; "Shortage of Small Help," *Commoner*, Apr. 20, 1907; "Pith of the Week's News," *Commoner*, Apr. 27, May 18, 1907.

77. "Small Help from New York City," *Commoner*, Nov. 20, 1909.

78. "Pith of the Week's News," *Commoner*, Apr. 8, 1905.

79. "The Child Labor Bill Discussed," *Commoner*, Feb. 9, 1907.

80. *Commoner*, editorial, Mar. 9, 1907.

81. "Glass Men at Harrisburg," *Commoner*, Mar. 23, 1907.

82. *Commoner*, editorial, Mar. 23, 1907.

83. Ibid.

84. *Commoner*, editorial, Mar. 27, 1909.

85. Ibid., Feb. 18, 1911.

Chapter 5. School Law and Compulsory
Education in Pennsylvania

The epigraph is quoted in Kelley, "Factory Inspection in Pittsburgh," 208 fn.

1. Finkelstein, "Casting Networks of Good Influence," 111–12; Cohen, "Child-Saving and Progressivism," 284. "Common English branches" refers to the type of courses normally offered in the common schools of the time and typically included orthography, reading, writing, English grammar, geography, and arithmetic.

2. Katz, "Origins of Public Education," 93–95.

3. Finkelstein, "Casting Networks of Good Influence," 127.

4. Kaestle, *Pillars of the Republic*, xi. The common school movement has been the subject of a number of important studies. For a still useful early study, see Cubberley, *Public Education in the United States*; for more recent work, see Kaestle, *Pillars of the Republic*, and McClellan and Reese, *Social History of American Education*.

5. Kaestle, *Pillars of the Republic*, 105.

6. Quoted in ibid., 104.

7. Commonwealth of Pennsylvania, *Journal of the House of Representatives* (1823–1824), vol. 1, 602.

8. Commonwealth of Pennsylvania, *Special Bulletin No. 27* (1934), 6.

9. Commonwealth of Pennsylvania, *Journal of the House of Representatives* (1827–1828), vol. 1, 48; Commonwealth of Pennsylvania, *Journal of the Senate* (1827–1828), vol. 1, 577.

10. Quoted in Cubberley, *Public Education in the United States*, 126.

11. Quoted in Commonwealth of Pennsylvania, *Special Bulletin No. 27* (1934), 6.

12. Commonwealth of Pennsylvania, *Special Bulletin No. 27* (1934), 6–7.

13. Ibid., 7.

14. The establishment of the common school system in Pennsylvania is beyond the scope of this book. The one element of that system that is of importance here and that will be discussed in depth is the compulsory attendance requirement.

15. Commonwealth of Pennsylvania, *Journal of the House of Representatives* (1874), 588–90.

16. There were other attempts at educational reform. One, House Bill No. 473, entitled "An act to provide for the maintenance and education of necessities of children of this Commonwealth," was committed to the Committee on Judiciary General. Commonwealth of Pennsylvania, *Journal of the House of Representatives* (1889), 470. A second, House Bill No. 646, labeled "An act to the better protection of women and children, regulating their employment and providing for the compulsory education of all

children in ... the Commonwealth," was committed to the Committee on Education. Commonwealth of Pennsylvania, *Journal of the House of Representatives* (1889), 644.

17. Quoted in Commonwealth of Pennsylvania, *Journal of the House of Representatives* (1893), 2102–3.

18. Commonwealth of Pennsylvania, *Journal of the House of Representatives* (1893), 913; *Journal of the Senate* (1893), 1078–79.

19. Commonwealth of Pennsylvania, *Journal of the House of Representatives* (1893), 1411–12.

20. Quoted in ibid., 2102–3.

21. Laws of Pennsylvania, Act no. 53, May 16, 1895, P.L. 72.

22. Commonwealth of Pennsylvania, *Journal of the Senate* (1895), 1100.

23. Laws of Pennsylvania, Act no. 53, May 16, 1895, P.L. 72.

24. See, e.g., the Factory Act of 1893, Laws of Pennsylvania, Act no. 244, June 3, 1893, P.L. 276, allowing children thirteen years and older to work, and the Elevator Act of 1893, Laws of Pennsylvania, Act no. 83, May 24, 1893, P.L. 131, allowing children fourteen years and older to work.

25. Laws of Pennsylvania, Act no. 192, art. IX, June 2, 1891, P.L. 176; Act no. 48, art. XVII, May 15, 1893, P.L. 52.

26. Ibid., Act no. 199, July 12, 1897, P.L. 248.

27. Commonwealth of Pennsylvania, *Journal of the Senate* (1897), 677, 699, 738, 792.

28. Commonwealth of Pennsylvania, *Journal of the House of Representatives* (1897), 575, 1195–96, 2682.

29. Laws of Pennsylvania, Act no. 199, July 12, 1897, P.L. 248.

30. Ibid., Act no. 123, June 14, 1897, P.L. 148.

31. Ibid., Act no. 143, May 11, 1901, P.L. 176.

32. Ibid., Act no. 335, July 11, 1901, P.L. 658.

33. Ibid., sec. 1, July 11, 1901, P.L. 658.

34. Ibid., sec. 3, July 11, 1901, P.L. 658.

35. Ibid., Act no. 182, Apr. 29, 1909, P.L. 283.

36. Ibid., Act no. 235, May 20, 1889, P.L. 243.

37. Ibid., Act no. 98, sec. 1, Apr. 10, 1905, P.L. 131.

38. Commonwealth of Pennsylvania, *Journal of the House of Representatives* (1905), 1443–44; *Journal of the Senate* (1905), 1312.

39. Laws of Pennsylvania, Act no. 237, May 29, 1907, P.L. 314.

40. Ibid., [School] Act, July 9, 1911, P.L. 309.

41. Ibid., secs. 1414–1416, July 9, 1911, P.L. 309.

42. Ibid., sec. 1417, July 9, 1911, P.L. 309.

43. Illick, *American Childhoods*, 71.

44. Ibid.

45. Mintz, *Huck's Raft*, 134.

46. Graff, "Literacy, Jobs, and Industrialization," 234.

47. Ibid., 240.

Chapter 6. Child Labor Laws in Pennsylvania

The epigraph is from the Laws of Pennsylvania, Act no. 226, sec. 3, May 2, 1905, P.L. 352.

1. Laws of Pennsylvania, Act no. 226, sec. 5, May 2, 1905, P.L. 352.

2. Trattner, *Crusade for the Children*, 35.

3. Laws of Pennsylvania, Act no. 226, sec. 5, May 2, 1905, P.L. 352.

4. See ibid., Act no. 182, sec. 6, Apr. 29, 1909, P.L. 283.

5. Harris, *Keystone of Democracy*, 128.

6. Laws of Pennsylvania, Act no. 227, Mar. 27, 1848, P.L. 278.

7. Ibid.

8. Ibid., Act no. 415, Apr. 21, 1849, P.L. 671.

9. Ibid., Act no. 501, May 7, 1855, P.L. 472.

10. Ibid., Act no. 172, June 1, 1887, P.L. 287.

11. Ibid., Act no. 415, sec. 2, Apr. 21, 1849, P.L. 671.

12. Ibid., sec. 4, Apr. 21, 1849, P.L. 671.

13. See, e.g., Commonwealth of Pennsylvania, *Journal of the Senate* (1848), 51, 95, 106, 133, 152, 160.

14. Ibid. (1849), 535.

15. Ibid., 284. The use of the word *foreign* is a bit ambiguous. Although, in general usage, it typically refers to a person or entity from a different country, in the law of corporations, for example, it may refer simply to a business incorporated in another state. Thus, the use of the term by the senator here may or may not be an early reference to what we might now see as economic globalization.

16. Commonwealth of Pennsylvania, *Journal of the Senate* (1849), 301–2.

17. Laws of Pennsylvania, Act no. 244, June 3, 1893, P.L. 276. The 1893 action may have been related to the economic panic of that year, with its mounting bank and business failures. Morison, *Oxford History of the American People*, 795.

18. Laws of Pennsylvania, Act no. 182, April 29, 1909, P.L. 283; Act no. 210, May 1, 1909, P.L. 375. In 1915, the state's child labor provisions received a massive overhaul, with the hours for child laborers further reduced, to nine per day and fifty-one per week. Ibid., Act no. 177, May 13, 1915, P.L. 286. Except for the fact that the 1915 legislation addressed the night work prohibition, it is beyond the scope of the present study.

19. Laws of Pennsylvania, Act no. 172, June 1, 1887, P.L. 287.

20. Ibid., Act no. 244, June 3, 1893, P.L. 276; and Act no. 83, May 24, 1893, P.L. 131, respectively.

21. Ibid., Act no. 226, May 2, 1905, P.L. 352.

22. Hall, "Child Labor Statistics," 115–16.

23. Laws of Pennsylvania, Act no. 415, Apr. 21, 1849, P.L. 671; and Act no. 235, sec. 19, May 20, 1889, P.L. 243, respectively.

24. Ibid., Act no. 206, sec. 4, May 29, 1901, P.L. 322.

25. Ibid., Act no. 226, sec. 5, May 2, 1905, P.L. 352.

26. Ibid., Act no. 182, sec. 3, Apr. 29, 1909, P.L. 283.

27. Ibid., Act no. 172, sec. 1, June 1, 1887, P.L. 287 (emphasis added).

28. Ibid., Act no. 169, June 30, 1885, P.L. 205; Act no. 170, June 30, 1885, P.L. 218; Act no. 192, June 2, 1891, P.L. 176; Act no. 48, May 15, 1893, P.L. 52.

29. Ibid., Act no. 235, May 20, 1889, P.L. 243.

30. For the subsequent legislation, see ibid., Act no. 244, sec. 1, June 3, 1893, P.L. 276; Act no. 26, sec. 1, Apr. 29, 1897, P.L. 30; Act no. 226, secs. 1 and 2, May 2, 1905, P.L. 352.

31. Laws of Pennsylvania, Act no. 182, secs. 1 and 2, Apr. 29, 1909, P.L. 283.

32. Ibid., sec. 3, Apr. 29, 1909, P.L. 283.

33. Ibid., sec. 4, Apr. 29, 1909, P.L. 283. Although this revision may have looked like a significant change in the way coverage of the law was defined, it did not seem to concern the legislators. In the Pennsylvania House of Representatives, the vote on the 1909 child labor bill occurred on March 31, 1909, when, with hardly a word of discussion, it was approved with a 187-to-3 vote. Commonwealth of Pennsylvania, *Legislative Journal* (1909), 2025. The Senate likewise had virtually nothing to say about the language of industrial coverage in the bill. The first four sections of the bill, all in the exact language contained in the final law, were presented at length to the senators on April 7, 1909, on the bill's second reading, and not a single comment or question was raised as they approved each. Commonwealth of Pennsylvania, *Legislative Journal* (1909), 2942.

34. Commonwealth of Pennsylvania, *Legislative Journal* (1905), 1213, 1365.

35. Ibid., 1951.

36. Ibid., 1956.

37. Ibid., 2048.

38. Ibid., 2215, 2419, 2606.

39. Ibid., 2606, 2612, 3402.

40. National Child Labor Committee, "Proceedings of the Second Annual Meeting," typescript, 10.

41. Ibid., 11.

42. Ibid.

43. Ibid.

44. Commonwealth of Pennsylvania, *Legislative Journal* (1909), 750, 1920–21.

45. Ibid., 2025–26.

46. Ibid., 2170.

47. Ibid., 3115–16.

48. Ibid., 3117.

49. See comments of Senator Charles A. Snyder, Commonwealth of Pennsylvania, *Legislative Journal* (1915), 2573.

50. Commonwealth of Pennsylvania, *Legislative Journal* (1909), 3435.

51. Ibid., 3434.

52. Ibid., 3434–35 (emphasis added).

53. Ibid., 3435.

54. Ibid., 3435 (emphasis added to first quote).

55. Jones, "Investigation of Glass Factories of Western Pennsylvania," 2.

56. Ibid.

57. Commonwealth of Pennsylvania, *Legislative Journal* (1909), 3435, 3564.

58. Ibid. (1913), 828, 1187–88.

59. Ibid., 1188.

60. Ibid.

61. Ibid.

62. Ibid.

63. Ibid.

64. Ibid. See also ibid., 828, 1186, 1821, 1816.

65. Ibid., 4006–7.

66. Ibid., 4098. The exception read as follows: "Provided, That when the usual process of manufacture or the nature of the business is of a kind that customarily necessitates continuous day and night employment, male minors not under the age of fourteen may be employed day and night . . . not exceeding nine hours during any twenty-four hours for minors under sixteen. And provided further, That in glass factories, male minors not under the age of fourteen years may be employed day and night."

67. Commonwealth of Pennsylvania, *Legislative Journal* (1913), 4100.

68. Ibid., 4442.

69. Ibid., 4446.

70. "Labor Fakir Deceived Labor," *National Glass Budget*, Apr. 12, 1913.

71. Commonwealth of Pennsylvania, *Legislative Journal* (1913), 4446, 4451.

72. Ibid., 4787.

73. Ibid., 5408.

74. Ibid., 5410.

75. Ibid., 5424, 5425.

76. Pennsylvania Constitution of 1874, Art. 3, sec. 4.

77. Commonwealth of Pennsylvania, *Legislative Journal* (1913), 5426.

78. Ibid. (1915), 400–401, 1138, 1358.

79. Ibid., 1289–1301.

80. Ibid., 1290, 1297, 1299, 1301.

81. Ibid., 2194, 2572–84.

Bibliography

Addams, Jane. "National Protection for Children." *Annals of the American Academy of Political and Social Sciences* 29, no. 1 (January 1907): 57–60.

Avery, Gillian. *Behold the Child: American Children and Their Books, 1621–1922.* Baltimore: Johns Hopkins University Press, 1994.

Binning, William J. "The Glass Industry of Western Pennsylvania, 1797–1860." Master's thesis, University of Pittsburgh, 1936.

Biser, Benjamin F. *Elements of Glass and Glassmaking.* Pittsburgh: Glass & Pottery Publishing Company, n.d.

Blumberg, Dorothy Rose. *Florence Kelley: The Making of a Social Pioneer.* New York: Augustus M. Kelley, 1966.

Butler, Elizabeth Beardsley. "Sharpsburg: A Typical Waste of Childhood." In *Wage-Earning Pittsburgh: The Pittsburgh Survey,* edited by Paul Underwood Kellogg, 279–304. New York: Survey Associates, 1911.

Campbell, James. *Annual Report of the Factory Inspector of the Commonwealth of Pennsylvania,* for the years 1895–1897 and 1899–1902. Harrisburg: State Printer of Pennsylvania, 1896–1898 and 1900–1903.

Catlin, Warren. *The Labor Problem: In the United States and Great Britain.* New York: Harper & Brothers, 1926.

Chute, Charles L. "The Enforcement of Child Labor Laws." *Child Labor Bulletin* 1, no. 2 (August 1912): 108–13.

———. "The Glass Industry and Child Labor Legislation: Report of an Investigation of the Glass Manufacturing Industry in Illinois, Indiana, Ohio, Pennsylvania and West Virginia." 1911. Commission Reports: Mills & Factories. Box 3, National Child Labor Committee Collection, Manuscript Section, Library of Congress, Washington, DC.

Cohen, Ronald D. "Child-Saving and Progressivism: 1885–1915." In *American Childhood: A Research Guide and Historical Handbook,* edited by Joseph M. Hawes and N. Ray Hiner, 273–309. Westport, CT: Greenwood Press, 1985.

Cohen, Steven R. "The Failure of Fair Wages and the Death of Labor Republicanism." In *Pittsburgh Surveyed,* edited by Maurine W. Greenwald and Margo Anderson, 50–68. Pittsburgh: University of Pittsburgh Press, 1996.

Commoner. Weekly newspaper published under various titles by the Glass Bottle Blowers' Association of the United States and Canada. Various articles, 1887–1914.

Commons, John R., and William M. Leiserson. "Wage-Earners of Pittsburgh." In *Wage-Earning Pittsburgh: The Pittsburgh Survey*, edited by Paul Underwood Kellogg, 113–88. New York: Survey Associates, Inc., 1911.

Commonwealth of Pennsylvania. *Journal of the House of Representatives*. Vol. 1. Harrisburg: State Printer, 1823–1824.

———. *Journal of the House of Representatives*. Vol. 1. Harrisburg: State Printer, 1827–1828.

———. *Journal of the House of Representatives*. Harrisburg: State Printer, 1874, 1889, 1893, 1897, 1905.

———. *Journal of the Senate*. Vol. 1. Harrisburg: State Printer, 1827–1828.

———. *Journal of the Senate*. Harrisburg: State Printer, 1848, 1849, 1889, 1893, 1895, 1897, 1905.

———. *Legislative Journal*. Harrisburg: State Printer, 1889, 1905, 1909, 1913, 1915.

———. Department of Labor and Industry. Bureau of Women and Children. *Special Bulletin No. 27: A History of Child Labor Legislation in Pennsylvania*. 1934.

Cubberley, Ellwood P. *Public Education in the United States*. Boston: Houghton Mifflin, 1919.

Davis, Allen F. *Spearheads for Reform: The Social Settlements and the Progressive Movement, 1890–1914*. New York: Oxford University Press, 1967.

———, and Mary Lynn McCree. *Eighty Years at Hull House*. Chicago: Quadrangle Books, 1969.

Davis, Edgar T. "The Difficulties of a Factory Inspector." 1906. *Proceedings of the Annual Meeting of the National Child Labor Committee, 1905, 1906*. Reprint, New York: Arno Press, 1974.

Davis, Pearce. *The Development of the American Glass Industry*. Cambridge, MA: Harvard University Press, 1949.

Delaney, J. C. *Annual Report of the Factory Inspector of the Commonwealth of Pennsylvania, for the years 1903–1909*. Harrisburg: State Printer of Pennsylvania, 1904–1910.

DeLeon, Daniel. "Playing Labor for Bass." *Daily People* (New York), editorial, July 18, 1901.

Dubofsky, Melvin. *Industrialism and the American Worker, 1865–1920*. 2nd ed. Arlington Heights, IL: Harlan Davidson, 1985.

Dye, Nancy S. Introduction to *Gender, Class, Race, and Reform in the Progressive Era*, edited by Noralee Frankel and Nancy S. Dye, 1–9. Lexington: University Press of Kentucky, 1991.

Finkelstein, Barbara. "Casting Networks of Good Influence: The Reconstruction of Childhood in the United States, 1790–1870." In *American Childhood: A Research Guide and Historical Handbook*, edited by Joseph M. Hawes and N. Ray Hiner, 111–52. Westport, CT: Greenwood Press, 1985.

Flanagan, Maureen A. *America Reformed: Progressives and Progressivisms, 1890s–1920s*. New York: Oxford University Press, 2007.

————. "Gender and Urban Political Reform: The City Club and the Women's City Club of Chicago in the Progressive Era." *American Historical Review* 95 (1990): 1032–50.

Foner, Philip S. *History of the Labor Movement in the United States: The Policies and Practices of the American Federation of Labor, 1900–1909.* New York: International Publishers, 1994.

Forbath, William E. *Law and the Shaping of the American Labor Movement.* Cambridge, MA: Harvard University Press, 1991.

Frank, Susan. *Glass and Archaeology.* London: Academic Press, 1982.

Freedman, Russell. *Kids at Work: Lewis Hine and the Crusade against Child Labor.* New York: Clarion, 1994.

Glass Bottle Blowers' Association of the United States and Canada (GBBA). Papers. Kheel Center for Labor-Management Documentation and Archives, Cornell University, Ithaca, NY.

Graff, Harvey J. *Conflicting Paths: Growing Up in America.* Cambridge, MA: Harvard University Press, 1995.

————. "Literacy, Jobs, and Industrialization: The Nineteenth Century." In *Literacy and Social Development in the West,* edited by Harvey J. Graff, 232–60. Cambridge: Cambridge University Press, 1981.

Greenwald, Maurine W., and Margo Anderson, eds. *Pittsburgh Surveyed: Social Science and Social Reform in the Early Twentieth Century.* Pittsburgh: University of Pittsburgh Press, 1996.

Hall, Fred S. "Child Labor Statistics." In *Child Employing Industries: Proceedings from the Sixth Annual Conference,* 114–26. New York: American Academy of Political and Social Sciences, 1910.

————. "Pennsylvania Child Labor Association." In *Child Employing Industries: Proceedings from the Sixth Annual Conference,* 184–86. New York: American Academy of Political and Social Sciences, 1910.

Harris, Howard, ed. *Keystone of Democracy: A History of Pennsylvania Workers.* Harrisburg: Pennsylvania Historical and Museum Commission, 1999.

Hindman, Hugh D. *Child Labor: An American History.* Armonk, NY: M. E. Sharpe, 2002.

Hoffman, Miles E. *A Contemporary Analysis of a Labor Union.* Labor Monograph No. 1. Philadelphia: Glass Bottle Blowers Association, 1959.

Hofstadter, Richard. *The Age of Reform: From Bryan to F.D.R.* New York: Vantage Books, 1955.

Illick, Joseph E. *American Childhoods.* Philadelphia: University of Pennsylvania Press, 2002.

Innes, Lowell. *Pittsburgh Glass, 1797–1891: A History and Guide for Collectors.* Boston: Houghton Mifflin, 1976.

Jones, Herschel H. "Investigation of Glass Factories of Western Pennsylvania." 1912–1913. Commission Reports: Mills & Factories. Box 3, National Child Labor Committee Collection, Manuscript Section, Library of Congress, Washington, DC.

Kaestle, Carl F. *Pillars of the Republic: Common Schools and American Society, 1780–1860.* New York: Hill and Wang, 1983.

Katz, Michael B. "The Origins of Public Education: A Reassessment." In *The Social History of American Education,* edited by B. Edward McClellan and William J. Reese, 91–107. Urbana: University of Illinois Press, 1988.

Kelley, Florence. "Child Labor Legislation and Enforcement in New England and the Middle States." 1905. Reprinted in *Proceedings of the Annual Meeting of the National Child Labor Committee, 1905, 1906,* 66–76. New York: Arno Press, 1974.

———. "Factory Inspection in Pittsburgh." In *Wage-Earning Pittsburgh: The Pittsburgh Survey,* edited by Paul Underwood Kellogg, 189–216. New York: Survey Associates, Inc., 1911.

———. "Obstacles to the Enforcement of Child Labor Legislation." *Annals of the American Academy of Political and Social Sciences* 29, no. 1 (January 1907): 50–56.

Kerber, Linda K., Alice Kessler-Harris, and Kathryn Kish Sklar, eds. *U.S. History as Women's History: New Feminist Essays.* Chapel Hill: University of North Carolina Press, 1995.

Kett, Joseph F. "Juveniles and Progressive Children." *History of Education Quarterly* 13, no. 2 (summer 1973): 191–94.

Larner, John William, Jr., "The Glass House Boys: Child Labor Conditions in Pittsburgh's Glass Factories, 1890–1917." *Western Pennsylvania Historical Magazine* 48 (1965): 355–64.

Laws of Pennsylvania. Published in *Laws of the General Assembly of Pennsylvania,* 1848–1915.

Link, Arthur S., and Richard L. McCormick. *Progressivism.* Arlington Heights, IL: Harlan Davidson, 1983.

Lovejoy, Owen R. *Children of the Glass Industry in Pennsylvania.* NCLC pamphlet no. 14. New York: National Child Labor Committee, 1907.

Madarasz, Anne. *Glass: Shattering Notions.* Pittsburgh: Historical Society of Western Pennsylvania, 1998.

Martins, William H. *Report of the Factory Inspector.* Harrisburg: State Printer of Pennsylvania, 1890.

McClellan, B. Edward, and William J. Reese, eds. *The Social History of American Education.* Urbana: University of Illinois Press, 1988.

McGerr, Michael. *A Fierce Discontent: The Rise and Fall of the Progressive Movement in America, 1870–1920.* New York: Free Press, 2003.

McKearin, George, and Helen McKearin. *Two Hundred Years of American Blown Glass.* New York: Crown, 1949.

Minton, Lee W. *Flame and Heart: A History of the Glass Bottle Blowers' Association of the United States and Canada.* Washington, DC: Merkel Press, 1961.

Mintz, Steven. *Huck's Raft: A History of American Childhood.* Cambridge, MA: Belknap Press of Harvard University Press, 2004.

Moore, N. Hudson. *Old Glass: European and American.* New York: Tudor, 1935.

Morison, Samuel Eliot. *The Oxford History of the American People.* New York: Oxford University Press, 1965.

Mowry, George E. "Progressivism: Middle-Class Disillusionment." In *Conflict and Consensus in Modern American History,* edited by Allen F. Davis and Harold D. Woodman, 187–98. 4th ed. New York: D. C. Heath, 1976.

National Child Labor Committee. "Child Labor Laws in All States." *Child Labor Bulletin* 1, no. 2 (August 1912): 1–77.

———. "Proceedings of the Second Annual Meeting." 1905. Typescript version. Box 2, National Child Labor Committee Collection, Manuscript Section, Library of Congress, Washington, DC.

National Glass Budget. Articles published between 1896 and 1913.

Parton, James. "Pittsburg." *Atlantic Monthly* 21, no. 73 (January 1868): 17–36.

Pennsylvania Constitution of 1874. www.paconstitution.duq.edu/con74.html [accessed August 2007].

Perry, Josephine. *The Glass Industry.* New York: Longmans, Green, 1945.

Phillips, C. J. *Glass: The Miracle Maker, Its History, Technology, and Applications.* New York: Pitman, 1941.

Rogers, Frances, and Alice Beard. *5000 Years of Glass.* New York: Frederick A. Stokes, 1937.

Scott, Anne Firor. *Natural Allies: Women's Associations in American History.* Urbana: University of Illinois Press, 1991.

Scoville, Warren C. *Revolution in Glassmaking: Entrepreneurship and Technological Change in the American Industry, 1880–1920.* Cambridge, MA: Harvard University Press, 1948.

Sklar, Kathryn Kish. *Florence Kelley and the Nation's Work: The Rise of Women's Political Culture, 1830–1900.* New Haven: Yale University Press, 1995.

———. "Two Political Cultures in the Progressive Era: The National Consumers' League and the American Association for Labor Legislation." In *U.S. History as Women's History,* edited by Linda K. Kerber, Alice Kessler-Harris, and Kathryn Kish Sklar, 36–62. Chapel Hill: University of North Carolina Press, 1995.

Spargo, John. *The Bitter Cry of the Children.* New York: Macmillan, 1906.

Steinfeld, Robert J. *The Invention of Free Labor: The Employment Relation in English and American Law and Culture, 1350–1870.* Chapel Hill: University of North Carolina Press, 1991.

Trattner, Walter I. *Crusade for the Children: A History of the National Child Labor Committee and Child Labor Reform in America.* Chicago: Quadrangle Books, 1970.

Trollope, Anthony. *North America.* New York: Harper and Brothers, 1862.

U.S. Senate. *Report on Conditions of Woman and Child Wage-Earners in the United States.* Vol. 3, *Glass Industry.* Washington, DC: Government Printing Office, 1911.

Walbridge, William S. *American Bottles Old & New: A Story of the Industry in the United States.* Toledo: Owens Bottle Co., 1920.

Watchorn, Robert. *Annual Report of the Factory Inspector of the Commonwealth of Pennsylvania,* for the years 1893 and 1894. Harrisburg: State Printer of Pennsylvania, 1894 and 1895.

———. *Report of the Factory Inspector.* Harrisburg: State Printer of Pennsylvania, 1892.

Weeks, Joseph D. *Report on the Statistics of Wages in Manufacturing Industries.* U.S. Department of Interior, Census Office. Washington, DC: Government Printing Office, 1886.

———. *Report on Strikes and Lockouts, 1880.* U.S. Department of Interior, Census Office. Washington, DC: Government Printing Office, 1886.

Who's Who in Pennsylvania. Edited by Lewis R. Hamersly. New York: L. R. Hamersly Company, 1904.

Wilson, Kenneth M. *American Glass, 1760–1930: The Toledo Museum of Art.* New York: Hudson Hills Press, 1994.

Wolman, Leo. *The Growth of American Trade Unions, 1880–1923.* 1924. Reprint, New York: Arno Press, 1975.

Zelizer, Viviana A. "From Child Labor to Child Work: Changing Cultural Conceptions of Children's Economic Roles, 1870s–1930s." In *Ideas, Ideologies, and Social Movements: The United States Experience since 1800,* edited by Peter A. Coclanis and Stuart Bruchey, 90–101. Columbia: University of South Carolina Press, 1999.

———. *Pricing the Priceless Child: The Changing Social Value of Children.* New York: Basic Books, 1985.

Zembala, Dennis Michael. "Machines in the Glasshouse: The Transformation of Work in the Glass Industry, 1820–1915." PhD dissertation, George Washington University, 1984.

Index

child labor laws (*cont.*)
  and required certificates for child workers,
    47, 158, 159–60, 172–73, 200n26; violations
    in certificates required by, 42–43, 51–52,
    168, 202n83
child labor reform: and characterization of
    glass house boys, 35–36, 38; education and
    (*see* education); evolving position of glass
    workers, their unions, and the *Commoner*
    on, 130, 135–44; glass houses' position on,
    99, 103–5, 136, 137; *National Glass Budget's*
    objections to, 99–102, 103–9; objections
    to night work by children, 2–4, 103–9, 116,
    175; parents' and boys' resistance to, 46,
    71–72, 149, 168; role of gender in, 10–17; in
    terms of specific ages, 36–37. *See also* National Child Labor Committee (NCLC)
Chute, Charles: Delaney's criticism of, 109; on
    enforcement of child labor laws, 57–58, 59;
    report on child labor, 62–65, 67, 71, 149, 188
City Club of Chicago, 13–14, 197n21
City Club of Pittsburgh, 105–6
Clansman, The, 205n21
Clay, Henry, 77, 81
cleaning-off boys, duties of, 8
Cohen, Ronald, 199n10
Commoner: coverage of wage negotiations,
    121–22, 124, 126, 127–28, 129, 130; downplaying of strikes by glass house boys,
    130–33, 135; evolving position on child labor reform, 135–41; gender-based attack on
    reformers, 143; on mechanization, 117–18;
    nativist and racist views of, 115, 205n21
Commons, John R., 15, 17, 28, 38
compulsory education legislation, 4–5, 147,
    149, 153–64, 172–73, 208n16
Connecticut, factory inspection in, 200n28
continuous tank system for melting glass,
    85–86, 174
contractual (free) labor, 79, 203n14
Cox, Edwin R., 193
Craig, Isaac, 75–76
Crawford, John C., 176, 180
Cunningham glass works, 131

daubing, 101, 134–35, 138
Davis, Edgar T., 47
de Forest, Robert W., 29, 198n27
Delaney, J. C.: criticism of Chute, 109; on

education, 55, 145, 173; removal from office
    as State Factory Inspector, 59; reports of,
    52, 53, 54–55, 56–57
Denny, Harmar, 82
Devine, Edward T., 27, 29
Dewalt, Arthur G., 180, 182, 183, 184
Druggist Ware Glass Blowers' League, 113
Dye, Nancy S., 10
Dyottville System, 152–53

Eastman, Crystal, 17
education: and child labor in nineteenth-
    century Pennsylvania, 40, 41, 42, 54, 149–
    53, 168, 170; compulsory education legislation, 4–5, 147, 149, 153–64, 172–73, 208n16;
    curriculum advanced by progressives, 146;
    Delaney on, 55, 145, 173; for social reformers, 24; support for vocational education in
    public schools, 14
Edward H. Everett Glass Works, 137
Eichbaum, William, 83
Engels, Frederick, 20, 26

factory inspection: in Connecticut, 200n28;
    in Great Britain, 58; in Illinois, 26–27, 139;
    in Massachusetts, 200n28; in New York,
    58; in Pennsylvania, 46–58, 59, 136, 160,
    200nn28–29
finishers, duties of, 7
Fitch, John, 17
Flanagan, Maureen A., 13
Fletcher, Harry, 48–49
foreign-born workers, 102–3, 115, 146
Fox, John E., 179–80, 182–84
free (contractual) labor, 79, 203n14
Freedman, Russell, 201n67

gatherers, duties of, 7
GBBA. *See* Glass Bottle Blowers' Association
    (GBBA)
gender: *Commoner's* gender-based attack on
    reformers, 143; and the NCLC's visible
    leadership, 29–30, 31; Progressive Era reform and, 10–17
glass blowers, master, 7, 111, 115
Glass Blowers' League, 113
Glass Bottle Blowers' Association (GBBA):
    affiliation with the AFL, 114–15, 116–17;
    antimechanization strategies of, 98, 119–21,

125, 126–28; concern about strikes by glass house boys, 130–33; conflict regarding daubing by glass house boys, 134–35; declining membership, 129–30; *National Glass Budget's* criticism of, 95–98, 100, 101; origins of, 112–14; position on child labor, 99, 116–17, 135–44, 179, 187, 189–90; role in wage negotiations, 121, 122, 124–29

glass house boys: conflict regarding daubing by, 134–35; consequences of night work for, 64–65, 67, 69–70; duties of, 7–9, 22–24, 44; and hand-blown methods of glass production, 99, 121, 130, 135, 139, 141; health of, 27, 44–45, 60, 63, 67; impact of labor-saving machines on, 85–86, 89; legal exception for night work by (*see* night work provision in child labor laws); *National Glass Budget's* portrayal of, 73, 99, 100–102; NCLC's investigative report on, 62, 68–71, 149, 188; and parents' resistance to reform, 71–72; participation in strikes, 100, 101, 130–33, 135, 199n2; *The Pittsburgh Survey's* analysis of, 38–46; power disparity between employers and, 77, 79–80, 203n14; prospects for apprenticeship, 40–41, 64, 101; reformers objections to night work by, 2–4, 103–9, 116, 175; sleep habits of, 65, 67, 69–70; strain of physical labor on, 64

glass houses: child-adult duality in, 35; continuous tank system used in, 85–86, 174; dangerous conditions in, 27, 40, 44; early history of, 75–77; factory inspections of (*see* factory inspection); growth patterns of, 80, 83–84, 203n15; legal exception for night work by boys in (*see* night work provision in child labor laws); mechanization in, 87–95, 98–99, 117–21; NCLC's critique of, 59–65, 67–72, 74, 184, 188, 199n9; nineteenth-century politics and, 80–84; Owens Automatic's impact on, 74, 91–92, 93, 94–95; position on child labor reform, 99, 103–5, 136, 137; pot system used by, 84–85, 86; power disparity between glass house boys and, 77, 79–80, 203n14; reformers' objections to night work by children in, 2–4, 103–9, 116, 175; specific positions in, 6–8; underreporting of child labor, 5; wage negotiations between unions and, 121–22, 124–29, 130

glassmaking: history of, 74–77; tradition of secrecy, 111–12

Goldmark, Pauline, 29, 30

Gompers, Samuel, 114–15

Graff, Harvey, 163, 164

Great Britain, 58, 137

Green Bottle Blowers, 113

Green Glass Workers' Association, 113–14

Greenwald, Maurine W., 17

Grim, Webster, 182

Haines bottle plant, 131

Hall, Fred S., 55–56, 172

Hall, George, 27–28

Hall, Henry, 49

Hastings, Daniel H., 155, 157

Hay, John, 83

Hayes, Denis A.: antimechanization strategies of the GBBA and, 98, 119–20, 121, 125, 126–28; conflict on daubing, 134–35; death of, 114; leadership role of, 112; *National Glass Budget's* criticism of, 95, 96–97, 101; position on child labor reform, 116–17; position on Owens Automatic, 96–97, 110, 118, 119, 120; role in wage negotiations, 121, 124–25, 126–29

Heinz glass-bottle factory, 131–32

Hemmingway Glass Company, 131

Henry Street settlement house, 11, 27

Hine, Lewis W., 17, 62, 201n67

Hulings, Willis James, 181, 183

Hull House, 11, 26

Hupp, Frank Le M., 67

Huyler, John S., 29

Illinois: factory inspection in, 26–27, 139; law on night work by children, 68; NCLC's report on glass houses in, 62; relocation of glass factories to, 74, 84; shortage of glass house boys in, 139

Illinois Glass Company, 27, 47, 102–3, 202n83

illiteracy, 54, 57, 163–64

immigrant workers, 102–3, 115, 146

indentured servitude, 77–78

Indiana: child labor in, 68, 200n26; objections to proposed child labor bill in, 140; relocation of glass factories to, 74, 84

Indiana Bottle & Glass Company, 132

inspection, factory. *See* factory inspection